Paper Knowledge

SIGN, STORAGE, TRANSMISSION

Edited by Jonathan Sterne and Lisa Gitelman

Paper Knowledge

TOWARD A MEDIA HISTORY OF DOCUMENTS

Lisa Gitelman

DUKE UNIVERSITY PRESS   DURHAM AND LONDON   2014

2/24/15
WW
$22.95

Designed by Amy Ruth Buchanan
Typeset in Garamond Premier Pro by
Tseng Information Systems, Inc.

DUKE UNIVERSITY PRESS GRATEFULLY
ACKNOWLEDGES THE SUPPORT OF NEW YORK
UNIVERSITY'S STEINHARDT SCHOOL, WHICH
PROVIDED FUNDS TOWARD THE PUBLICATION
OF THIS BOOK.

Library of Congress Cataloging-in-Publication Data
Gitelman, Lisa.
Paper knowledge : toward a media history of
documents / Lisa Gitelman.
pages cm — (Sign, storage, transmission)
Includes bibliographical references and index.
ISBN 978-0-8223-5645-5 (cloth : alk. paper)
ISBN 978-0-8223-5657-8 (pbk. : alk. paper)
1. Communication and technology. 2. Written communication—Social aspects. 3. Communication and
culture. 4. Authors and readers. I. Title. II. Series: Sign,
storage, transmission.
P96.T 42G56 2014
302.2'244—dc23   2013030269

CONTENTS

Death certificates are serious documents. They look so official. At least in New York City each death certificate attests to its own veracity, explaining that it "is a true copy of a record on file." Each bears a number, the printed signatures of a doctor and a city official, two seals, a barcode, and multiple carefully filled-in boxes that together elaborate the particulars regarding a specific decedent, a death, and the disposition of the bodily remains. The back of each death certificate is blank — or it would be, except for a list of security features to look for should you wish to reassure yourself that the truth-claiming document you hold is genuine. The seals and borders have raised intaglio printing. (Run your finger over them to check.) The bottom of the document contains a microprinted legend. (Hold the document very close or use a magnifier.) The paper has an elaborate watermark. (Hold it up at arm's length with a light behind it.) And there's a logo printed with thermochromic ink. (Warm it by rubbing your finger over it quickly to make sure it will change color.) One doesn't so much *read* a death certificate, it would seem, as perform calisthenics with one, holding it out and then holding it close, flipping it one way and fingering it another.

Death certificates look official, then, but looking official is both a tall order and a moving target. The baroque complexity of security features employed for today's death certificates shows just how worried New York City must be about counterfeits and possums. The variety of production and reproduction techniques employed — generalizable somehow as "printing" — implies an arms race, an ongoing contest between unscrupulous parties who might play dead and city officials, their contractors, and agents. That contest in turn implies an ever growing, ever more intricate scriptural economy, today characterized in part by the availability of digital tools and so-called prosumer electronics. "Scriptural economy" is a phrase coined decades ago by Michel de Certeau in order to refer to what he identified as the "endless tapestry" of writing and writings that works as both discipline and myth: discipline because writing is a form of socialization and control, and myth because writings accumulate with (that is, as) the weight of history itself.[1]

I adopt the phrase here to refer to that totality of writers, writings, and writing techniques that began to expand so precipitously in the nineteenth century. It is a dynamic totality that has in general eluded scholarly attention because of the ways that contemporary disciplines construct and divide their subjects. Not only did advancing literacies, the proliferation of print formats, and the widespread adoption of new media help complicate nineteenth-century experiences of writing and writtenness—of "-graphy" and graphism—but the specialized labors of printing and the look of printedness were also reframed by the eventual use of new devices for the production and reproduction of writing as well as new media for the inscription of sounds, sights, and other sundry phenomena.

This book addresses selected, specific moments in the expansion of the scriptural economy. These moments are important less because of the technological innovations associated with them than because of the enlarged and enlarging constituencies that those innovations had a role in enabling. The scriptural economy is an ever expanding realm of human expression, even if its reigning conditions have typically been harnessed to the interests of officialdom. De Certeau was looking for isolated threads within his endless tapestry that might give voice to an anonymous hero he called "the ordinary man."[2] It is a project that still appeals today, if in different terms, yet it is a project that first requires a thoroughgoing history of the scriptural economy in recent times, a history that must correctively exceed the contrastive generalities used to describe the so-called Gutenberg revolution—or, for that matter, the Internet one. This book takes one step toward that end.

....

Each of the four chapters that follow my introduction was developed in conversation with colleagues amid the long-standing, if informal, open peer review process that consists of conference presentations, invited talks, animated conversations, and the e-mail circulation of rough drafts for comment. The kernel of chapter 1 was written as a talk delivered at the

University of Rhode Island, where I was invited by Carolyn Betensky and her colleagues. It was reworked for presentations at American University, where I was invited by Despina Kakoudaki, Erik Dussere, and their colleagues; the Re:Live conference in Melbourne, Australia, hosted by Sean Cubitt and others; a workshop at the Radcliffe Institute for Advanced Study, organized by Leah Price and Ann Blair; and a workshop at Yale University, where I was invited by Jessica Pressman and Michael Warner. I was able to improve this chapter further thanks to readings by Ben Kafka, Dana Polan, Michael Winship, and numerous others, as well as a timely conversation with Mary Poovey about the exchange function.

Chapter 2 started when Rick Prelinger turned me on to Robert Binkley's "New Tools for Men of Letters" and has benefited from a cycle of presentations and revisions that has taken me to the Society for Textual Studies; McGill University's Department of Art History and Communication Studies; the Department of Information Studies at the University of California, Los Angeles; the Department of English at the University of California, Santa Barbara; the Stanford University Program in Science and Technology Studies; Carnegie Mellon University's Center for the Arts in Society; the Material Texts Seminar at the University of Pennsylvania; and Ohio State University's Department of English. My generous hosts and interlocutors at these locales included Matt Kirschenbaum, Will Straw, Johanna Drucker, Rita Raley, Alan Liu, Fred Turner, Paul K. Eiss, Jamie "Skye" Bianco, Peter Stallybrass, and Jared Gardner. This chapter also benefited from careful readings and corrections offered by Mary Murrell, Kathleen Fitzpatrick, Laura Helton, and Brian Murphy.

Chapter 3 started longest ago, as a conference paper for the first meeting of the Humanities, Arts, Science, and Technology Advanced Collaboratory (HASTAC) and then for an uproarious panel (really, it was) at the Society for the History of Authorship, Reading, and Publishing's meeting in Minneapolis. That paper was subsequently enlarged, revised, and presented at the Maryland Institute for Technology in the Humanities; the University of Uppsala, Sweden; and Harvard University's Department of the History of Science, where my short exile in Cambridge was so significantly enriched by Stephanie Athey, Jimena Canales, and Craig Robertson, among others.

Chapter 4 started as a job talk for the Department of English at New York University (NYU) and a presentation at Texas A&M University's Glasscock Center, where I was invited by Eric Rothenbuhler and hosted by James Rosenheim. The talk subsequently benefited from additional airing at the John Hope Franklin Institute for the Humanities at Duke University, where I was invited by Ellen Garvey and her seminar mates and hosted by Srinivas Aravamudan, as well as a careful reading by Alex Csiszar and discussions with John Willinsky, Elena Razlogova, Carlin Wing, and others. Along the way I tried to articulate what was holding these emerging chapters together in talks delivered at the Canadian Communication Association, where I was invited by Sandra Gabriele, and Indiana University's Department of English, where I was hosted by Jonathan Elmer. Additional presentations at Concordia University (at the invitations of Darren Wershler and Jason Camlot) and the Texas Institute for Literary and Textual Studies (where I was invited by Matt Cohen) helped me to collect my thoughts and—as at any such meetings—probably to collect the thoughts of others too. I remain grateful to these and other hosts, copanelists, readers, interlocutors, critics, and event sponsors. I'm sorry that I can't name you all or make explicit where so many of your thoughts have so granularly and enjoyably influenced mine.

My introduction benefited from generous readings by Andy Parker, Marita Sturken, Dana Polan, Jennie Jackson, and Rita Raley. My afterword evolved in fits and starts and benefited from the encouragement of Lara Cohen as well as exposure to audiences at Berkeley, the Newberry Library in Chicago, North Carolina State University, and the University of Wisconsin in Madison. I remain grateful for invitations from David Bates and the Berkeley Center for New Media; Paul Gehl and the Caxton Club; Carolyn Miller and the Program in Communication, Rhetoric, and Digital Media at N.C. State; as well as Mary Murrell at the Center for the Humanities and Jonathan Senchyne of the Center for the History of Print and Digital Culture, both in Madison. I would additionally like to thank the anonymous reviewers—generous and smart—who were deployed by Duke University Press to read the entire manuscript. I have learned a lot from them and probably filched a little. In addition, this project has benefited from incalculable support—both intellectual and moral—from a core group of friends and colleagues, many of them already named above. Jonathan Sterne and Meredith McGill have been supporters, collaborators, friends, and interlocutors of the first water, while I have also found that it is no fun—and thus no use—thinking without Pat Crain, Andy Parker, Jennie Jackson, Martin Harries, Gayle Wald, Carolyn Betensky, Lisa Lynch, Stephanie Athey, Rita Raley, or Terry Collins. My sisters, Hillary and Alix, learned what I did about death certificates while this book was in preparation, and my hat is forever off to them in thanks and in love.

A few paragraphs from the introduction and a few ideas from chapter 1 have appeared previously as part of "Print Culture (Other Than Codex): Job Printing and Its Importance," in *Comparative Textual Media*, edited by N. Katherine Hayles and Jessica Pressman (University of Minnesota Press, forthcoming); and an earlier version of the first section of chapter 3 has appeared as "Daniel Ellsberg and the Lost Idea of the Photocopy" in *The History of Participatory Media: Politics and Publics, 1750–2000*, edited by Anders Ekström, Solveig Jülich, Frans Lundgren, and Per Wisselgren (Routledge, 2011). Any overlap between those publications and this one appears by permission, and I have benefited gratefully in each case from editorial suggestions as I have more recently from the professional attentions of Ken Wissoker, Courtney Berger, and the staff at Duke University Press. Timely fellowship support aided in the preparation of this book, both when I was a Beaverbrook Media@McGill Visiting Scholar in 2012 and when I was an NYU Humanities Initiative Fellow in 2011–12. The Steinhardt School at NYU helped defray the cost of illustrations. The American Antiquarian Society supported me with a short-term fellowship in the summer of 2007 to research something different, but that's when I first encountered a copy of Oscar Harpel's wacky *Typograph*, so thank you as ever to the AAS.

The document is a particularly important vernacular genre, both sprawling and ubiquitous. We know it by its diverse subgenres — the memo, for instance, or the green card and the promissory note — as well as by its generalized, cognate forms, like documentary and documentation. This book is about the genre of the document glimpsed selectively in four episodes from media history. Each episode concerns a different medium for the reproduction of documents, since reproduction is one clear way that documents are affirmed as such: one of the things people do with documents is copy them, whether they get published variously in editions (like the Declaration of Independence, for instance), duplicated for reference (like the photocopy of my passport that I carry in my suitcase), sort of or semipublished for internal circulation (like a restaurant menu), or proliferated online (mirrored and cached like the many documents in Wikileaks).

Although reproduction is one of the functions that have helped people to reckon documents as documents — as I hope to elaborate below — the core function of the document genre is something else entirely. The word "document" descends from the Latin root *docer*, to teach or show, which suggests that the document exists in order to document. Sidestepping this circularity of terms, one might say instead that documents help define and are mutually defined by the know-show function, since documenting is an epistemic practice: the kind of knowing that is all wrapped up with showing, and showing wrapped with knowing. Documents are epistemic objects; they are the recognizable sites and subjects of interpretation across the disciplines and beyond, evidential structures in the long human history of clues.[1] Closely related to the know-show function of documents is the work of no show, since sometimes documents are documents merely by dint of their potential to show: they are flagged and filed away for the future, just in case. Both know show and no show depend on an implied self-evidence that is intrinsically rhetorical. As John Guillory notes, "persuasion is implicit in *docer*."[2] If all documents share a certain "horizon of expectation," then, the name of that horizon is accountability.[3]

A quick word on genre: As I understand it, genre is a mode of recognition instantiated in discourse. Written genres, for instance, depend on a possibly infinite number of things that large groups of people recognize, will recognize, or have recognized that writings can be for. To wit, documents are for knowing-showing. Schoolbooks have long suggested, by contrast, that genre is a question of ingredients or formal attributes — sonnets have fourteen lines, for instance, while comedies end in marriage and tragedies in death — so I'm urging a different perspective by focusing on recognition that is collective, spontaneous, and dynamic.[4] As an analogy, consider the word search, that pencil puzzle that newspapers sometimes print next to the crossword. In the word search, your task is to recognize and circle words amid a two-dimensional grid of random letters. You recognize the different words that you do because words are conventional expressions and because you know how to read. The words don't just lie there on the page waiting, that is; they are also already inside you, part of the way you have learned (and been schooled) to communicate with people around you. Likewise genres — such as the joke, the novel, the document, and the sitcom — get picked out contrastively amid a jumble of discourse and often across multiple media because of the ways they have been internalized by constituents of a shared culture. Individual genres aren't artifacts, then; they are ongoing and changeable practices of expression and reception that are recognizable in myriad and variable constituent instances at once and also across time. They are specific and dynamic, socially realized sites and segments of coherence within the discursive field.

But what *is* a document? Bibliographers and other information specialists have persisted in puzzling over this question for at least the last hundred years. Most famously, the French librarian and "documentalist" Suzanne Briet proposed in 1951 that an antelope running wild would not be a document, but an antelope taken into a zoo would be one, presumably because it would then be framed — or reframed — as an example, specimen, or instance.[5] She was pushing a limit case, as Michael Buckland explains, drawing attention to the properties of documents: they are material objects intended as evidence and processed or framed — if not always caged —

as such.[6] Although I think it is probably best to remain agnostic on the question of antelopes, Briet and Buckland help underscore the context-dependent character of the know-show function. Any object can be a thing, but once it is framed as or entered into evidence—once it is mobilized—it becomes a document, an instance proper to that genre. What is notably obscured by the exoticism of Briet's instance is just how intricately entangled the genre and the thing can be and have become over the last several centuries.[7]

Written genres in general are familiarly treated as if they were equal to or coextensive with the sorts of textual artifacts that habitually embody them. This is where media and formats enter the picture. Say the word "novel," for instance, and your auditors will likely imagine a printed book, even if novels also exist serialized in nineteenth-century periodicals, published in triple-decker (multivolume) formats, and loaded onto—and re-imagined by the designers and users of—Kindles, Nooks, and iPads. Not all written genres are subject to the same confusion with the same intensity (say "short story," for instance), but documents familiarly are, descendant of a long and varied tradition that forever entangles the material form of an expression with its linguistic meanings or incompletely distinguishes the two—confusing "the text" and "the work," to put that more succinctly.[8] So tickets, receipts, and business cards count as things at the same time that they count as subgenres of the document; they are patterns of expression and reception discernible amid a jumble of discourse, but they are also familiar material objects to be handled—to be shown and saved, saved and shown—in different ways. When it comes to documents, it should be clear, a thing made of paper and bearing semiotic traces is not merely the most typical case, it is also the most salient, since the affordances of paper and the function that defines documents have become inextricable from one another during the many centuries in which paper has been in general use, whether under conditions of scarcity, plenitude, or excess.[9]

The ways that paper works have become part of what documents are for, and vice versa, though the workings of paper are admittedly complex and even paradoxical. Consider that paper is a figure both for all that is sturdy and stable (as in, "Let's get that on paper!"), and for all that is insubstantial and ephemeral (including the paper tiger and the house of cards).[10] Likewise, paper is familiarly the arena of clarity and literalism—of things in black and white—at the same time that it is the essential enabler of abstraction and theory, as in mathematics and theoretical physics.[11] Paper serves as a figure for all that is external to the mind—the world on paper—as well as all that is proper to it, the tabula rasa. Contradictions like these hint at the complexities that documents may present as paper things, while digital things admittedly help destabilize many of the foregoing generalizations in additional and interesting ways. (What is digital thingness, after all?[12]) That said, the genre of the document and the commonsensicality of its life on and as paper have both been crucial to the designers and users of digital media, partly in the negative sense—via the structuring myth of the paperless office, for instance—and partly in the positive.[13] Think of the "My Documents" folder on every PC, for instance, or the "Documents" on every Macintosh. The e-ticket is another good example; a familiar subgenre of the document that is today variously reckoned on screen: bought and sold, uploaded and downloaded, sent and saved, known and shown.

Documents are important not because they are ubiquitous, I should be clear, but rather because they are so evidently integral to the ways people think and live. The epistemic power of the know-show function is indisputable, and the properties of documents matter in all kinds of far-reaching ways. As Geoffrey Nunberg describes it, information is understood today to come in discrete "morsels" or bits partly because of the way the concept of information reifies the properties of paper documents; they are separate and separable, bounded and distinct. Likewise, information has an objective, autonomous character partly because of the way it reflects the authoritative institutions and practices to which documents belong.[14] What this reflection of authority suggests is that documents—unlike information, interestingly enough—are importantly situated; they are tied to specific settings. Again, the know-show function is context-dependent in space and time: consider the poor antelope, trapped within the zoological garden. Or consider the 1839 *American Slavery as It Is*, a key document in the history of the abolitionist movement in the United States. Compiled in part from Southern newspapers, it altered the contexts of advertisements describing runaway slaves by recognizing their value for republication in the North.[15] Republication turned the ads into a powerful indictment of slavery because they so frequently described runaways in terms of bodily mutilations. Embedded in local newsprint these advertisements had been documents, to be sure, but collecting them and reproducing them in another context for another audience made them know-show with much greater force. What had been published first as instruments calling the slave system into complicity, to aid in slaves' recapture, were now republished as instruments of moral suasion whereby the slave system became paradoxically enrolled in the antislavery cause: slavery "as it is" condemns itself. Because it implies accountability, knowing and showing together constitute an epistemic practice to which ethics and politics become available, even necessary.

Documents are integral to the ways people think as well as to the social order that they inhabit. Knowing-showing, in short, can never be disentangled from power—or, more properly, control.[16] Documents belong to that ubiquitous subcategory of texts that embraces the subjects and instruments of bureaucracy or of systematic knowledge generally. "The dominion of the document," Guillory notes, "is a feature of modernity," though documents of course predate the modern and exceed modernity.[17] They were part of the way that medieval subjects, for instance, expressed distrust amid the anxious contexts of uncertain power relations.[18] In the modern era documents have cultural weight mostly according to their institutional frames—the university, the corporation, and the state, for example—however remote the contextual framework can sometimes seem. As a growing literature in anthropology, sociology, and literary and cultural studies now elaborates, documents are at once familiar "props in the theater of ruling [and] policing" and the fetish objects "of the modern economic era," while bureaucracies don't so much employ documents as they are partly constructed by and out of them.[19] Thus the colonial subjects of British South Asia once called their government the Kaghazi Raj, or document regime, while today in the United States we live in an age of "undocumented" human beings at the same time that errors and malfeasance in "document execution" have helped exacerbate and extend a housing foreclosure crisis.

Some readers may rightly sense a connection between the genre of the document so described and Bruno Latour's interest in inscriptions. "Inscription" is the broader term, but favoring the document genre in this book aims both at particular contexts—the institutional and the everyday—and at substance, substrate, or platform: typically, if not necessarily, paper and paperwork. Latour follows inscriptions in order to explain "our modern scientific culture" and its power, without recourse either to overarching "mentalist" explanations (as if you could climb inside people's heads to see what makes them modern) or overarching materialist ones. Better instead, he argues, to pursue what he calls a strategy of deflation—to look, that is, for more mundane phenomena, not in the brain or in abstractions like the Social or the Economy, but rather in the everyday things that people do and handle when they are modern: They mobilize inscriptions.[20] This book seconds Latour's move. My interest in the genre of the document is deflationary in the very least because documents may be distinguished from more elevated uses of text, as in "the literary," and from more elevated forms of text, like "the book" — the former residing as it does closer to the mentalist end of the spectrum and the latter closer to the materialist end. The literary is a category of imagined and imaginative works evident across materialized instances: Shakespeare's *Hamlet*, famously, is a work existing across multiple editions, countless productions, and infinite appropriations.[21] It doesn't exist in any one place as much as it exists anywhere and everywhere its interpretations do. The book, meanwhile, is a category of material goods, an object of commerce as well as of librarianship and pedagogy, the focus of scholarly domains (especially bibliography and the history of the book) as well as a powerful metonym within the popular discourse that so incessantly debates the supposed death or future of printed books and reading.

The document, in contrast, lives at a larger, lower level. Its study earns a more catholic sociology of text and enables a view of disciplines and disciplinarity turned "inside out" and disciplines thought from scratch.[22] Documents have existed longer than books, paper, printing, or the public sphere, and certainly longer than the literary has been described as such. Thinking about documents helps in particular to adjust the focus of media studies away from grand catchall categories like "manuscript" and "print" and toward an embarrassment of material forms that have together supported such a varied and evolving scriptural economy.[23] Focusing selectively on the last 150 years, the pages that follow consider documents that are handwritten, printed, typed, mimeographed, microfilmed, photocopied, scanned, and more. They consider how these different sorts of documents were themselves considered amid the contexts of their production, reproduction, and use, as well as what such considerations might tell us about documents and the contexts of their circulation more generally. Like Jonathan Sterne's recent book on a particular format (the MP3) or Bonnie Mak's recent book on a particular interface (the page), my focus on a particular genre works to decenter the media concept precisely in order to evolve a better, richer media studies.[24]

There are several arguments lurking here, two of which may be stated simply as goals of this book. The first is that a more detailed account of documents in the past will without question facilitate more nuanced accounts of documents in and for the future. That said, teleology is not my stock in trade. I do not wish to render the past narrowly in terms of or service to the present any more than I would deny that present "adventures" with technology — as Jacques Derrida puts it — promote "a sort of future anterior," enriching our sense of the past.[25] In what follows I have aimed to open the question of digital text — or to allow readers to open that question — in what I hope are original and productive ways, inspired in part by the work of Matthew Kirschenbaum, Richard Harper, and David Levy, among numerous others.[26] Readers may find in the end that this book hops toward digital media and then refuses to land there, or at least refuses to plant a proper flag on arrival. Chapter 4 concerns a digital format for documents — the portable document format or PDF file — but it is a peculiarly backward-looking format, characterized by what Marshall McLuhan might have called an acute rearview-mirror-ism.[27] ("Warning: Objects in mirror . . .") A second, related argument advanced here is that the broad categories that have become proper to the history of communication and that increasingly have a bearing on popular discourse are insufficient and perhaps even hazardous to our thinking.[28] I refer in particular to the concept of "print culture," and one aim of what follows is to discourage its use.

The history of communication typically defines print by distinguishing it from manuscript, yet there is considerable poverty in that gesture. Far from being a simple precursor, manuscript stands as a back formation of printing. (That is, before the spread of printing there wasn't any need to describe manuscript as such.[29]) Meanwhile print itself has come to encompass many diverse technologies for the reproduction of text, despite its primary, historical association with letterpress printing à la Johannes Gutenberg. Until the nineteenth century every "printed" text was printed by letterpress, using a process of composition, imposition, and presswork very like the one that Gutenberg and his associates and competitors developed in the mid-fifteenth century, although saying so admittedly overlooks xylography (woodblock printing) and intaglio processes like printing from copperplate engravings. Since 1800, however, multiple planographic, photochemical, and electrostatic means of printing have been developed and variously deployed, to the point that in the twenty-first century virtually nothing "printed" is printed by letterpress. With the tables turned, the term "print" has floated free of any specific technology, if indeed it was ever securely moored in the first place. Instead "print" has become defined—as if in reflexive recourse to its own back formation—by dint of "a negative relation to the [writer's] hand."[30] Any textual artifact that is not handwritten or otherwise handmade letter by letter (typed, for example) counts as "printed," and lately even the printer's hand has gone missing, since today "printers" are usually not human: now the term more familiarly designates machines proper to the realm of consumer electronics. (Curiously—and unlike human hands—office printers have been almost without exception beige in color, although that norm appears to be changing.) The fact that Gutenberg's bible and the assortment of drafts and documents rolling out of my laser printer all count as "printed" only goes to show how difficult it can be to speak or write about media with any great precision. This is partly due to the poverty of terminology, but it is also partly due to the persistent if idiosyncratic power of the media concept.

If "print" is tricky, "print culture" is problematic in an entirely different way. As Paula McDowell explains, the term was coined by McLuhan in the 1960s and then earned its broad utility with the 1979 publication of Elizabeth L. Eisenstein's *The Printing Press as an Agent of Change: Communications and Cultural Transformations in Early-Modern Europe*. Eisenstein's version of print culture, which includes a useful critique of McLuhan, has itself been the subject of sustained critique for its apparent suggestion that there is a logic inherent to print—the "soft" determinism, if you will, of calling the printing press itself "an agent of change"—yet even the notion's harshest critics have tended to redefine or reinstall "print culture" rather than reject the idea that there is any such thing.[31] Adrian Johns, for instance, points toward "sources of print culture" that are less technological than social, tracing the "conventions of handling and investing credit in textual materials" that emerged during the sixteenth and seventeenth centuries in Europe—mutual and coincident, as it happens, with the knowledge making of early modern science.[32] For his part, Michael Warner tries to avoid writing of "'print culture,' as though to attribute a teleology to print," while he traces the eighteenth-century development of what he calls "republican print culture" in Anglo-America, which, as it happens, came to double as the logic of the bourgeois public sphere.[33] In both cases print culture is something that developed according to the uses of printing, as those uses became widely shared norms.

Used in this way, the concept of print culture works as a gaping catchall that depends on "the steadily extending social and anthropological use of [the term] *culture*"[34] to suggest a pattern of life structured to some degree by what Warner calls "the cultural meaning of printedness."[35] But how widely, how unanimously, and how continuously can the meanings of printedness be shared, and what exactly are their structuring roles? How best to find out? How would we know? With science and the public sphere as its mutual cousins, print culture starts to seem related in scale to Western modernity itself and thus to jeopardize explanation in all of the same ways that concept does. Jonathan Crary signals some of this jeopardy at the beginning of *Techniques of the Observer: On Vision and Modernity in the Nineteenth Century*, when he writes: "What happens to the observer in the nineteenth century is a process of modernization; he or she is made adequate to a constellation of new events, forces, and institutions that are together loosely and perhaps tautologically definable as 'modernity.'"[36] So print culture and the cultural meanings of printedness risk chasing each other, cart and horse, explanation and *explanandum*, like modernization and modernity.[37]

This is not to deny the importance of printing or to disparage the works of Johns or Warner, on which I gratefully rely. It is only to argue against the use of print culture — or even print cultures, plural, as an analytic set loose from the very specific histories of printing, print publication, regulation, distribution, and circulation.[38] We might likewise be wary of recent claims that "the Age of Print is passing" because "print is no longer the default medium,"[39] a notion promoted in 2009 by none other than the Modern Language Association of America (MLA), which "no longer recognizes a default medium" in the *MLA Handbook for Writers of Research Papers*.[40] (Current MLA style directs researchers to label works cited as "Print" or "Web," as appropriate.) Not only do statements like these tend to reify (to default to?) print as one thing instead of many, but they also impute a generalized cultural logic for print and — by extension — other media, at the same time that they fall back on the old Romantic trick by which Western modernity forever periodizes itself as modern.[41] Better instead to resist any but local and contrastive logics for media; better to look for meanings that arise, shift, and persist according to the uses that media — emergent, dominant, and residual — familiarly have.[42] Better, indeed, to admit that no medium has a single, particular logic, while every genre does and is. The project of this book is to explore media history further, not just by juxtaposing one medium with another but also by working a selective history of one especially capacious genre — the document — across different media.

The histories of genres and the histories of media don't so much overlap as they intersect, constituting partial and mutual conditions for one another. Unless they focus on the political economies of print publication, accounts of written genres usually understate this point, stressing instead the importance of broad social patterns or dwelling on developments in intellectual history. So—thinking about subgenres of the document—the memorandum is descended from the business letter, catalyzed by the managerial revolution of the nineteenth century amid the forgetting of rhetoric; while the passport is descended from the diplomatic letter, catalyzed by modern governmentality and its construction of personal identity.[43] The genres of the credit economy, similarly, emerged within and into a dynamic genre system for "mediating value."[44] Stories like these, it almost goes without saying, involve words and images and an extensive repertoire of techniques (devices, structures, practices—in short, media) for producing and reproducing them for circulation: letterpress printing and typewriting, carbon paper and photocopying, steel and copperplate engraving, photography and lithography, penmanship and rubber stamps, and so on. Media and genre support each other, as shared assumptions evolved amid the proliferation of related instances serve dynamically to underwrite and articulate the know-show function. The genre and its subgenres are recognizable by dint of repetition with variation, conditioned in part—at least in this present extended age of technological reproducibility—by the diverse media of their production and reproduction.

....

The pages that follow begin an inquiry into documents with an episode from their maturity, when the document genre had already flowered into numberless subgenres of increasing variety and specialization, and when its institutional contexts were already legion. Not only did the nineteenth century witness a radical diversification in what counted as writing—think of its many "-graphies"[45]—but the postbellum social order in the United States also became increasingly diversified and bureaucratic, one part Max Weber's iron cage and another part a conflicted jangle of aspirations, allegiances, and demands. It was an extended moment now familiar to media history, when industrial print production and the additional subjectivities of increased literacy and access to print were increasingly supported and framed by photography, phonographs, and the new electronic communications media. Numerous earlier episodes are also fascinating,[46] but starting an inquiry into documents around 1870 helps put the techniques and practices of mechanized textual reproduction and the ever expanding scriptural economy at center stage. The new sonic and electronic media of the late nineteenth century will not cut much of a figure in my account, yet their proliferation was (and is) admittedly what has helped to consolidate "print"—and, eventually, "print culture"—so bluntly as such. Each of the four chapters that follows argues for a more nuanced account of print by attending to the recent history of documents and the means, meanings, and methods of their reproduction in necessary detail.

Chapter 1 operates in a deflationary mode, both by taking up documents and by considering the often neglected work of commercial or "job" printers. Job printing was a specialization that accounted for roughly a third of the printing trades in this period, and for this reason alone its output must have contributed largely to the meanings of letterpress printing (and the by then allied engraving and lithographic processes), even though it does not fit neatly within the framework of "print culture" as print has traditionally been described by the history of communication. Indeed, because nineteenth-century job printing has so seldom been studied on its own in any significant detail, it has never been clear the extent to which job printers sidelined the time-honored subjects and agencies that have come to populate generalizations about print media and the history of the book, including authors, readers, publishers, booksellers, and editors. Considered as an admittedly heterogeneous class, telegram blanks, account book headings, menus, meal tickets, stock certificates, and the welter of other documentary forms that issued in such profusion from jobbing houses in the nineteenth century suggest a corrective addition to—or perhaps an additional negation of—the histories of authorship, reading, and publishing. It would seem that a—maybe even *the*—significant amount of the bread and butter of the printing trades was the printing of documents that were merely printed, not edited or published. These were documents that didn't—as chapter 1 will elaborate—have readers or create readerships, nor did they have authors or entail authorial rights. Nor in many cases were printed documents of this sort produced in the interests of cultural memory or even meant to last for very long, despite the storied self-regard of nineteenth-century printers themselves for printing as "the art preservative of all arts," to use a phrase common in the trade literature.

With some exceptions, the documents produced by job printers in the later nineteenth century were instruments of corporate speech proper to the conduct of businesses of every sort, as well as to the operations of institutions such as schools, churches, voluntary associations, and municipalities. These were contexts in which the know-show function might hinge triply on what documents said, on their format (the size, weight, and folds of the paper on which they were printed), and on their formatting (their layout and typographical design) created by the compositors who set them in type.[47] The meaning of documents thus inheres symbolically, materially, and graphically, according to the contexts in which documents make sense as visible signs and/as material objects.[48] A multitude of forms — some of them literally fill-in-the-blank forms — helped to shape and enable, to define and delimit, the transactions in which they were deployed. In their sheer diversity and multiplicity, documents originating with job printers point toward a period of intense social differentiation, as Americans became subject to a panoply (or, rather, a pan-opoly) of institutions large and small, inspiring a prolific babble of corporate speech. Beyond the simple logic of spheres — public and domestic — job printing indicates an intersecting tangle of transaction, as individuals used printed and written documents variously to negotiate — with greater and lesser success, one must imagine — their everyday relationships to and amid many institutions and institutionalized realms all at once.

Chapter 1 argues for the neglected importance of the jobbing press and its centrality within "the dominion of the document," while describing the extended moment at which printers were about to lose their monopoly on the means of documentary reproduction. Widely recognized to have undergone a process of industrialization in the later nineteenth century, the printing trades also for the first time faced the possibility of competing, amateur print production, as smaller jobbing presses were marketed to young adults and other amateurs. Still more significant competition emerged as part of the so-called managerial revolution, as new imperatives for "control through communication" inspired new labor patterns and new technologies for writing and copying that both dramatically expanded and diversified the scriptural economy.[49] Soon secretaries (edging out clerks) in offices produced and reproduced documents as means of both internal and external communication, working at typewriters and a parade of other mechanical Bartlebies. Rather than dwell on this "control revolution," described so ably by JoAnne Yates, James Beniger, and others,[50] chapter 2 jumps forward in time to the 1930s, when new media for the reproduction of documents — among them photo-offset, mimeograph, hectograph, and microfilm — were celebrated as alternatives to letterpress printing with the potential to transform publishing and publication. Rather than continuing to pursue documents sketchily and speculatively across the increasingly differentiated social order, chapter 2 investigates a single social subsystem in detail. Other scholars have followed documents within specific government bureaucracies, nongovernmental organizations, and modern corporations.[51] I focus instead on the admittedly more diffuse realm of scholarly communication, where enthusiasts noted the power of new media to transform scholarship by changing the ways that documents might be reproduced for circulation. One result of this focus is a turn away from documents that are created to operate in an indexical register that is primarily identitarian — like the travel visa, birth certificate, or theater ticket — and toward the related, vast, and inarticulate arena of un- and semipublication in which documents simultaneously enable and delimit both institutional memory and system-specific or system-oriented communication. This is not a distinction as much as an emphasis, one that helps underscore the increasing scale and diversity of modern institutions.

Whether glimpsed in titles such as Martha Graham's *American Document* (1938) or in the better-known work of documentary photographers sponsored by the Farm Securities Administration or the guidebooks produced by the Federal Writers' Project, the 1930s was a decade of intense "documentary expression," of Americans trying to know and show themselves to themselves.[52] Different documentary forms possessed different "aesthetic ideologies,"[53] while the project of knowing and showing — although scattered and diverse — worked persistently to beg "the question of how [or, indeed, whether] representation can have agency."[54] Could — can — the knowing-showing of social documentary really make a difference? Will documenting an inconvenient truth for public consumption prompt any real action? Against this backdrop of more familiar documentary forms and impulses, chapter 2, like chapter 1, takes a deflationary tack. Instead of pursuing the documentary representations of dance, cinema, theater, or other arts arising — as Michael Denning explores — along the cultural front, this chapter considers the lowly typescript document. Even as feminized secretarial labor remained strangely invisible, a structuring absence,[55] the look of typescript carried important connotations in the 1930s, marking documents that were internal to the workings of business, journalism, corporate and state bureaucracy, education, and scholarship. Typescript documents were unpublished or prepublished, subject to correction, revision, versioning, and obsolescence. Reproducing typescripts, whether by mimeograph, photo-offset, or other means, retained the look of the bureaucratic process and associated secretarial labors, while it also successfully ended the monopoly that printers had so long possessed — the monopoly that had lasted for the four centuries during which print publication had required letterpress printing. Letterpress printing continued, of course, now with the aid of linotype and monotype typecasting machines, but something of the look and distributive functions of print could now be had by other means.

Chapter 2 pursues the work of a committee convened jointly by the American Council of Learned Societies and the Social Science Research Council. The Joint Committee on Materials for Research, as it was eventually called, responded both to the promise of new media for documentary reproduction and to what was widely perceived as a crisis in scholarly communication exacerbated by the Great Depression. More and more intensive specialization across the humanities and social sciences made the publication of scholarly resources unappealing to commercial publishers — readerships were small — at the same time that other avenues for publication were fragile and few amid the global economic downturn. The Joint Committee equated reproduction with access: if the appropriate media of reproduction were deployed, scholars might gain access to necessary source materials, no matter how rare, and they could have better access to each other's works as well. The committee imagined new tools as a solution, but its members saw that structural changes were also required: new responsibilities for librarians and archivists; new cooperation among scholars and publishers; and new technical and institutional structures for the collection, preservation, organization, and dissemination of materials for research. At the same time that the historical profession was worriedly debating its own relevance to American society, the Joint Committee and its president, Robert C. Binkley, were able to imagine everyday Americans as amateur historians and nonprofessional archivists engaged productively in the collective recognition and preservation of the historical record.[56]

The reproduced typescript documents considered in chapter 2 are interesting and important partly because so many of the related concerns — like the ongoing crisis in the humanities and desirable new tools — remain provokingly relevant today. The work of the Joint Committee assumed an implicitly liberal political philosophy that coincided with New Deal reform. Self-improvement abetted social welfare, while the hoped-for transformation of scholarly communication was contradictorily imagined both as the canny evasion of market forces and as a calculated triumph over them. The academy in general and the humanities in particular sought to reject the commercial logic of publishing at the same time that they adopted the language of cost-effectiveness and Fordist coordination and control. New sorts of for-profit publishers—such as University Microfilms International, better known as UMI—would prosper, while state sponsorship and philanthropy helped underwrite—modestly and tenuously—the crucial values of liberal intellectual inquiry. Meanwhile, amateur cultural production appeared ascendant, and popular awareness of documents, documentation, and documentary ran particularly high. Then as now, crisis might harbor opportunity—*might*—if only the path forward were not so variously fraught and so obscure.

Chapter 3 jumps thirty years forward in time to describe a different episode in media history, one that offers some additional points of contrast. Rather than consider documents in a single social subsystem (loosely called "scholarly communication," and its institutions that are discussed in chapter 2), chapter 3 considers documents that transgress the borders between different systems, documents that leak beyond the structures of the scriptural economy designed to maintain secrecy, for instance, or to protect intellectual property at the expense of the public domain. In the place of mimeographed or microfilmed documents, chapter 3 considers the photocopy. It begins by dragging photocopies back into the past. Henry Jenkins and others have celebrated self-published fanzines as an early gesture toward today's online sociability. Like so much Web content, tattered old zines—whether by science fiction fans, East Village poets, or coffeehouse radicals and riot grrls—are evidence of the power and persistence of "grassroots creativity."[57] Yet there is a lot still to learn about the ways that old textual duplication technology stands as an antecedent of today's new participatory media. Chapter 3 seeks to fill in some of the missing details by offering an account not of fans or zines but rather of the xerographic medium so many of them have deployed since the 1960s. What did photocopied documents mean—on their own terms—before the digital media that now frames them as old or analog? It seems clear that tacit knowledge of things digital has worked retrospectively to alter the meanings of xerography, not in the least as a result of technological and corporate convergences and mystifications. Today photocopy machines scan digitally rather than not, while laser printers work xerographically, printing according to the electrostatic principles adapted first for making copies on the photo-copy machines that were originally marketed in 1959.

Like the chapters before it, chapter 3 focuses on a few exemplary — if not exactly typical — human actors, yet unlike them it considers actors who were more clearly concerned with "transverse *tactics*" than with the "tech-nocratic (and scriptural) *strategies*" that their actions inhabit and poten-tially subvert. The tactic-strategy distinction is Michel de Certeau's, born of cultural conditions that he describes in *The Practice of Everyday Life* as a "productivist economy" — capitalism plus mass media — relegating "the non-producers of culture" to a pervasive margin, a silent majority.[58] So-called tactics reside in everyday practices like reading, cooking, or walk-ing, and they work as modest victories or tricks that deviate from the im-posed (strategic) order of an author's meaning, another cook's recipe, or a planner's built environment. In these terms photocopy machines of the 1960s and 1970s became sites of cultural production — of documentary reproduction as cultural production — that were introduced as corporate strategy and yet quickly became broadly available to a multiplicity of tacti-cal uses and users. By focusing on Daniel Ellsberg, who Xeroxed and leaked the Pentagon Papers, and on John Lions, who wrote and Xeroxed a well-known guide to the UNIX operating system, this chapter addresses admit-tedly idiosyncratic users and uses, yet it does so in confidence that idio-syncrasy points inversely if speculatively toward more typical uses and the conditions that structure them.

More clearly than either job printing or scholarly mimeographs and microforms, photocopied documents form the site and substance of mod-ern bureaucracy, part of its strategic repertoire. Ellsberg in particular works as something like a latter-day addition to the colorful cast of historical actors described in Ben Kafka's *The Demon of Writing: Powers and Failures of Paperwork*. Like Charles Hippolyte Labussière, for instance — who is said to have saved hundreds of people from the guillotine by surreptitiously destroying the relevant paperwork during the Reign of Terror — Ellsberg risked much in acting against the Vietnam War. He worked from a position inside the machinery of state — or at least inside the scriptural economy of the military-industrial complex — while he did so in ways that gestured as much toward the contradictory "psychic reality" of bureaucracy, in Kafka's terms, as toward its specific material features.[59] Whereas tactics à la Labus-sière involved the misdirection and destruction of documents, Ellsberg's tactics involved their proliferation through photocopying.

Photocopies emerged within 1960s and 1970s bureaucracy as modest sites of self-possession — one could finally keep one's own files — at the same time that they hinted at the inevitable documentary logic of accountability — copies collected and saved, just in case — that helped beg the question of openness or transparency that proved of particular moment in the era of Watergate and the Vietnam War. Ellsberg aired the Pentagon's dirty laundry, while on and around college and university campuses, other forms of openness prospered. As if in answer — finally — to the Joint Committee's dreams, library materials entered circulation as photocopies, while coursepacks sidestepped commercial publishing. Against this backdrop, the efforts of Lions and others to install and improve the UNIX operating system — a storied chapter in the history of open-source software — connect emerging digital forms with the photocopied documents that aimed to describe them. Computing was in the midst of what Levy calls its "huge step," a conceptual shift from "seeing text just as an *input* to the computer" to text as "the *primary object* of the user's attention."[60] Digital documents and photocopied or otherwise in-house and "gray literature" software manuals emerged as overlapping and mutually defining textual forms, versioned and versioning in a reciprocating interplay.[61] Thus, even if digital media today make it difficult to recuperate the original meanings of xerography, I argue that xerographic copying ironically worked partly in the construction of digital documents as such.

The biggest difference between digital and analog documents, according to Buckland, is that digital documents exist "physically in digital technology as a string of bits, but so does everything else in a digital environment."[62] Digital documents in this sense have no edges. They are materially, bibliographically the same as the windows that they appear in and the programs that manipulate them, so that "any distinctiveness of a document as a physical form" fades away, and "there is no perceptible correlation between the boundaries of the texts we read on a computer and . . . the display itself."[63] Visual cues and interface conventions help make digital documents legible as such, though there is of course a lot more going on than that when we call a document to the screen. Thinking about the digital environment recalls my earlier analogy between genre systems and word search puzzles. Remember, like words hidden in a random grid of letters, genres get picked out contrastively amid a jumble of discourse because of the ways they have been internalized by members of a shared culture. So documents, for instance, are recognized according to the context-dependent structures and practices of knowing-showing. For digital documents—as for digital objects generally—the jumble of discourse isn't a two-dimensional grid as much as a three-dimensional one, the layered and diverse writings that recursively make platforms, operating systems, and applications intelligible to each other in an architecture of processes that works to generate the textual event, the "interface effect," that we recognize on screen.[64]

In turning to consider digital documents, chapter 4 focuses on what Wikipedia as of this writing calls "the de facto standard for printable documents on the web," the PDF file.[65] In doing so it admittedly forecloses two orders of complexity, leaving questions for others to pursue. First, I will not be explicitly concerned with the ontological complexity of digital text—in other words, with the question of what digital text fundamentally is. The answer to that question seems on the face of things far from clear, when one considers that some digital text—"code"—is considered "executable," for instance, or that some electronic circuits are printed and ink conductive.[66] Likewise I will not be explicitly concerned with the mutually transitive relations among medium, format, and genre. The PDF is an interesting digital format partly because it is so completely sutured to the genre of the document: all PDFs are documents, even if all digital documents are not PDFs. It turns out that PDF technology is an outcome of a second, related "huge step" in computing, the "elegant idea" that the texts forming the primary object of the user's attention might be represented not directly as strings of characters or maps of pixel values but indirectly as programs, the execution of which will generate pages of a document either on screen or at the printer.[67] Chapter 4 asks how the know-show function has been mobilized in the design and implementation of the PDF format. What are the assumptions about documents that have been built into PDF technology, and how does using that technology help reinforce or reimagine the document? How is the history of PDFs a history of documents, of paper and paperwork, and how is it also a history of the computational and corporate contexts from which PDF technology emerged? If the PDF format is disparaged as clunky and backward looking—as it is in some circles—what's so new or special or consequential about it? How should we explain its success?

Readers will have gleaned that each of the episodes of media history presented here is concerned with a relatively brief moment in time as well as with events that occurred primarily, although not exclusively, in the United States. This remains the context that I know best as well as the one for which published and archival sources—my documents—have been most readily at hand. The brief chronological windows and the jumps between them represent both a more calculated methodology and a strategic appreciation of media archeological perspectives that have been so productive—and so fashionable—in recent scholarship.[68] I have aimed to make each episode exacting in its detail while also reaping the benefits of its contrastive separation from the other episodes. A contrivance, perhaps, yet one that productively displaces to the level of method the breaks or ruptures in media historical narration that must forever warrant our concerted critical attention: every supposedly new medium is only ever partly so. Being self-conscious about the ways that historical narratives work is essential to media studies, especially because of the reflexive burdens of studying documents by means of documents, for instance, or of understanding media from within an always already mediated realm. As W. J. T. Mitchell puts it, none of us "only think *about* media, we think *in* them," too.[69] Just as Romanticism and its afterglow have had us "dreaming in books" lo these many years—to use Andrew Piper's resonant phrase—so we have been thinking variously in the handwritten, typed, mimeographed, and photocopied document, some of us across generations as well as throughout lifetimes.[70]

Each chapter works by recuperating documentary forms and actors who have been neglected by media studies, arguing by example that the field must consider "little tools of knowledge" in addition to larger, glitzier—that is, more intensively capitalized—forms.[71] Media studies must continue to aim at media, in short, not just "the Media" as such. Organizing chapters partly around unsung and offbeat heroes[72] seconds the work done by Siegfried Zielinski to populate what he terms the "deep time of media" with illuminating dead ends, gee-whizzery, and what-ifs, while it also aligns with Guillory's observation that documents raise "questions about writing in modernity that cannot be answered by asking these question only of figures such as Joyce, Freud, or Heisenberg."[73] One might, it is true, identify certain canonical documents and their authors—the Declaration of Independence? Franz Kafka's office writings? Thomas Edison's papers?—but documents are properly a vernacular form for which Foucault's author function in general does not apply.[74] The compositors, typists, microfilm technicians, and xerographers rendered below may be notable and even noteworthy, but they are hardly authorial in any familiar sense. If I have warmed toward several of my subjects — a talented if hapless printer named Oscar Harpel, an idealistic young historian named Robert C. Binkley, and an antiwar activist named Daniel Ellsberg — this is not to reproduce an old, great-men style of history but rather to deflate it. Harpel, Binkley, and Ellsberg appeal to attention here because each is so charmingly eccentric, if, I argue, revealingly so.

So many of the popular stories we continue to tell ourselves about what we refer to as print are big-boned affairs that rely on gross analogies. McLuhan probably locked this pattern in, with his 1962 account of a "Typographic Man" who is woefully "unready" for the electronic media of his day. Readers today may be shocked at having to slog through so much about classical antiquity and medieval Europe in *The Gutenberg Galaxy*, because McLuhan proceeds with such certainty that letterpress printing in the Renaissance "was an event nearly related to the earlier technology of the phonetic alphabet."[75] The connection starts to seem typological. It has similarly become a commonplace of late to compare the ascendance of digital networks and the World Wide Web with the rapid dissemination of letterpress printing in Renaissance Europe and the supposed emergence of print culture. Clay Shirky, for instance, has suggested that the "mass amateurization of publishing" on the Internet could be likened to the mass amateurization of "literacy after the invention of moveable type."[76] Three analogical revolutions by these lights, one vast historical arc: if one accepts this premise, then the history of the West may be figured as a self-celebrating page, written first in phonetic characters, printed next by movable type, and finally and triumphantly generated and published online. What the media of documents and the fortunes of characters like Harpel, Binkley, and Ellsberg offer instead are a lode of smaller bones to help enrich this tale, and not a little gristle to complicate its tenor. Following documents reveals both the abundant diversity of the scriptural economy and its ever widening scope, as knowing-showing has again and again been worked by new and different means as well as by additional and increasingly diverse actors. Following documents hints further at intricate and proliferating techniques of control, as subjects know and show within and against the demands of an increasingly dense overlay of institutions and institutionalized realms.

ONE

A Short History of _____

In 1894 the *American Dictionary of Printing and Bookmaking* offered examples in its entry on blank books:

> Address-books, bank-books, bankers' cases, bill-books, blotters, books of design, buyers' price-books, card albums, cash-books, check-books, collection-books, composition, exercise and manuscript books, cotton-weight books, day-books, diaries, drawing-books, engineers' field-books, fern and moss albums, flap memorandums, grocers' and butchers' order books, herbariums, hotel registers, indexes, invoice-books, ledgers, letter-copying books, lumber and log tally-books, manifold-books, memorandum-books, miniature blanks, milk-books, money receipts, notes, drafts and receipts, notebooks, order-books, package receipts, pass-books, pencil-books, perpetual diaries, pocket ledgers, portfolios, receiving and discharging books, rent receipts, renewable memorandums, reporters' note-books, roll-books, salesmen's order-books, scrap-books, scratch-books, shipping receipts, shopping-lists, tally-books, travelers' ledgers, trial-balance books, tuck memorandums, two-third books, visiting-books, writing-books and workmen's time-books.[1]

The list points variously to the workplace, marketplace, school, and home, while it belies the assumption that books are for reading. Books like these were for writing, or at least for incremental filling in, filling up. Fillability in some cases suggests a moral economy (diaries and fern and moss albums, for example), and in many others it suggests the cash economy with which nineteenth-century Americans had grown familiar.[2] Filling up evidently helped people locate goods, map transactions, and transfer value, while it also helped them to locate themselves or others within or against the sites, practices, and institutions that helped to structure daily life. Roll-books and workmen's time-books might be the incremental instruments of power — locating as they do the schooled and the laboring — while hotel registers, rent receipts, and visiting-books point toward the varied mobility of subjects who stayed over, resided, or stopped by. Letter-copying books helped businessmen keep at hand the very letters they also sent away, while cotton-weight, milk-, lumber and log tally-books offered space to record one moment — and always again the same moment — in the life cycle of a bulk commodity. Some examples (flap memorandums? two-third books?) are obscure today. The general picture, however, is one of motion — a confusion of mobilities, really — whereby things, value, and people circulate: they move through space and across borders, from and to, out and in; they get caught and kept, or they pause and pass. Moving faster or slower, they also move in time, recorded in increments and thus amid intervals.

Yet for all of the mobilities the list suggests, it also suggests stasis or inertia.[3] Things (cards and fern fronds, for example) and — more typically — records of things stopped forever as they filled the waiting blankness of books like these. Writing is mnemonic, the history of communication tells us; it is preservative. And so are printing and bookmaking: each of the books listed formed a class or category of blank because each catered to the repetition of certain kinds of writing. If writing is preservative, these books preserved preservation. Their design, manufacture, and adoption worked to conserve patterns of inscription and expression. A blank blotter catered to the repetition of inked inscription only — no matter what was written or drawn — but most blank books would have worked however modestly to mold, to direct and delimit expression. Order and invoice books, for instance, like ledgers and daybooks, catered to inscriptions accreted according to the vernacular habits of trade and the long-standing formulas of accountancy. Habits and formulas can change or be changed, of course, but inertia is their defining characteristic. Checkbooks and receipt books called for perfunctory expressions according to legal necessity, or at least according to shared standards of proof attending the transfer of funds ("Pay to the order of _____"). Entries made in exercise books, composition books, and reporters' notebooks would have been far less constrained, less formulaic, yet they too were loosely microgenres, repetitive expressions in some sense shaped according to the inertial norms and obligations that attended the specific settings or callings in which they and the books that contained them were habitually deployed. These blank

FIGURE 1.1. Ruling machine, W. O. Hickok's *Illustrated Catalogue of Ruling Machines &c.* (1875). Courtesy of the New York Public Library.

books were meta-microgenres, one might say, documents establishing the parameters or the rules for entries to be made individually in pencil or ink. Rules, like habits, were broken, of course—as notebooks became scrapbooks, for instance, or as ledgers became the illustrated chronicles of indigenous tribes—but rules there were; that is what made one class of blank book distinguishable from another.

To write of "rules" for filling them up is likely to exaggerate the constraints hinted at or imposed by different types of blank books, but it also appeals obliquely to conditions of their design and manufacture to which it is crucial to remain attuned. Many blank books—though not all—were ruled, their pages lined in expectation of particular uses, as if in standing reserve for the document they are to become. Like blank forms generally, the pages of many blank books had ink on them. That ink—whether applied by a specialized ruling machine (figure 1.1) or printed on a printing press—was paradoxically what made most blanks blank. Each type of blank was designed and manufactured for its own purpose, like a primitive information technology, Martin Campbell-Kelly has suggested, suited to the organization and control of knowledge according to what Charles Babbage—writing in 1835—called "the division of mental labor."[4] Though the first blanks were ancient or medieval documents rather than modern ones, and thus predate printing (think, for example, of papal indulgences[5]), the nineteenth century witnessed a proliferation of preprinted blank forms. The people who designed and deployed them were thinking ahead to their filling in. The labor of filling was divided from the labor of planning what filling was for and directing how filling should happen: a "managerial revolution" wrought in miniature and *avant la lettre*.

Take a quick look at that list again. The sheer diversity of forms — of blank forms or of forms of blank — hints first at the broad purview and intricate specialization of the printing trades in the nineteenth century, but it hints more particularly at the diversity of knowledge work to which job printers and their associates catered. So-called job printing was a porous category used to designate commercial printing on contract — often small jobs — standing in habitual distinction from the periodical press and "book work," in the nineteenth-century printers' argot. Job printers were printers who catered to bureaucracy, knowledge work of and for the state, but also of and for other residual and emerging forms of incorporation. Job printing fed the paperwork addiction of managerial capital, in particular, as it expanded into national and then multinational enterprises. But plenty of the work of job printing had little or nothing to do with the overarching logics of government or the fortunes of the modern corporation. Think of those butchers' order books and rent receipts. Printed forms were documents that inhabited the interstices of American life at a much more mundane level, too, as job printers produced everything from diplomas and playing cards to a profusion of tickets, posters, and labels.

Rather than a thoroughgoing history of blanks from A to Z — or from address-books to workmen's time books — this chapter seeks to sketch preliminarily what such a history might entail and imply. In particular, it raises the question of how blanks, and job-printed documents more generally, may have worked to structure knowledge and instantiate culture in the United States during the second half of the nineteenth century. My title, "A Short History of," alludes to and appreciates a different work on structures of knowledge and the instantiation of culture, Patricia Crain's *The Story of A*, which considers the alphabet and the culturally and historically specific conditions of the acquisition of literacy in the early United States. Just as American children were schooled partly by dint of print genres like alphabet books and spellers, so American adults became subject to a profusion of printed forms in association with institutions of every stripe. Elsewhere Crain describes the ways the word "literacy" itself gets thrown around—in phrases like "literacy acquisition" and "literacy rates"—as the expression of "everything that is left out when one speaks solely of reading and writing." The surplus meanings of the word "literacy" point off the page, toward, "among other things, ideology, culture, identity, power, [and] pleasure."[6] One of the arguments I make here is that the topic of nineteenth-century job printing works in something of the same fashion, or as a sort of inversion, the site of surplus meanings otherwise left out by the history of communication as well as by "print culture studies" or "the history of the book." These last two scholarly subfields are usually organized around accounts of authors, editors, booksellers, publishers, and readers: cohorts notably missing from the world of blanks. Blanks are printed and used, not—as I hope will become clear—authored or read.

Before the nineteenth century job printing was a lucrative staple of the printing house, something that printers like Benjamin Franklin relied on for bread and butter amid newspaper and book work. Later it became a sideline in some cases, for newspaper offices and businesses dependent on printed matter (think of mail-order concerns, for instance, which might produce their own catalogs), but it was also increasingly recognized as a separate or sometimes separable division of the printing trades, a specialized labor practice requiring its own machinery, material, and expertise. The increasing specialization of job printing inspired—and was partly inspired by—innovations in printing technology: smaller iron hand presses, particularly versions of the platen press or "jobber" (after 1850), as well as specialized borders, fonts (especially what are known as display fonts) and furnishings, like the American job case (after 1838).[7] It was perhaps ironic, then, that job printing remained specialized at the end of the century in part because it was not as susceptible as either newspaper or book work to the incursions of linotype and monotype. (At the annual meeting of the International Typographical Union in 1894, the union's president expressed a concern that the affinity among branches of the industry "will be greatly lessened by the reason of the almost total dissimilarity of working methods.")[8] Though I dwell on examples from the 1870s through the 1890s, the best reckoning we have of job printing is from a later time, since the 1904 Census of Manufactures analyzed the size and structure of the printing and publishing industry. The Census Bureau found that the value of newspapers and periodicals produced in the United States represented fully 52 percent of the total for the industry. Job printing accounted for another 30 percent, while books and pamphlets were worth just 11 percent (a mere smidgen of them were literature), leaving 7 percent for other work, like music publishing, lithography, and — in this tally — the manufacture of blank books as distinguished from forms and other job work.[9] Looked at in this light, job printing has been weirdly invisible — a hole in the past the way the budget of the Central Intelligence Agency is a hole in the U.S. balance sheet — despite its giant footprint. Something like a third of this sector of the economy has gone missing from media history, encountered if at all in that most unglamorous and miscellaneous of bibliographical and archival designations, ephemera.

Although the subject of nineteenth-century job printing thus stands to amplify and enrich our knowledge of the history and uses of printing as well as of documents, it may also open some important questions for comparative media studies. Printed blanks point toward tensile connections among media forms. For one thing, they are print artifacts that incite manuscript, as James Green and Peter Stallybrass have noted.[10] For another, the script they incite can be prompted by oral communication, as census enumerators write down on forms what they are told by people, for instance, or as corporate managers — in the name of scientific management — learned in the early twentieth century to direct their underlings on memo blanks with printed headings like "Verbal orders don't go" and "Don't say it, write it." And if blanks help to demonstrate as well as to ensure the continued interdependence of the oral, the written, and the printed, then they also raise questions about the digital. Today blanks are increasingly encountered online, where the interface is often designed to look like nineteenth-century job printing on paper, notwithstanding the data architecture and manipulability that lie behind or beneath that interface. Going still further, Alan Liu has suggested that we might think of every online text object as an already filled-in blank, because of the ways that metadata necessarily direct and delimit (that is, encode) the appearance and behavior of text on screen: Metadata make the blank, and data are poured in.[11] By this account nineteenth-century job printing and its fillable blanks offer a glimpse of an extended history of information, presenting one context (certainly among many) for the supposed distinction between form and content — for the imagination of data as such — on which contemporary experiences of information technology so intuitively rely.

In what follows, I begin by describing nineteenth-century job printing in terms of its missing cohorts, especially readers and authors. Job printing must have escaped our attention for so long partly as a result of these curious fugitives, since without them job printing stands strangely at odds with the usual accounts — familiar schematics by now — of print publication and the bourgeois public sphere, those mutually constitutive formations of the late seventeenth and the eighteenth centuries. Before I can address how job-printed blanks don't fit narratives of the public sphere, however, I should admit and elaborate that there are other printed blanks that do. I refer to the typographic representation of missing indexes — the dates, places, and particularly people who are so ostentatiously not named in English letters of the eighteenth century. Again it would probably be fruitless to search for the precise origins of this kind of blank, but there was fertile ground for such typography in the political satire and pamphleteering of the early century, when authorship — like so much of the literary marketplace — remained in formation. "We are careful never to print a man's name out at length; but, as I do, that of Mr. St — le," Jonathan Swift writes, "although everybody alive knows who I mean."[12] Swift suggests that this is an evasion of authorial liability aimed at dodging prosecution for libel, but common recourse to not printing precisely what was commonly known also served to indicate the presence of potentially libelous statements, calling attention to them.[13] These are nominal blanks in both a modern grammatical sense — they are missing names — and in the contemporary, Swift-era sense that they are not really blank but only virtually so: they are sites of transaction between a knowing author and a knowing reader within the public, published world of print. The same public knowledge that made names supposedly unprintable made them known to all and unnecessary to print, when "all" refers to the selective "everybody" of the public sphere.

Nominal blanks are complicated fictions, one might say, where the author gets to pretend or perform discretion within an elaborate game of "I know you know I know you know I know." Meanwhile the reader gets to identify with the author in the process of identifying the author's referent. Essential to this game are multiple social actors — authors, readers, publishers or booksellers — as well as a corresponding centripetal logic of printedness, the logic whereby publics are self-organized and communities self-imagined by dint of shared experiences of print publication. In short, readers and reading produce readerships. This is the familiarly ritual character of communication in operation; the characters of "I" and "you" enact a drama of shared presence inspired in part by a tacit understanding of the circulations of print.[14] Sounds simple, but it's not.

The fictionality of nominal blanks was complicated, of course, by their appearance in fictional works of the eighteenth and nineteenth centuries. The pamphleteers' fictions of absence become fictional presences, as the same typography works as a fulcrum on which questions of referentiality — and therefore fictionality — turn. This accounts for a lot of the fun in Edgar Allan Poe's "The Purloined Letter" (1845), for example, a story explicitly about "identification" with one's opposite: the author and the reader of a crime. An unnamed narrator — call him "I" — and C. Auguste Dupin receive a visit from "G —, the Prefect of the Parisian police." He is on the trail of the villain, Minister D —, who has purloined a letter and is using it to blackmail a "certain royal personage." Of course plenty of blanks in the story are what one might call elocutionary, not nominal; they suggest pauses in speech rendered in print. When Dupin says, smoking his pipe, "Why — puff, puff — you might — puff, puff," these are elocutionary blanks, here bracketing the onomatopoetic functions of the word "puff" and thus pointing to a complex phonologic field. When G — tells "I" and Dupin about his insanely exhaustive search of D —'s furniture, he notes that "any disorder in the gluing — any unusual gaping of the joints — would have sufficed to ensure detection" of a secret compartment. These are elocutionary blanks, too, with an additionally rebus-like function, since they are gaping joints in the sentence. It's no stretch at all to say that "The Purloined Letter" is about letters — epistles, yes, but also typographic characters, like *D* and *G* and *I*, missing or not, as phonologic, idiographic, and logographic signs, all testament to Poe's intense self-consciousness about what happens on the surface of a written, printed, and reprinted page.[15]

In the end, Dupin manages to purloin the purloined letter — hidden in plain sight — replacing it with a blank sheet he has inscribed with a motto, while D — is momentarily distracted by a crazy man in the street below shooting off blanks. "The pretended lunatic," Dupin says, "was a man in my own pay." The missing letter is located because Dupin has fully identified with — so he says — the "daring, dashing, and discriminating" D —. How could he not? G — and "I," who can't, of course, identify with D —, are both astonished. Dupin takes out a blank checkbook and directs G —

to "fill me up a check" for the reward money. The check is signed, one must imagine, "G—," by a fictional character who is not allowed to know his own name in full because he doesn't have one.[16] "The indirect lighting" of narration, as Jacques Derrida puts it,[17] doesn't let the reader glimpse a signature. The nominal blanks of fictions like Poe's are nominal primarily in the grammatical sense that they work as names. They are otherwise non-referential—they do not refer to actual people the way Jonathan Swift's blanks do—except to the extent that their typographic presence is itself a reference to the sort of referential practices that writers of the eighteenth century made such a commonplace. (They don't refer to names, that is; rather, they refer to referring to names.) Nominal blanks may offer a complicated fiction in political satire and critique, but in fiction they point toward the real world without entirely arriving there. When truth inhabits fiction, Derrida asks, does it "make fiction true or truth fictive?"[18]

I'm suggesting in part that there is an unnoticed typographical register—hidden in plain sight—to the deconstructions of Poe's tale offered in turn by Jacques Lacan, Derrida, and Barbara Johnson, for all of whom there is a metaphorical blankness at the center of things—the eponymous purloined letter, for one—but not a printed blank as such.[19] To the extent that other scholars have focused on Poe's typography, they redirect attention toward the marketplace for print. As Meredith McGill notes, "Poe's minimal use of temporal markers," like his typically vague settings and other habits of abstraction, often "seems like a careful attempt to hold open a tale's potential field of address."[20] The events of "The Purloined Letter," its narrator reports, happened "in the autumn of 18—." Such openness may have helped get Poe's tales and poems (including lyrics such as "To _____") published, and they would not have hindered getting them republished, effectively providing Poe with a flexible or "mobile form of capital."[21] Seen in this light, the typography of "The Purloined Letter" does work something like the typography of a job-printed checkbook, since both facilitate monetary exchange. One difference is that Poe's typography works in part because his blanks can't be definitively filled in, while a checkbook works presumably because its blanks can be. More, the hectic "culture of reprinting" that McGill illuminates hints at a countervailing centrifugal logic for printedness in tension with the centripetal genesis of the public sphere, a logic whereby different readers and readerships may not have been drawn together as much as they were held apart in the varied experience of respective situations and localities.[22]

My purpose in these pages cannot be to argue on behalf of either the centrifugal or the centripetal vectors of force discerned in recent accounts of American letters. Did print circulation of the nineteenth century work to pull Americans together into a single conceptual realm, an imagined community, or did it work to hold or push them apart along sectional or other lines? My suspicion is that there are better questions to ask, particularly about the postbellum era, both because job printing reveals structures of a much finer and more pedestrian grain and because job printing offers a glimpse of pull and push — of Jürgen Habermas and Niklas Luhmann, one might say — that may more accurately reflect the complexities of nineteenth-century life. Apart from public or counterpublic, nation or region, nineteenth-century job printing served — and thereby entailed and articulated — the functional sites and institutions of daily life, among them settings like the marketplace, workplace, and municipality, as well as organizations like the company, the voluntary and trade association, the church, and the school.[23] Increasingly differentiated and diverse sites and institutions such as these were organized in part by the inter- and intramural circulation of documents, written notes, and printed jobs, and thus by the elements of petty bureaucracy that form a systemic integument of sorts for the associated circulations of things, value, and people with which this chapter suggestively began.

By dividing mental labor, blanks make bureaucracy, directing and delimiting fill-in entries that form the incremental expressions of the modern, bureaucratic self. And it should be clear that, as the instruments of innumerable petty bureaucracies, blank forms and other job printing, like paperwork generally, cannot inspire the sorts of readerly subjectivity that Poe — through Dupin — calls "identification" and "identifying with." Indeed, who ever really reads receipts, bills, tickets, bonds, or certificates? Yes, there is writing printed on them, and filling in blanks requires attention to prompts, but their textual qualities have become "naturalized" through the social processes that have made them useful as the impersonal instruments they are, so that the printing on them "has seemed to disappear."[24] They wouldn't function if they didn't have printing on them, yet few people would describe their functioning in terms of reading, unless in the context of controversy, where a counterfeit is discovered or a lawsuit seems likely; then both reading and forensic analysis enter the picture.[25] Notably, whatever reading is entailed by genres like bills of lading and stock transfers, it is not reading that has very much to do with the sort of readerly subjectivity that came to such special prominence in the course of the eighteenth and nineteenth centuries, the subjectivities of literature in general and the novel in particular. Nor can genres like these strictly be said to have inspired identification among communities of readers in the way that newspapers are said to have done because of the ritualized character of their consumption.[26] Job-printed forms didn't have readers, then; they had users instead. Users have subjectivities too, without question, but they are not exactly readerly ones.

Blank forms work on their face to rationalize work, but they are also one small part of the way that bureaucracy assumes an objective character. Bureaucracy, Max Weber writes, "is increasingly perfected the more it becomes objectified or 'dehumanized.'" Bureaucracy works through what Weber calls "the successful exclusion of love, hate and all of the purely personal, irrational, and emotional elements to which calculation is alien."[27] Because blank forms help routinize, they dehumanize. Agency, as Ben Kafka puts it, gets "refracted through the medium" of paperwork,[28] and along the way, affect drops out. Filling in blank forms offers a kind of negative supplement to what Michael Hardt generalizes as "immaterial labor" of the "affective" sort.[29] When a nurse or doctor annotates a patient's chart—a form of blank that dates to the mid-nineteenth century—she or he turns away from the affective labor of health care to the documents that help medicine reduce phenomena to data and treatment to bureaucracy. The medical professional identifies with her or his patient—one hopes—but the medical chart merely objectifies the patient. When practitioners insist, as some do today, that the paper chart is an instrument of subjective identification, it is usually a way of condemning digital charts as the ultimate objectification, a contrast reminiscent of Darren Wershler-Henry's observation that "once, typewriting symbolized all that was antithetical to poetry; it was cold, mechanical, awkward. Now, however, through the misty lens of nostalgia . . . we believe that typewriting *is* poetry: precise, clean, elegant in its minimalism."[30]

Even blank forms that have to do with identity do not entail identification. Identifying oneself on a form may involve a modicum of self-possession, even uncomfortably self-divided self-possession—as when checking a box for one and only one race, gender, or religion—but it typically doesn't involve an affective relationship with bureaucracy. One doesn't identify with the bank to write a check, or with the Department of Motor Vehicles to get a driver's license, or with the insurance company to file a claim. Chat with a teller, mollify the clerk, and commiserate with the agent—by all means—but that's precisely what one doesn't do on paper, filling in the blanks. The drama of shared presence has become a drama of solicitation, if not subordination. The game of "I know you know I know you know" played or gestured toward by the authors, publishers, and readers of nominal blanks cannot happen in settings such as these, because the bank, the Department of Motor Vehicles, and the insurance company do not know what their clients know. They are "they," endowed with agency in part according to the bureaucratic processes of knowing that they don't have the information they need. Filling in and filing away are the ways that bureaucracies collect and connect; like the micrologics of enclosure and attachment, they are part of a repertoire of techniques through which bureaucracies come to know.

Admittedly, it is difficult to generalize, particularly about blanks. Taking the example of letterhead, for instance, where is the line between letterhead and stationery, between a blank and (blank) paper? How does using official letterhead work like filling in a blank form, and how may it work differently? Because letterhead is for official use only, many bureaucracies have spelled out policy statements. The U.S. House Committee on Standards of Official Conduct even offers some Poe-eque examples for members of the U.S. Congress, who are not allowed to use congressional letterhead for personal business: "Example 18. A social acquaintance of Member E, who has not previously worked with E in any official capacity, asks E to write a letter of recommendation to Federal Agency in support of his application for a competitive service position. E may prepare a letter of recommendation but must do so on personal stationery."[31] Personal stationery by dint of being personal is not the same as letterhead. This is perhaps less about what's printed at the top of letterhead than it is about the bureaucratic frame of its authorization. Stationery too can include preprinted elements, as of course do greeting cards. Sending a personal letter or a birthday card certainly involves the subjective identification of sender and recipient. Still, stationery and greeting cards also work as blank forms, at least to the extent—however modest—that senders have been purchasers who therefore supplement an impulse of subjective identification with another of commercial relations.[32] The ultimate implication of this—that the blank paper you buy is always at some low level a blank, meaningful in triangulation with you, your writing, and a paper mill or stationery store—is probably not all that useful. Though it is possible to find letter writers like Emily

Dickinson who pause self-consciously to consider "the man who makes sheets of paper," most writers understandably remain oblivious.[33]

To look at the same subject from a slightly different vantage point, even the fact that there's something printed on a blank might not be the thing that makes it one. When Great Britain imposed a stamp tax on its American colonies in 1765, it sought to control many uses of paper — everything from almanacs to bills of lading, from liquor licenses to newspapers, from diplomas to playing cards. For these purposes colonists were required to use paper that was specially stamped: blank paper turned into blanks, interpellated within the bureaucratic purse strings of an imperial regime. The tax was a hardship, particularly for publishers. When stamped paper arrived in Boston in February 1766 it was paraded through the streets, declared guilty at a mock trial, strung up on a "tree of liberty," and then burned to death.[34] Bureaucracies objectify in part by controlling and mobilizing blanks, but that's not to say that blanks can't inspire real passions.

There were at least two arguments about blanks that made it all the way to the U.S. Supreme Court during the nineteenth century. One involved telegram blanks and Western Union's practice of indemnifying itself in what later came to be called "the fine print." Senders handwrote telegraphic messages on blanks for transmission, and telegraph offices handwrote messages on blanks for delivery to recipients. Both ends used preprinted forms that disclaimed — lawfully, as it turned out — liability for garbled messages.[35] Those blanks offer an interesting prehistory for EULA (end user license agreement) of today, since one had to opt in to send a telegram the way one has to opt in to use — or, in many cases, buy — the software being licensed. It's a yes-or-no question that one can't really say no to. Or, crucially, it's a yes-or-no question to which one can't answer, "Yes, but. . . ."[36]

The other Supreme Court case involved blank bookkeeping forms and cuts a grander figure in American legal history. All counties in Ohio were required to have auditors and treasurers to keep orderly accounts of receipts and disbursements, and Charles Selden from Cincinnati came up with his own system for doing so. He received copyrights for *Selden's Condensed Ledger, Or, Bookkeeping Simplified* (published in 1859) and several related texts. His system offered a way to cut down on the cumbersome back-and-forth between bound ledgers and journals by locating accounts and transactions on facing pages of the same little book. He invented a set of blank forms and described how to use them. Things went well for a while, it seems: Selden promoted his system to counties in Ohio and Indiana, and there were plenty of takers. His home county of Hamilton even licensed the system, paying $6,600 for twelve years. The abolitionist, spiritualist, and well-known reformer Robert Dale Owen wrote a pamphlet with Selden vaunting the benefits of the system, which were "moral as well as pecuniary." It saved time and money, yes, but it also gave such a clear and transparent accounting that it was bound to reduce the graft that so threatened "to sap by slow degrees the very foundations of our government fabric."[37] In fact, *Selden's Condensed Ledger* was such an "aid in correcting public morals" that Owen and Selden announced their intention to depart shortly for Washington, D.C., in order to promote the system to Congress.[38]

It is unknown whether they went through with this plan. The pamphlet is dated a month before the surrender of General Robert E. Lee at Appomattox and the assassination of President Abraham Lincoln. Owen was in Washington the following spring helping to draft the Fourteenth Amendment, but Selden's whereabouts remain obscure. He died in Indianapolis in 1871. Meanwhile, a bookkeeper named William C. M. Baker was promoting a rival set of blank forms in counties across Ohio. Some counties switched from *Selden's Condensed Ledger* to *Baker's Register of Receipts and Disbursements*. In 1872 Selden's widow, Elizabeth, sued Baker for copyright infringement.

The case—on appeal it was named *Baker v. Selden*—is important in American copyright law as the origin of what lawyers call the idea-expression dichotomy. Ideas are free to all; a copyright protects not the ideas, but the way they are expressed.[39] Or, as Justice Joseph Bradley held, "the use of [an] art is a totally different thing from a publication of [a] book explaining it"; "the description of [an] art in a book, though entitled to the benefit of copyright, lays no foundation for an exclusive claim to the art itself." One can copyright a manual on how to do something (an expression), but that doesn't make one the owner of doing that thing (the idea). The confusion here had arisen because Selden's "art" or idea was a method of bookkeeping, so "the illustrations and diagrams employed [in his description] happen to correspond more closely than usual with the actual work performed by the operator who uses the art." The manual for doing something included the actual instrument used to do it. Selden had described his method of bookkeeping. His copyright was for the description, the court said, not the method. Sorry, Mrs. Selden, blanks don't have authors.[40]

During the original trial both sides had presented testimony and affidavits from bookkeepers. Those using Baker's forms preferred them to Selden's, and those using Selden's forms preferred them to Baker's—even though the forces of Selden were wont to argue that Baker's forms were too close a copy of Selden's. Different witnesses dilated differently on similarities and differences between the two systems and the forms they used. Into this demimonde of county functionaries and green eyeshades entered one stooge. E. F. Williams, a witness for Baker, was a thirty-four-year-old "ruler of blank books" at a bookbindery and job house in Columbus, Ohio. He called himself "an expert in the business of ruling." He testified that Baker's and Selden's forms were not alike: "They are of a different pattern." But when he was pressed to explain what, in the trade, is considered the same pattern, he answered, "If they are both alike they are the same." With some difficulty Baker's attorney was able to determine that two forms are "the same" if the arrangement and number of columns are the same, but that the width of the columns—the amount of blank space—was incidental, and the specific wording of column heads might not matter either. In cross-examination, Selden's attorney caught Williams out in an exaggeration about the extent of his experience as a ruler and then got him to admit that if he had to use the forms he ruled, he "probably could not fill them up."[41] Apparently one did not have to understand anything but ruling in order to rule.

If the *Baker v. Selden* decision created the idea-expression dichotomy by locating its nebulous frontier—where blank forms are the incidental yet strangely instrumental illustrations of the idea of their own filling in—then the Williams testimony was a tonic in its simplicity. Like the court, Williams inhabited with full confidence the "distinction between the book as such and the art which it is intended to illustrate." Selden may have vaunted his accounting system as self-explanatory, but Williams ruled blanks without understanding how they were to be filled in, or filled up.[42]

Williams's testimony also offers a reminder of the obvious, that from the perspective of bookkeepers and other users, blanks are filled in or not, labored over or left blank; but from the perspective of printers, rulers, and their paying customers, blanks are always the calculated result of labor. Notably, at the job printer's office there was little need to distinguish blanks from other jobs. The *American Dictionary of Printing and Book-making* lists some of the most common types of job work:

> Account-book headings, ball tickets, bank notices, bonds and coupons, billheads, bills of lading, bills of fare, blank-books, business cards, cer-

tificates of deposit, certificates of stock, checks, commutation tickets, deposit tickets, drafts and notes, printed envelopes, election tickets, fare tariffs, handbills, hotel registers, indexes, inland bills of lading, insurance notices, labels, law blanks, leaflets, letter-circulars, letter headings, manifests, memorandum billheads, money receipts, monthly statements, newspapers, note circulars, note headings, order-books, orders of dancing, pamphlets, pamphlet covers, passage tickets, programmes, price currents, policies, posters, railroad blanks, restaurant tickets, shipping cards, shipping receipts, show-cards, time-tables, transfers of stock, working lists, wedding cards and wrappers.[43]

There are blanks and plenty of nonblanks in this list. Whether the job in question was a run of blank billheads or a set of (not blank) business cards, job printing, as the *Dictionary* puts it, "is very much more open than either book or newspaper work. . . . There are great blanks scattered through much of it." The same authority observes that "bountiful provision should be made for slugs, leads and metal furniture thus required, as well as for brass rule."[44] Brass rule was used for making borders and ruling blanks on the job press. Furniture was the term of art for pieces of wood or metal used to fill "blank spaces both within the matter itself and between the matter and the sides of the chase."[45] That is, when printers set type (the "matter") and then made up what they called the forme or form, they had to put in spacers — the "furniture" — to create blank space in and around the ultimate printed material. Job printing involved a lot of "fat," or "phat" as typographers had it: in a trade where many workers were paid according to the amount of copy they set in type, job work involved a lot of juicy — that is, bulky — elements, often with big, em*phat*ic typefaces that could be rapidly set.[46]

Any space within the printed page is — effectively — printed, the result of specific labors in composition, imposition, and presswork. Each specialization of letterpress printing involved a different balance of concerns and a different spatial economy. Job printers filled up space with furniture, while in newspaper work an editor might be anxious to fill up space with copy. There's a moment in one of William Dean Howells's novels about publishing, *The World of Chance* (1893), in which the main character — having failed to get his Great American Novel published — swallows the cold hard facts: "His career as an author was at an end; he must look for some sort of newspaper work; he ought to be very glad if he could get something to do as a space man."[47] He gets hackwork and is paid to write filler by the column inch.

The niceties of job printing point toward a whole cluster of highly specialized labor practices behind the scenes as well as to the fact that the items printed were obviously tailored to different, specialized labors of almost infinite variety. Indeed, we might speculate that job-printing offices in the nineteenth century played something of the same role in the maturation of modern bureaucracy that machine-tool manufacturers played in the maturation of mass production. (Machine tools are the task-specific machines used in manufacturing.) According to historians of technology, "the machine tool industry was the main transmission center for the transfer of new skills and techniques" among industries in the important machine-making sector of the economy: firms that made firearms, sewing machines, typewriters, bicycles, and eventually automobiles. Production techniques that were developed in one industry spread to other industries when people changed jobs, and also when machine-tool makers transferred their own developing expertise among their customers.[48] So too the job printer — like the scientific management guru in the twentieth century[49] — must have served as a locus of transmission, where the designs and genres produced for one client might inform the work produced for another. "Printers are rapidly educating the business community," the trade magazine *Printers' Circular* noted hopefully in 1870.[50] That claim may be impossible to prove, but the coherence of job printing as a specialty in a sense testifies to the emerging coherence of bureaucratic methods within the broader cultural economy. The increasing use of standardized forms throughout this period has been widely remarked, yet the multivalent agencies of standardization remain largely unspecified.

The speculative resemblance of machine tools and job printing may even be pushed a little further, since by one measure they formed part, respectively, of the first- and second-largest industries in America that were oriented toward specialty production: "Printing and Publishing" and "Foundry and Machine Shops," as the U.S. Census of Manufactures designated them.[51] Though standardization in general and standardized mass production in particular — the assembly line — have long captured the attention of economic historians and management consultants, specialty production — custom or batch manufacturing — was still a common approach to production in the nineteenth century, and it was *the* approach that ultimately enabled standardized mass production to emerge as the paradigmatic mode of industry in the twentieth century. Printed forms and machine tools could not be manufactured assembly-line style; they were made to order in batches of varying size. Rather, it was *using* forms and *using* machine tools that introduced or increased standardization. Specialty manufacturing was manifestly diverse, really a whole "battery of production approaches ubiquitous in postbellum America," according to Philip Scranton.[52] Yet specialist producers shared certain characteristics, particularly when burdened with fixed costs in similar proportions. Both printers and machinists would have "utilized extensive contracting networks, rather than investing in integrated production. They shed labor or shortened hours in slow periods and ran overtime when orders jammed their ledgers." For businesses like these, "there was no better location than an urban industrial district filled with firms practicing comparable strategies."[53] Despite their obvious differences, then, the products of foundries and job-printing offices — machine tools and "little tools of knowledge"[54] — had much in common.

....

Trade literature helps to render job printing with greater specificity than generalizations about production can allow, and the remainder of this chapter considers specimen books published by the job printers Oscar H. Harpel and John L. Phillips, using them to glimpse the fascinating and checkered career of Harpel, in particular. *Harpel's Typograph, Or Book of Specimens* (1870) and Phillips's *"The Art Preservative"* (1875) are both framed as works of pedagogy, modeled after earlier generations of printers' manuals.[55] In their elaborate subtitles, Harpel's book is explicitly "Arranged for the Assistance of Master Printers, Amateurs, Apprentices, and Others" (figure 1.2) and Phillips's is "for the Use of Job Printers and Apprentices." Front and back matter offer instructional material, while the center — and bulk — of each volume contains specimens of job printing ostensibly collected and compiled "in the regular run of work," as Phillips puts it, and "in the order of their occurrence" at the shop, Harpel explains, because "the necessity to use the material in the type forms [while they were standing, prevented] the possibility of systematic arrangement." The happenstance accumulation of job work is thus vested with renewed purpose, the stated purpose of educating job printers in fine or fancy work, as well as an implied purpose of providing potential customers with samples to which to refer. In printing, the term "specimen books" usually refers to the catalogs

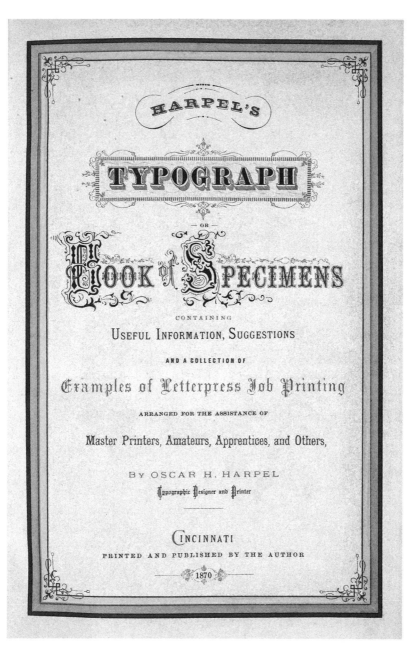

FIGURE 1.2. Title page in four colors and many typefaces, Oscar H. Harpel, *Harpel's Typograph* (1870), courtesy of the American Antiquarian Society.

of type founders, who offered different fonts and supplies to the trade. Harpel and Phillips likewise addressed themselves to the trade, but to the extent that their printed specimens worked as goods or services on offer, both of their books were also aimed at employees who might execute jobs and customers who might commission them. It is so much easier and less annoying than "verbal instruction," Harpel notes, to have "a convenient means of reference at hand."[56] The *Typograph*—better known and more widely circulated by far than Phillips's book—had the even grander purpose of representing American excellence in printing. It won a rare medal for "good taste" at the international exposition held at Vienna in 1873.[57]

The *Typograph* and *"The Art Preservative"* are weird books. Blank books notwithstanding, job printing stood in distinction from book work, so that a codex formed from the regular work of a job printer and published on the open market represents a contradiction in terms. The three specializations in nineteenth-century printing—job work, book work, and newspapers and periodicals—overlapped in intricate ways: novels were first serialized in the periodical press and then published as books; newspapers could do job printing on the side, and job printers might be hired to print a publisher's books or periodicals. (In the nineteenth century the U.S. Bureau of the Census divided the industry it called "Printing and Publishing" into four sectors, probably for this reason: book, newspaper, job, and "not specified.") But for a job printer himself to publish something (rather than just print) was atypical, and to assemble individual specimens as a codex was anomalous, reminiscent of specimen books used to sell type, sample books used to sell stationery, dummies used to sell books by subscription, or scrapbooks compiled by readers. As such, the codex form of the *Typograph* and *"The Art Preservative"* serves to countermand the habitual ephemerality of job printing: Books are for keeps, but job printing—if it survives—tends to reside in collections of ephemera, the "minor transient documents of everyday life."[58] Like the paradox of describing surviving documents in relation to their transience, the *Typograph* preserves an ephemerality it thereby refutes.

And if the codex form of these works is peculiar, so is their substance. When it came to specimens, neither Harpel nor Phillips was responsible for his own copy—that is, the matter they set in type—though both exerted control over innumerable details of layout and design, working within constraints that are impossible to identify in retrospect. Which spacing, which fonts, and which colors were the printers' choices and which the customers' choices? Which were nonchoices dictated by certain documentary subgenres or formats—because that's what an invoice looks like, for instance—or other habits and imperatives of the trade? Indeed, the "content" of these books is difficult to identify because of the ways that their codex form occludes the habitual formats of the job printer. What do these books actually contain? Certainly not the book plates, cards, dodgers (small handbills), and envelopes that Harpel's index of specimens lists: in producing sheets to be bound into books, Harpel and Phillips separated their impressions from the usual paper or card stock of job printing. There are no book plates or envelopes in these books, only printing ink that would have marked and made them functional. The specimens as such rest on top of the paper, calling attention to its surface with the delicacy of their impressions. They are unused, unusable specimens of ink shaped by specimens of labor. They adhere to the pages of these books in the way that dead butterflies might be pinned gently to a board.

As specimens of specialized labor, the items compiled in these books are particularly obscure in retrospect, as they would have been to any but Harpel's and Phillips's associates in the trade. The instructional material that surrounds the specimens identifies the labor involved, but—as the presence of specimens itself attests—can hardly be sufficient to explain it. (This is another version of Mrs. Selden's lament.) And even if knowledgeable users of these books could figure out what was done, knowing who did it was another matter. By Harpel's own report, the *Typograph* required 476,000 impressions on his Globe "half-medium" press "to complete less than three thousand copies of the book." Harpel styles himself a "typographic designer and printer" on the title page, noting that the book, for which he claimed copyright, was "printed and published by the author." Yet in the end he acknowledges "presswork, under the supervision of Mr. David Cohen," as well as other employees for "much patient extra manipulation" and composition while he also acknowledges the contributions of many people outside of his employ, "for much intricate mitring [*sic*]," engraving work, electrotyping, and various "cuts," and special care in binding, the supply of inks, and so forth.[59] These books were showing the trade to the trade, showing how good relief printing—even in color and as opposed to lithography—could be, "to promote the interests of all concerned."[60]

More particularly, the specimens that Harpel and Phillips offered were specimens of their own discernment, both as knowing constituents of the trade and as compositors (figure 1.3). They had the unique fortune (or mis-

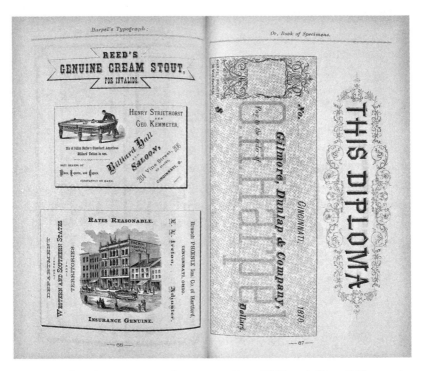

FIGURE 1.3. Sample specimens on facing pages, Oscar H. Harpel, *Harpel's Typograph* (1870), courtesy of the American Antiquarian Society.

fortune?) to be working in the extended moment before the concept of "graphic design" existed. As Harpel hyped his book, the *Typograph* was "fresh, elegant, demonstrative of new ideas, thoroughly practical for utilitarian purposes, and, at the same time, fit to be preserved in any library."[61] It was original and ornamental, but not art in any modern sense. When the *Printers' Circular* celebrated Harpel's "art," just as when John L. Phillips entitled his specimen book *"The Art Preservative,"* it followed nineteenth-century usage in which "art" meant what today we call "craft," and the fineness of the "art" denotes both a level of skill and one of taste, along with the showiness of their mutual elaboration. When Harpel died in 1881 at the age of fifty-three, obituaries appearing across the country noted his excellent taste and all that he had done to raise "job printing to a fine art." His work was "of a fine, or perhaps it may be said a fancy character"; the *Typograph* was called "suggestive, progressive, and elaborate," though at the time of his death Harpel was out of the business, having declined to compete "in the suicidal warfare with 'cheap and nasty' work, which [had] latterly become so universal."[62] The subsequent Arts and Crafts movement and sympathetic modern eyes would soon react equally against the "fancy" and the "cheap and nasty." With all the benefits of hindsight — and of Modernism — *Harpel's Typograph* is an artifact of an overwrought, unreasoned aesthetic, a time capsule of unnecessary curlicues, clashing display fonts, and other technical gimcracks, all executed with extraordinary — indeed, by now unfathomable — skill.[63] Where Harpel was an artist in something like the modern sense — as the author of several lyrics in a collection he made of the *Poets and Poetry of Printerdom* — his work now seems just as dated, only through somewhat different cultural channels.

If *Harpel's Typograph* is very much of its time, it is also of its place. In 1870 Cincinnati was the industrial powerhouse and largest population center in Ohio, a hotbed of bookkeeping systems, shorthand promoters, and other schemes and schemers. With more than a quarter of a million residents, the city had just been eclipsed in size by St. Louis and Chicago in the decade after 1860. Meatpacking was the chief industry in Cincinnati — known as "Porkopolis" — which produced some $9.2 million worth of pork products in 1870. (Hog butchery was also the leading industry in Cook County, the home of Chicago, already producing $19.2 million worth of products.) It was far from the only industry, however; the census reveals an economy that was both robust and diverse, with something of a specialty in machine tools. Cincinnati's printing and publishing sector was split into job printing (twenty-seven establishments) and "not specified" (twenty-two establishments), with a total value of goods produced of approximately $2.7 million. This does not include lithography, bookbindery, and other allied trades. (Chicago, in contrast, had job, newspaper, book, and "not specified" printing and publishing, producing just $2.2 million worth of products.) Harpel was one of sixty-seven individual "Book and Job" printers listed in *Williams' Cincinnati Directory* for 1870, all of them clustered within a short walk of one another downtown. Eight of them were job-printing offices run by the city's daily newspapers — there were six papers in English and two in German.[64]

These details are important because *Harpel's Typograph* speaks so powerfully of the geographies of job printing. It contains approximately 311 specimens printed on 232 numbered pages, with additional unnumbered pages tipped in. (The number of specimens is approximate because of clusters, multiples, and impressions meant to form a unified recto and verso pair.) There are only three specimens in German and nothing to do with hog butchery, yet 74 percent of the specimens that include information about the location of the business for which they were printed (or for which the city directory establishes a location) are from Cincinnati and its environs. This number is probably lower than the norm for job printing due to an accident during the book's production.[65] In comparison, *"The Art Preservative"* was printed in Springfield, the capital of Illinois, and of the specimens it contains that include information about the location of the business for which they were printed, 91 percent are from Springfield; only one out of Phillips's 125 specimens gives a location outside Illinois.[66] Job printing was an intensely local business. If Harpel could walk easily to the shops of all his Cincinnati competitors, he could also walk easily to the shops or offices of the vast majority of his clients, and the same was likely true for his competitors and the clientele that they served. Typical for specialty production though it may have been, this organization all but ensured intense price competition and tiny profit margins. Harpel's several fulminations on the subject of price suggest that his business suffered on this score. He decried "the greed of incompetent parties" and "the suicidal disposition to underbid," even as he sought to differentiate himself from his competitors as a man of particular taste and accomplishment.[67] Like others, Harpel thought the trade should establish prices, but he also hoped that quality would pay.[68]

Rubbing elbows in Cincinnati is not the only geography that *Harpel's Typograph* entails, however. A number of Harpel's repeat clients were local agents for insurance companies from Hartford, Connecticut, and Cincinnati distributors or dealers for other out-of-town concerns. In short, the intense localism of job printing was framed by the extra- and inter-local growth of the modern corporation — of regional, national, and global markets as well as the nascent entertainment industry, since touring amusements needed tickets, programs, handbills, and posters. Even job printing that did not directly express relations between the local and extra-local participated in that idea, to appeal again to the idea-expression dichotomy. A job printer's billheads, checks, bookkeeping forms, envelopes, and labels may typically have borne (that is, expressed) local street addresses, but they were intended as instruments within the broader commercial economy in which local concerns participated, to be filled in with far-flung transactions (in the case of bookkeeping forms) or circulated to enact them (in the case of checks, bills, envelopes, tags, and labels). Just as *Harpel's Typograph* preserves an ephemerality it thereby refutes, Harpel's many Cincinnati specimens testify to a localism that they were designed partly to transcend. These complex geographies of job printing were unique if nonetheless related to the intricate geographies of American newspapers. Both were emphatically local, yet each marked and was differently marked by the extra-local. Newspapers juxtapose local and nonlocal content, of course, while in the immediate antebellum years patent insides (sheets sold to local papers with some nonlocal content preprinted on them) and the beginnings of syndication emerged as extra-local sources beyond the already familiar exchange desk (reprinting items from other papers across the country), out-of-town correspondents, and telegraphic or wire service reports.

At the same time that job printing offered a powerful local index of and local instrument for extra-local forces, printers exemplified the sorts of commercial relations that their products indexed and instrumentalized. Harpel included a small separate section of advertisements, half- and full-page notices for fifteen concerns that had supported his efforts—five of which were companies in Cincinnati and ten of which were spread across the country—involved in the manufacture or sale of printing presses and printing supplies, including type, ink, paper, rollers, glue, and printing-house furnishings. The existence of a national market for producer goods like these and the existence of trade papers like the Philadelphia-based *Typographic Advertiser* (founded in 1857) and *Printers' Circular* (1866) and the Chicago-based *Inland Printer* (1883) hint at an emerging nationwide printing and publishing industry, which the Census Bureau clearly sought to encapsulate and the International Typographical Union sought to organize.[69] Printing-house labor was still marked by a high degree of itinerancy—this was the age of the fabled "tramp" printer—so that even apart from the printed materials produced, printers' supplies, printers' literature, and printers' labor circulated effectively to produce a coherent trade, a partly imagined and partly enacted integration of localities according to both ideology and economics. Harpel—who had worked in Philadelphia, Baltimore, Wilmington, St. Louis, and Galveston before Cincinnati—called it "Printerdom" when he entitled his 1875 anthology *Poets and Poetry of Printerdom*. If Benedict Anderson's "print capitalism" gestures toward the efficacies of print circulation in the centripetal construction of a national and nationalist consciousness, then "printerdom" is its trade practice. Harpel's coinage gestures toward the efficacies of print production—not just circulation—in the construction of an occupational consciousness. That consciousness was powerfully marked by class as well as gender and race, but "printerdom" included members of the bourgeois like Horace Greeley as well as strivers like Harpel. (Greeley was among the "poets of printerdom" whom Harpel anthologized.)

It is difficult to judge with any precision how typical or atypical Harpel may have been as a job printer. Despite the success of his *Typograph*, he was out of business by sometime in 1875, and a projected sequel to *Poets and Poetry of Printerdom*—titled "Inside Glimpses of Printerdom"—never appeared.[70] Surviving records of one of Harpel's contemporaries in Worcester, Massachusetts, offer some additional context and a point of contrast. Unlike Harpel, Charles Hamilton was hardly itinerant. Born the same year as Harpel, in Barre, Massachusetts, Hamilton did his apprenticeship in Worcester, worked briefly in Boston, and in 1849 returned to Worcester, where he worked as a book and job printer for the next forty-seven years, mostly as the owner of his own firm. In 1880 the firm had gross receipts of $16,416, offset by $14,041 in expenses for an annual net of $2,375. The business grew over the next twenty years (it was continued by Hamilton's sons), though annual profits remained quite modest.[71] Hamilton printed newspapers in three languages, "but newspaper printing was actually a small part of his work," which was extraordinarily varied.[72] For example, Michael Winship notes that Hamilton did 193 jobs for seventy-one different customers in March 1896: "Thirty-six of those jobs cost less than $1.00; half of them less than $2.75. On the other hand, eight jobs cost more than $25; two more than $100. The largest charge was $972.44 for printing the Worcester City Directory."[73] Indeed, Hamilton's success—the longevity of his firm in contrast to that of Harpel's—probably depended on this variety as well as on Hamilton's regular or repeated engagement by local institutions and concerns, such as the American Antiquarian Society, Worcester's Music Hall, and the Worcester and Nashua Railroad Company.[74] Hamilton even had out-of-town clients for book work. In October 1893 Hamilton or his representative wrote to one potential customer in Wisconsin: "I have carefully measured and estimated the cost of printing a work in the style of the Parker Genealogy ... and find that it can be done at the rate of one dollar and sixty-five cents per page for 500 copies. ... If we should have the order I should want to have the paper made soon, before the water is rendered muddy by the fall rains."[75] Thanks to the American Antiquarian Society, some of Hamilton's business records as well as some of his print jobs have survived.

Apart from *Harpel's Typograph* and *Poets and Poetry of Printerdom*, Harpel's work survives only in fragments: an envelope has been catalogued at the American Antiquarian Society, as have an envelope and a couple of political cartoons at the Library of Congress. (EBSCO's new database of American Antiquarian Society periodicals contains several contributions by Harpel to trade publications and a song about baseball.)[76] Some of the most interesting specimens of Harpel's career, however, almost certainly do not survive. In 1871, after he had published his *Typograph*, Harpel was arrested in Cincinnati for counterfeiting and passing counterfeit meal tickets at "Macdonald's new eating saloon on Vine Street," around the corner from his printing house and a short walk from his home. Roughly two years before he had apparently been arrested for counterfeiting tickets to the street railway and then let go, but this time charges would be pressed.[77] A newspaper account tells us a little about Harpel—that he begged to be let go, "declared that he must have been insane," and promised to leave town—but it tells a good bit more about job printing: "The genuine tickets are quite elaborately gotten up, with complicated scrollwork. . . . The counterfeits are wonderfully perfect save in two minor points, which would escape any scrutiny but the very closest."[78] Meal tickets were a convenience in a cash-poor economy. (*Harpel's Typograph* includes a specimen meal ticket for the Central Restaurant on Vine Street in Cincinnati.) They had a promotional function for their issuer, no doubt, while they also allowed customers to prepay for meals when cash was on hand and could be used as scrip in a pinch. As with other, more formal and familiar sorts of commercial paper, the intricacy of their printing made them look valuable because it made them harder to forge. That said, there is no knowing Harpel's motivation. Was he going hungry or desperate for a drink? Was this a streak of malevolence or of mental imbalance? Was it hubris, another demonstration of his excellent workmanship, but this one gone horribly awry? Had he gotten away with other counterfeiting? Are any of the specimens in *Harpel's Typograph* fake—that is, fiction—referring only to the process of referring? There is simply no way to know.

Whatever his impulses, Harpel seems to have been done in partly by local geography: he went repeatedly to a saloon around the corner, passing fakes "for the staff of life and various other substantials and luxuries."[79] It was as if he had misperceived downtown Cincinnati as a fully anonymous zone of transaction, despite his own residence and business there. On that score, David Henkin has proposed that everyday reading in public helped to rearticulate the American cityscape as a public sphere, a zone "in which subjects could be addressed anonymously, impersonally, and without reference to particularities of status." He argues persuasively that nineteenth-century reading in public helped generate an "impersonal public discourse" partly out of cacophonous commercial messages addressed indiscriminately to all.[80] Job printers—like sign painters, billposters, newspaper publishers, and their advertisers—were instrumental in this process, but that didn't exclude them from public scrutiny. Successful counterfeiting—like the capitalism it corrupts—is typically a distributed geographic practice, depending on an attenuated chain of transactions "from hand to hand," which serves in the aggregate to affirm a common faith both in the value of the paper being passed and in the underlying principles of the credit economy.[81] After all of his own itinerancy, Harpel had stayed too close to home, as if he had mistaken "printerdom" for a hideout or disguise.

Job printers, it turns out, are a bit like locksmiths. That is, they are part of a small yet special class of tradesmen who serve as functionaries, skilled and relatively independent labor within the socioeconomic fabric that connects the sanctity of personal property to the abstract, impersonal capitalist marketplace. Finance capital "works" to the extent that it does on credit, but not without the help of creditable agents—bankers and brokers, yes, but also locksmiths and job printers. The difference is that while locksmiths are supposed to facilitate or ensure value in situ, or under lock and key, job printers facilitate the pure exchange function. That is, they ensure value that exists in and only because of exchange, exchangeability, and circulation. Certainly this is true for business instruments such as paper currency, stock certificates, and meal tickets: they work the way they do because they can be transferred from one bearer to another based on a shared confidence in their value. Ancillary yet essential to that confidence (and thus that value) is a little-noticed, seldom-remarked confidence that the right printers—printers hired for the job, instead of counterfeiters—have made the instruments in question. When job printers produce items that are less obviously instrumental—say, a concert program, a millinery label, or a piece of letterhead—they are nonetheless creditable agents, crucial if modest contributors to the value that is transferable when a concert gets produced, a hat purveyed, or some matter of business put in writing. Job printing is part of the figure someone cuts, the capital someone enjoys in transaction, whether issuing bonds or inviting guests to a fancy party.

Like the analogy of job printing to machine tools, the comparison of job printers to locksmiths helps underscore the basic, functional, even infrastructural role that job-printed documents clearly played within the postbellum social order. Many of the same genres exist and function similarly today, even if the media of their reproduction have changed. Preprinted forms offer a modest technique of entry, one might say, which trades on the role of individuals within that broad and various discourse that attends (that is, produces) both the public and the market as shared abstractions. It is a discourse dependent on the private uses of paper—by a customer, in a workplace, at a school—as well as on the public frame that makes those uses viably and knowably more private. By this account, the liberal subject may have emerged according to the subjectivities of reading, but she or he also emerged according to a sort of global positioning system enacted and entailed by job-printed documents. More clearly than other forms of printing, preprinted blank forms help triangulate the modern self in relation to authority: the authority of printedness, on the one hand, and the authority of specific social subsystems and bureaucracies on the other hand. To be sure, the point is not that anything printed is authoritative, or that all bureaucratic power is legitimate. The postbellum social order was an order cruel and rickety at best, with plenty of losers like Harpel. Though familiarly the era in which managerial capital matured, maturation came amid what Walter Benjamin would later call "the brutal heteronomies of economic chaos."[82] Graft, swindling, inequity, failure, and uncertainty abounded.[83] Job printing in general and blank forms in particular offer a glimpse into the incidental, everyday occasions on which the authority of printedness was and is continuously and simultaneously produced, deployed, tested, reconfigured, and reaffirmed in reflexive relation to the competing and imperfect structures of social differentiation—the credit economy, civil procedure, municipal governance, medical practice, institutionalized education, voluntary association, and so on. Those evolving structures, one must imagine, work as so many loose and chaotic cross-stitches over and against the public sphere, helping to tack it together even as they also potentially worry it apart.

....

Starting with John Moxon's *Mechanick Exercises on the Whole Art of Printing*,[84] generations of printers' manuals "appear to reveal to the world some of the secrets of the trade" at the same time that they articulate an "orderliness" and regularity more wished than lived.[85] The trade literature of the nineteenth century tended to express this conflict between order and actuality in terms of an unexamined contradiction between tradition and progress. Tradition helped to suggest the taint of mere "novelties,"[86] while progress required continually adapting to changes. Printers were caught between looking backward and looking ahead; the former earned them a solidarity that the latter might help to jeopardize. Progress was typically conceived of in technological terms, and its inescapable yet largely unspoken costs were the havoc it would certainly wreak on the orderly specialization and division of labor that every manual helped iterate. Mechanical typesetting was only the most obvious transformation that loomed by 1890. Ultimately even the role and designation of "printer" would be up for grabs. As David McKitterick notes, today "we have become accustomed to speaking or writing of 'printers' not as people but as machines" attached to our computers.[87] Like computers, that is, printers used to be humans only before they became machines as well.

With all of the myriad changes between Harpel's day and ours, it has become too easy to overlook the monopoly lost by printers on the work of printing and the look of printedness. Publications like Harpel's *Poets and Poetry of Printerdom* and the earlier *Voices from the Press: A Collection of Sketches, Essays, and Poems by Practical Printers* were in one sense elaborate statements to the effect that — crudely speaking — printers, like other people, might be authors.[88] There is an implied corollary: no one but printers could print. Exceptions only help prove this rule. *Voices from the Press* includes a sketch by a young Walter Whitman, printer of Brooklyn, whose later involvement with the printing and publication of his own poetry remains exceptional. Of course, the distance between printing and authoring — between printerdom and any journalistic or belletristic expression — was highly variable, if judging only from the inclusion of editor-writers like N. P. Willis (in *Voices from the Press*) and Lucy Larcom (in *Poets and Poetry of Printerdom*) in these volumes of occasional writings by printers: they weren't printers, but they were close enough.[89] Highly variable though it was, the distance between printing and authoring was definite and distinct, a bright line by dint of the fact that authors of necessity wrote everything in longhand. In short, authors only penned while only printers printed. Edgar Allan Poe, for one, felt this handicap keenly and dabbled in ways to reproduce text without printing.[90] Charles Babbage too chafed mightily at the necessity of dealing with printers and publisher-booksellers.[91] Not until typewriters became common toward the end of the century would writers finally be able to produce copy that, because typed, looked *almost* printed. Reproducing that typed copy would remain the printer's domain into the next century.

The look of printedness meant something to Poe, Babbage, Harpel, and their contemporaries, though the eventual erosion of the printers' monopoly has made its meanings difficult to discern in retrospect. Or maybe those meanings are all too obvious. As Thomas MacKellar put it in his manual, *The American Printer*, "sentiments in print look marvelously different from the same ideas in manuscript."[92] He was warning printers that authors receiving proof sheets (seeing their "mental products" in print for the first time) were wont to make annoying and costly alterations. Printedness had clarity, a keenness and transparency that handwriting did not — of course, this was because of its regular letterforms, but it was also because of the uniformity of spacing, spelling, grammar, and punctuation that instructors like MacKellar directed compositors and proofreaders to ensure. Theodore DeVinne urged the compositors in his shop to follow copy scrupulously, because "it is the author's undoubted right to go before the public in his own way." Yet at the same time, compositors "should not follow copy that has been carelessly prepared, without system in the use of points and capitals, and by a writer who spells badly."[93] Messages were mixed; composition of one sort intermingled with composition of another. As N. P. Willis wrote in an appendix to *Voices from the Press*, "there is no such effectual analysis of style as the process of type-setting."[94] From the point of view of printers, at least, mental products went through printerdom as through a mold or a lathe or filter, on the way to becoming thinkable by others. This was probably particularly true in job printing. Harpel had no qualms about changing "words and phrases, when they do not mar the original sense." He assured his readers that "it not frequently happens that patrons expressly desire and expect this from the intelligent printer," in order "to render a device more complete" or a design more "handsome."[95] Printing had an intellectual purpose as well as an aesthetic and a duplicative one.

Yet by 1870 and with increasing intensity, the same small, platen hand presses that were helping make job printing a specialization in the printing trades were also helping erode the printers' monopoly on printedness. The title page of *Harpel's Typograph*, addressed to "Master Printers, Amateurs, Apprentices, and Others," admits as much. Marketed intensively to shopkeepers who might print trade cards, price cards, and handbills, the smaller lever presses were soon also marketed to children, young adults, and other amateurs. The same contexts that made "printerdom" intelligible also produced "amateurdom," a term used as amateur printers formed voluntary associations and articulated a collective identity.[96] Elizabeth Harris remarks that "it is hard to explain the depth of hostility expressed in the trade journals" to amateur printing and printers, since "the real damage done [to the trade] by amateurs must have been negligible." But printing by amateurs was an "insult,"[97] an invasion of printerdom and an erosion of the printers' monopoly. The hostility of the trade press was matched or even exceeded by the enthusiasm of amateurs. The American Antiquarian Society—with its one envelope printed by Harpel and its several hundred examples by Hamilton—owns a collection of approximately 50,000 amateur newspapers produced between 1805 and 1900, and the collection reflects a tenfold increase in production after cheap presses for amateurs became available after the Civil War.[98] The Smithsonian Institution archives contain many additional examples as part of the records of the Kelsey Press Company (founded in 1873), a major producer of printing presses for amateurs.[99] Any connection between amateur printing and the later phenomenon of "zines," has not, to my knowledge, been adequately explored.[100]

Of course, at the same time that amateur printing eroded the printers' monopoly, printing itself ceased to be the only way that writing could be mechanically produced or reproduced. A variety of technological innovations—of which typewriters would prove the most important—offered writers the means of authorial expression in standardized letterforms with standardized spacing. A revolution in business communication was at hand, and the scriptural economy correspondingly grew in scale and complexity.[101] The next chapter jumps forward in time to consider documents of a different sort than those considered above: not typescripts themselves, but rather typescripts reproduced without letterpress printing and sometimes even without (human) printers, the printers' monopoly broken. In doing so, the next chapter focuses not on the blank forms and formulas of everyday life but on the realm of scholarly communication. This shift is partly expedient, attuned to the archival record and exemplified by a book wholly unlike *Harpel's Typograph* and a man wholly unlike Oscar Harpel. But the shift is also strategic, since the next chapter delves into a single arena rather than speculating across so many. It considers documents amid the internal workings of scholarship, while it also offers glimpses of the ways that the scholarly arena may relate to other realms—to government and business—and to society at large in an era when new media and new forms of amateur cultural production captured the attention of scholars and others.

Few people as yet, outside the world of expert librarians and museum curators and so forth, know how manageable well-ordered facts can be made, however multitudinous, and how swiftly and completely the rarest visions and the most recondite matters can be recalled, once they have been put in place in a well-ordered scheme of reference and reproduction. . . . There is no practical obstacle whatever now to the creation of an efficient index to *all* human knowledge, ideas and achievements, to the creation, that is, of a complete planetary memory for all mankind.

—H. G. Wells, *World Brain*

In 1931 Edwards Brothers, Inc., of Ann Arbor, Michigan, published a slim volume titled *Methods of Reproducing Research Materials*, by Robert C. Binkley. As may be guessed from such a title, it made no splash. Indeed, to describe the volume as "published" at all is generous on at least three counts. The edition was minuscule, its substance was admittedly provisional or "tentative," and the book was photo-offset from the author's own double-spaced typescript.[1] Many unpublished documents have appeared in greater numbers and in grander garb. Nor were the economics of publication in this case anything like the norm. Edwards Brothers had produced only one hundred copies, and most were going to be given away for free, "promised to persons who have furnished information toward" the completion of the work itself.[2] Yet author and publisher both had a certain stake in *Methods of Reproducing Research Materials* as an item of public issue. The method of its reproduction might be reminiscent of in-house production and glorified office technology, but its subject bespoke a public: it was about research materials, and hence it *was* research material, directed toward members of the scholarly community and thereby toward the broad public for which scholarship exists and — in its own peculiar way — prospers. Of Robert Binkley this chapter will have much more to say directly. Of Edwards Brothers it may be enough to note for now that its director of publications would eventually leave to create another company called University Microfilms International, later simply UMI, which would eventually create another company called ProQuest. Today ProQuest publishes scholarly resources in the form of online subscription databases.[3]

Binkley was a Stanford-trained historian of modern Europe and a decorated veteran of World War I, a member of a generation that had fought for peace and yet would eventually realize the inevitability of another war. One of his scholarly research interests was peace studies — he wrote about the Treaty of Versailles — and another was the conduct of research itself, hence his work on *Methods*. More so than most of his peers, Binkley had a keen sense of living amid a continually accumulating and imperfectly preserved historical record, a sea of documents, the great recent accumulation of which was in jeopardy both because the necessary commitment to stewardship was lacking and because of the nineteenth-century switch from rag-based paper to less durable stock. Cheap paper had enabled "the development of the culture" over the previous half-century, supporting the institutions of a healthy civil society: a robust publishing industry and universal literacy as well as governmental and nongovernmental bureaucracies and scholarly subspecialization.[4] But the same cheap paper boded ill for future historians. "The records of our time are written in dust," Binkley warned in a talk at the First World Congress of Libraries and Bibliography in Rome in 1929.[5]

Binkley's *Methods* was a preliminary survey he prepared shortly thereafter at the behest of the Joint Committee on Materials for Research, which was formed in January 1930. The committee was "joint" because it had been convened jointly by the Social Science Research Council, or SSRC (founded in 1923), and the American Council of Learned Societies, or ACLS (founded in 1919). The SSRC had been the catalyst of the Joint Committee, whose baptismal name was the Committee on Enlargement, Improvement, and Preservation of Data, but the cooperation of the ACLS ensured that the humanities as well as the social sciences would share in its attentions. The committee had five convening members, moonlighting from full-time positions at the University of Minnesota, Harvard University, the New York Public Library (NYPL), the American Museum of Natural History, and the ACLS. The Joint Committee renamed itself at its first meeting in February 1930, and then Binkley's name came up as the logical person to tackle one of its several interests, the "problem" of reproducing "rare or unique materials."[6] He was added to the committee that fall, served for a time as its secretary, and then held the position of committee president from 1932 until his untimely death in 1940 at the age of forty-two. Binkley was a professor at Western Reserve University (now Case Western Reserve University) during most of his tenure as president of the committee, with one stint at Harvard (1932–33) and a visiting professorship at Columbia University (1937–38). Among his diverse accomplishments, he would briefly become the world's leading authority on the methods of reproducing research materials.[7]

This phrasing may sound awkward to twenty-first-century ears, but the notion that there are "methods of reproducing" that may be appropriate to "research materials" is hardly passé. Today's digital humanities constitute a scholarly domain framed in similar terms, asserting the relevance of digital media — digital "methods of reproducing" — to humanistic inquiry. Scholars working in the digital humanities "are tool-makers and students of their effects," seeking to apply computers to the text-centered, interpretive work of the humanities while also grappling with the persistent yet changeably perceived intersections between computation and interpretation.[8] The field had "a very well-known beginning" in 1949, when Father Roberto Busa sought to use computers in preparing a concordance of the works of St. Thomas Aquinas.[9] More recently the field has had the primary, practical result of designing scholarly resources and publishing them online: editions and collections, certainly, but also tools for data mining, analytics, and visualization. The intellectual results of these resources for their many users remain grossly understudied, but the intellectual payoffs for their designers have been immense, as detailed in a growing literature that addresses the core concerns of the humanities — everything from its terms of analysis (for example, what is a text?) to its changing role in and against the culture of information more broadly. I am thinking of works like Jerome McGann's *Radiant Textuality* and Alan Liu's *Laws of Cool*,[10] among many others, as well as ongoing publications like *Digital Humanities Quarterly* and *Digital Humanities Now* with its *Journal of Digital Humanities*.

This chapter pursues the largely forgotten work of Binkley and the Joint

Committee for two reasons: first, to gently suggest a deeper history of sorts (there must be other such histories) for the digital humanities, and second, to sketch a more ample and more specific account of typed documents and their reproduction than has yet been rendered either by scholars in media studies or by accounts of what William Stott called "documentary expression" in the 1930s.[11] However paradoxical it may seem, finding a pre-digital history for the digital humanities stands to open for scrutiny precisely the connections between "methods of reproducing" and "research materials," between media and the modes and substances of inquiry in the domains of history, arts, and letters. Like Liu's predigital history of encoded discourse — the standards and meta-standards of scientific management applied to knowledge work in the early twentieth century — such a history is one of surprising continuities rendered against obvious and admitted discontinuities.[12] That such a project must involve typescripts will I hope become clear. By adding the subject of job printing back into media history, the previous chapter revealed the many and varied organizational structures of modern life that printed jobs helped to articulate. Typing and typists, once they became ubiquitous, helped articulate many of these same organizational structures at a different level, as the clacketty mechanical production and — in many cases — reproduction of texts helped mark the writings internally important to them. If job-printed documents frequently expressed a localism they were designed partly to transcend, typescripts, too, carried the look of secretarial production — of the office — beyond its purview for a dizzying range of purposes.

It is to the internal workings of scholarship in particular that this chapter turns. Notoriously removed from practical, everyday concerns — the fabled ivory tower occupied by its absent-minded professoriate — scholarship depends on its own norms of communication, themselves changeable if notoriously inertial. These norms vary by discipline and according to an innumerable host of variables, everything from publication format (article or book?) to pedagogic practice (seminar or lecture?), from habits of written expression to habits of oral presentation. Most important, scholarly publication stands at odds with marketplace demands, as scholars publish for credit, earned in the circulation of their work among peers, and the academic rewards such as promotion and tenure that ensue, rather than for profit. The media of scholarly communication can be exclusive to the academy, too — a physicist's collider, a bibliographer's collator — but more typically the media of scholarship overlap and connect scholars and their students to the world beyond the ivied halls. Of course, other material conditions also connect and impinge. For instance, the Joint Committee on Materials for Research got down to business in the face of a global economic crisis and mass unemployment. Within the academy that meant a troubling dearth of positions for new PhDs and an apparent breakdown — a crisis, it was called — in the system of academic publishing on which the production and dissemination of new knowledge and the accrual of professional credit relied. Many in the humanities in particular felt beleaguered, as their disciplines lost prestige in relation to the sciences and the new social sciences. It felt, one must imagine, like time for something new.

....

Though published partly as an object lesson, in order to show the feasibility of small-run, specialty publication for scholars, Binkley's *Methods* was also "in effect, an internal document," aimed at the leadership of the Joint Committee's parent bodies, the SSRC and the ACLS.[13] It ends with ten pages of recommendations, many of them describing further work that ought to be coordinated, undertaken, or considered by the committee. As it happened, the work of *Methods* did continue, and Binkley brought out an expanded version in 1936 under the slightly more elaborate if no more alluring title *Manual on Methods of Reproducing Research Materials*. Again it was photo-offset from typescript, but this time the edition ran to 1,500 copies, with a cover price of $3.50. It was published on spec by Edwards Brothers (which seems to have at least come close to recouping costs), while the Joint Committee chipped in around $500 for secretarial and administrative work as well as for "illustrative material."[14] Like the first edition, the *Manual* sought to offer a detailed analysis of scholarly publication and the processes involved in the preservation and accessibility of scholarly resources. Unlike the first edition, it was lavishly illustrated, containing fifty-five charts and tables and seventy-three illustrations. The charts and tables were drawn and typed along with the body of the text, while the illustrations were tipped in and appear as unnumbered pages scattered throughout the book. This time Edwards Brothers prepared the final typescript manuscript for offset and then reproduced the work at 25 percent, so every four pages of typescript made a single, two-column page of the finished book. The *Manual* lacks a "Recommendations" section but is full of insights, and Binkley developed many of his arguments further in letters and memoranda prepared in connection with the work of the Joint

Committee, as well as in talks and articles such as the visionary "New Tools for Men of Letters," published in the *Yale Review*.[15]

What were the "materials for research" at which the Joint Committee was aimed? The term was used in three different ways. To begin with, materials for research were simply source materials, and the committee grappled with the difficulty of defining sources as a group. Norman Gras, a Harvard business historian, and Clark Wissler, an anthropologist at the American Museum of Natural History, solicited information from scholars in numerous fields, asking in a form letter about "needed source materials (such as newspapers, manuscripts and physical objects)." But they were frustrated, they reported to the committee, by the fact "that a number of scholars had never thought of the possibility of there being materials for their studies that were not being collected or utilized." A later attempt to define and consider "fugitive" source materials would itself remain fugitive, Binkley noted wryly.[16] With the best of intentions, the committee had run up against the problem of trying to know what is not known and therefore not easily knowable. Scholars could tell the committee what sources they did use, but they had a harder time identifying — or indeed caring about — what sources they didn't use, since they didn't use them. They "had never thought of" what they had never thought of. The committee was left with its own cares and assumptions. "We know already that our national machinery for collecting and preserving records is inadequate," it asserted in its "Circular Number I" in December 1930, noting in particular that newsprint was perishable, business records treated as disposable, and ephemera haphazardly kept.[17] Another early publication of the committee sounds a folksier note, defining materials for research as "tangible primary sources of information, usually the byproducts of the actual business of living, back of which the scholar cannot go in his search for new facts and truths."[18] The byproducts in question were familiarly known as documents.

The logical dilemma of trying to think about what has not been thought — or maybe in today's terms, of trying to search Google for what you haven't conceived of yet — suggests a second sort of material for research with which the Joint Committee would be concerned: materials that inventory, describe, catalog, or otherwise facilitate control over other materials. If scholars knew that source materials existed, and where, they would be much more likely and able to use those materials. The committee was keenly interested in the work being done by learned societies, historical societies, museums, and libraries in this direction — it would prepare and publish a survey of these activities—and discussion returned repeatedly to the idea of instigating or "making a bibliography of bibliographies."[19] It was a dream that jibed with international efforts initiated more than a generation earlier to produce comprehensive bibliographical systems—notably that of the Institut International de Bibliographie (founded in 1895)—and thus a dream that imagined the American academy on the world stage at the same time that it imagined the humanities and social sciences in relation to the natural and physical sciences, bibliographically controlled as those were by projects such as the International Catalogue of Scientific Literature (begun in 1896).[20] Materials for research of this type might include mundane "lists, inventories, calendars," but there was a grandiosity lurking in their conception.[21] The European bibliographical movement already existed, but there were plenty of American projects yet to be begun. In 1930 there was still no National Archives (a building was under construction; President Franklin D. Roosevelt would sign legislation creating the agency in 1934), and there was no national union catalog of books or manuscripts, which would tell scholars where the sources they needed were held (there was a union list of serials). Sources for many disciplines were available only in Europe, and no coordinated acquisitions plan existed among American research libraries, which as yet had no reliable capacities for interlibrary loan.

The third and final kind of material for research that the Joint Committee considered was the actual output of scholarship in the form of journal articles, dissertations, and books. Its central focus would be the scholarly monograph, which would eventually mean its work had greater relevance to the humanities than to the social sciences, where journal articles became the norm. (Most of the scholars who served on the committee were historians of one kind or another, and the discipline of history in general possessed an uneasy relationship with the ascendant social sciences.[22]) The reason for this focus was the widely perceived crisis in scholarly book publishing, still strangely current in the twenty-first century. Greater and greater specialization in the academy meant smaller, more specialized readerships. Yet the circulation of books to and within readerships was being constrained as scholars were caught between the limited acquisition budgets of their libraries and the motives of the publishing industry, whose policies were "not only valueless to the scholar, but even hostile to his purpose."[23] With their eyes set on titles that could sell in the tens of thousands, publishers had no interest in monographs or other titles aimed at

a few hundred specialists. Without subsidies of one kind or another —
harder and harder to come by in the Great Depression — scholarly publication was doomed. The same conditions constrained the publication of the
other materials for research — primary sources, finding aids, and finding
aids for finding aids — but the scholarly monograph was key. Binkley and
the Joint Committee repeatedly proposed that the SSRC and the ACLS
initiate their own publication service of some sort, but to no avail.[24] Now
new media for textual reproduction offered hope that the whole system
of scholarly communication might be reimagined. The *Manual* would be
one part experiment and one part argument about the feasibility of what
Binkley called "the typescript book."[25]

Calling three such varied "materials for research" by the same term indicates how much of a piece they must have seemed. Binkley and the Joint
Committee didn't confuse or conflate sources with finding aids or monographs — the three were easy to tell apart — but the way they knit together
demonstrates the conceptual strength that reproducing possessed. The
methods or media of mechanical reproduction — printing, microfilm,
photo-offset, mimeograph, ditto, blueprinting, and so on — might vary,
but the work of research requires reproducing because scholars everywhere
need access to materials. Reproducing means access. Access enables the
scholarly production of knowledge. The phrase "materials for research" or
"research materials" also worked to buttress the interests of scholarship by
consolidating the hierarchy of activities, needs, and conditions that runs
from the identification and collection of sources to the publication of
books. Granular particularities on the one hand were semantically aligned
with critical syntheses on the other. Interestingly, a similar semantics inhabits the more widely used term "documentary," which designates the
genre — or metagenre, in Jonathan Kahana's helpful formulation[26] — that
was so characteristic of the 1930s. The Great Depression made "a documentary approach" seem compulsory somehow,[27] and social documentary
in particular emerged as a cardinal form of cinema, photography, literature, dance, theater, and other arts, both with state sponsorship — under
the aegis of the Works Progress Administration (WPA) and the Farm
Security Administration — and without. "The power of social documentary comes," Kahana writes, "from its allegorical displacement of particular details onto the plane of general significance" — that is, its alignment of
granular particularities and critical syntheses, along with its persistent in-
terrogation of the effects and conditions of such an alignment.[28]

"Documentary" — like "document" — is of course a capacious term. When Binkley eventually declined to publish an updated supplement to his *Manual*, he continued its work by helping found the short-lived *Journal of Documentary Reproduction*, published by the American Library Association from 1938 to 1942. (It was replaced after World War II by *American Documentation*, a title that aligns with the European bibliographic movement called Documentation; the related American Documentation Institute was founded in 1936, with Binkley as vice president.) The social documentary form and the interests of the Joint Committee were hardly identical, but they ran parallel: part of the same culture of the 1930s characterized by the concept of culture as such, as well as by "the idea of commitment," illuminated in Warren Susman's fruitful analysis.[29] Underlying both documentary reproduction and the production of social documentary is a general interest in documents, with documents frequently doing national — if not nationalist — work at the same time they pointed toward tensions surrounding what Mark Goble terms "the mediated life of history itself."[30] The past slips away, while modern media ironically make the present seem more historic. A "new permanent record" was accumulating on shellac disk and celluloid film, as Lewis Mumford observed, while perishable paper and the lack of both system and commitment were threatening the archival record and additional diverse items in the historical fabric — arts, artifacts, architecture — that might offer Americans access to their own past.[31]

In *Documents of American History*, one of the earliest and most influential readers or editions of primary sources designed as college textbooks, Henry Steele Commager regretted the scarcity of documents beyond those "of an official or quasi-official character." Official documents give neither the "whole" nor the "real" story, he was sure. Needed in addition are documents of a social historical significance: "To discover [the undercurrents of our social life] it would be necessary to go to church records, school reports, the minutes of fraternal organizations, the records of labor organizations and agricultural societies, the records of probate courts, etc." (Commager would have been a godsend to Gras and Wissler had they polled him for their Joint Committee report in 1930). "American historians have been distressingly backward," Commager continues, "in their appreciation and publication of such material. These records therefore are not readily available, nor would a lifetime be sufficient to canvass them."[32] The same sort of thinking consumed the Joint Committee, as it assessed the work being done and the work proposed by various individuals, institutions, and learned societies. And the same thinking would soon animate — with Bink-ley's help — the Historical Records Survey or HRS (1936–42), a late WPA project that intended to produce something like the canvass of documents of which Commager despaired. Instead of relying on a single historian's lifetime, the design of the HRS sent an army of white-collar relief workers turned amateur archivists to scour county, church, and other records across the United States.

The recent preeminence of the social documentary as a cultural form has tended to focus attention on questions of representation. For instance, how are the human subjects of a documentary film represented? But the work of the Joint Committee favored questions of reproduction rather than questions of representation. Related questions of reproduction are certainly relevant in the sphere of the social documentary — Dorothea Lange manipulated her famous "Migrant Mother" (1936) in the dark-room; James Agee wanted the text of *Let Us Now Praise Famous Men* (1939) to be published on newsprint[33] — but they usually remain second-ary, part of the way that message tends to swamp medium as a focus of attention in popular as well as scholarly discourse. By focusing on repro-duction at the expense of representation — false dichotomy though that may be — the Joint Committee could sidestep questions of keen interest in the ongoing formation of disciplines in the social sciences and humani-ties. In history, for instance, it didn't matter where one stood on questions of objectivity or relativism (do historians seek a single truth, or is histori-cal knowledge a matter of perspective?) since positivists and pragmatists alike need access to research materials.[34] The Joint Committee could be unrelentingly empiricist without roiling these waters and without vouch-safing an opinion on the current political scene, fraught as it was by con-tests over the New Deal and anxieties about the Popular Front. Questions of reproduction so often seem safer and more neutral than questions of representation, though Binkley — like many of his contemporaries, Wal-ter Benjamin notably among them — did consider the broad social politics of mechanical reproduction. Modern media such as cinema, radio, and television, as Binkley explains in "New Tools for Men of Letters," "tend to concentrate the control of culture," which has its risks, if the lesson of "Germany to-day" be heeded.[35] The great promise of newer media, such as microphotography and photo-offset, is that they are "capable of working the other way — as implements of a more decentralized" culture.[36]

The combined result of Binkley's and the Joint Committee's focus on reproduction and their broadly heterogeneous notion of "materials for research" was a sometimes strategic disinterest in what Benjamin so famously apprehends as aura: the uniqueness of a work of art that withers as a result of technological reproducibility, so that the cultic functions of art give way to its exhibition or what might be called its access value.[37] Fine art was not the Joint Committee's concern, of course, but Benjamin himself gestures "beyond the realm of art" in order to extend the *general formula that the technology of reproduction detaches the reproduced object from the sphere of tradition*."[38] Binkley was writing in the same year as Benjamin, but from a very different place. Instead of sharing Benjamin's interest in the mass existence of new forms that might revolutionize the character of art, Binkley was interested in innovations within and an expansion of the scriptural economy that might transform the work of scholars. Instead of finding inspiration in cinema and the photographic image, Binkley was inspired by the documentary record. He asserts at the beginning of the *Manual* that "all the documents of which [the scholar] makes use are for him 'materials for research,'" and as "long as they are legible" and available on demand, the scholar "does not care whether they are printed or typewritten or in manuscript form, whether durable or perishable, whether original or Photostat."[39] The scholar is necessarily an opportunist, an interpreter, interested only in meanings that are assumed to be self-identical with written symbols available to his eye. By extension, primary sources may be loosened from "the sphere of tradition" represented by wealthy collectors—Henry E. Huntington, Henry Clay Folger, and Pierpont Morgan come to mind—and the isolated rare book rooms and archives that have to an extent become their surrogates and successors, now supplemented by expensive proprietary databases that disseminate collections only to subscribers.

There is a very contemporary, "informatic" sensibility lurking here, albeit a conflicted one.[40] Binkley writes with confidence that an original and its reproduction are interchangeable to the scholar. Only the custodians of research materials—archivists and librarians (and their allies on joint committees)—must fetishize material forms by dint of their interest in collection, organization, and preservation. Yet this was a self-contradicting position for Binkley, who explained his plans in a letter to the head of SSRC: "The finished [*Manual*] will contain illustrative material—illustrations, samples of paper, etc.—making it much more valuable than mere text."[41] It *did* matter that the *Manual*'s illustrations each took the material form they did because—like Harpel's specimens in relation to his instructional matter—what they illustrated could not be rendered in purely linguistic terms. The illustrations of the *Manual* would have a presence, an aura, that the "mere text" surrounding them could not. Other documentary projects of the period were conflicted on similar grounds. The Index of American Design, for instance, was a WPA project that would eventually produce 18,257 watercolor renderings of objects of American material culture, many drawn from photographs.[42] As Goble put it, "the Index wants to show us a massive accumulation of material as only a machine could view it, and yet let us know each object as only a human being could tell its story."[43] There is an unresolved tension between a machinic or an informatic sensibility, with its faith that content is fully separable from medium or form, and a more humanist or Modernist sensibility in which media matter and "content" does not—cannot—exist purely as such, or in which reproduction is always also representation.

The *Manual* is a bizarre book. Each copy contains individually prepared, unique illustrations, the purpose of which is to illustrate methods of mechanical reproduction. Chapter 5, for instance, considers "The Typescript Book or Memorandum: Reproduction Techniques." Here Binkley offers a comparative analysis of carbon paper, mimeograph, hectograph (later known as "ditto" in the United States and ultimately generalized as "mimeograph," which became a blanket term), and photo-offset as methods of reproducing typescript. How many copies can each process make of a single typescript and at what cost? What are the initial costs and respective requirements for preparing the typed manuscript? What implications does each process have for page layout and legibility? In order to illustrate his analysis, Binkley includes multiple samples. Three of his figures are dittos, pages of typescript reproduced in purple ink by three different versions of the hectograph process. His figure XXII begins: "This sample page has been made on a Standard Rotary Duplicator, a gelatin machine. It is claimed that as many as 200 legible copies may be obtained from one master sheet. This is the _____ copy from the master sheet." In my copy of the *Manual* the number 124 has been hand stamped into the blank in the text, indicating that I am looking at the 124th copy from a master. Binkley's figure XXIV is another ditto made with a different brand of machine; in my copy it is the 220th printed from a master sheet (figure 2.1). For 1,500 copies of the *Manual* there must have been at least a handful of figures XXIV numbered 220, since dittos edition differently than photo-offset, a point Binkley is at pains to make in his chapter 5. After being bound in

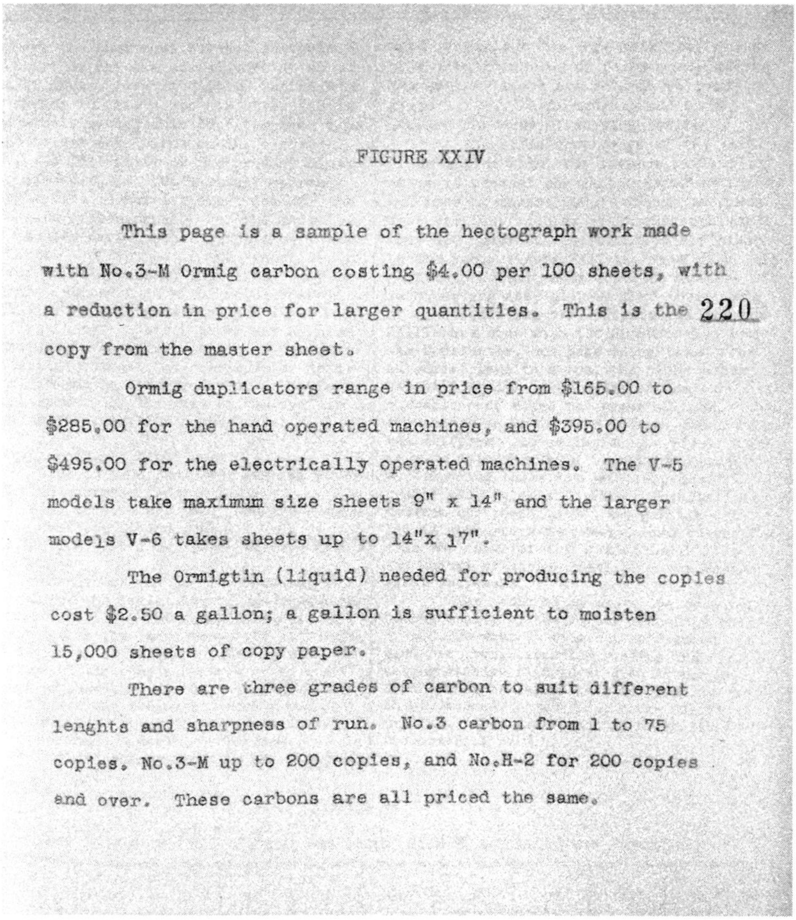

FIGURE XXIV

This page is a sample of the hectograph work made
with No.3-M Ormig carbon costing $4.00 per 100 sheets, with
a reduction in price for larger quantities. This is the 220
copy from the master sheet.

Ormig duplicators range in price from $165.00 to
$285.00 for the hand operated machines, and $395.00 to
$495.00 for the electrically operated machines. The V-5
models take maximum size sheets 9" x 14" and the larger
models V-6 takes sheets up to 14"x 17".

The Ormigtin (liquid) needed for producing the copies
cost $2.50 a gallon; a gallon is sufficient to moisten
15,000 sheets of copy paper.

There are three grades of carbon to suit different
lenghts and sharpness of run. No.3 carbon from 1 to 75
copies. No.3-M up to 200 copies, and No.H-2 for 200 copies
and over. These carbons are all priced the same.

FIGURE 2.1. Figure XXIV, a hectograph (purple ink) with rubber stamp (black),
Robert C. Binkley, *Manual on Methods of Reproducing Research Materials* (1936).

the *Manual* for seventy-five years, these figures do not have the distinctive ditto smell that some of today's readers may remember. Their paper has yellowed, particularly near the top and fore edge, and it is of a poorer quality than the pages of surrounding text. The four figures do still vary in the sharpness and darkness of their ink — as they must have in 1936 — though their variation in relation to one another may itself have varied over time.

Binkley's other illustrations are not as explicit as these about being unique examples of reproduction processes, though a good number possess the same self-captioning quality. They are self-descriptive pages of text composed by Binkley or a vendor he hired that have been reproduced for publication by Binkley, his assistants, or a vendor with whom they made arrangements. For example, they say: "This is a sample page demonstrating Multilith direct typing," "This is a sample page done with micro-elite type," or "This page illustrates a photo-offset format that has been designed to conform to the cost levels of medium-priced mimeographing." Each illustration of this sort speaks its own difference from the surrounding text, reporting the performative logic of its own material self-evidence in a simple, declarative mode. Occasionally a similar self-evidence is performed by supplemental material. Two figures each explain a different format of microfilm (16 and 35 mm) and include a sample of actual film attached by a staple. (Different copies of the *Manual* presumably have the same explanation attaching different frames of the same sample film.) Elsewhere the self-referring qualities of the *Manual* are even more complex: for example, its figure III consists of two columns of printed text (that is, letterpress, labeled "courtesy of R.R. Donnelley & Sons") that consider a two-column page as "an economical print-face format" but that also refer to "the typescript pages of this book," which are in a two-column format as well. Figure III is thus evidence of and caption for itself at the same time that it points toward the text it illustrates as an illustration.

Nor is the self-referring tangle of the *Manual* and its illustrations a fully closed system. The Joint Committee sponsored a number of experiments and pilot projects, and Binkley takes advantage of a few of them in the *Manual*. Chapter 8, "A Study of Paper Permanence," explains that the Joint Committee convinced the publishers of the *Dictionary of American Biography* (*DAB*) to produce twenty-five special copies of volume 8 of that work in 1934, each using three different kinds of paper. Binkley lists twenty-five libraries across the United States and Canada where "the reader is advised to examine them."[44] The NYPL owns copy number five. It contains an explanatory page labeling it as such and giving paper specifica-tions for each third of the volume. In order not to encourage handling that would damage the text, "two sample sheets of each stock are bound at the end of the volume to permit later checking or testing." (The three differ-ent papers do indeed look and feel different, though I declined to perform a fold-endurance test on the library's copy when I examined it in the Rose Main Reading Room in July 2010.) Readers of the *Manual* must examine the *DAB* according to a logic entirely out of keeping with the alphabeti-cally arranged text (Mills to Oglesby, in the case of volume 8). And they must examine one particular copy of the *DAB* uniquely identified among a group of twenty-five, itself unique amid an edition of many thousands.

The *DAB* experiment appeals to an unknown future, a future sketched in part many years later by Nicholson Baker's *Double Fold*, which inciden-tally demonizes Binkley as a promoter of microfilming.[45] Despite some forward-looking experimentation, the general result of the illustrative material within the *Manual* is a baggy temporality, with multiple forms and frames of self-reference emphasizing an extended present in which authorial production, mechanical reproduction, and reading might all take place. "This is," the *Manual* asserts again and again, deploying the obsessive present-mindedness of the documentary genre with its matter-of-fact sen-sibility: *These Are Our Lives*, *You Have Seen Their Faces*, *Let Us Now Praise Famous Men*, and *Why We Fight*, for example.[46] For all of this presentness, however, currency remains elusive. "It has seemed almost impossible to close the book," Binkley writes, "because the rush of innovation makes a chapter out of date almost as soon as it leaves the typist's hands."[47] Techno-logical change and perennial fluctuation in prices make the *Manual* out of date even as it comes into being. The many instances of "This is" in the illus-trations and text work to assert a minutely divided present — divided even into a typist's individual keystrokes — the moments of which can linger together as one only when they are collected in the hands and minds of readers. If the *Manual* is a documentary of sorts, then its method is one of participant observation, in which the author, his informants, and his assis-tants have all participated in the reproduction of research materials, which it seeks to document. Readers are drawn in and made party to its documen-tary work; they become conscripted to the cause of the typescript book.

The typescript book of 1936 was something like the electronic book of today. "Typescript" and "electronic" each denominate form in terms of process, a process of production (typing) on the one hand and processes of storage, delivery, and reception (downloading or displaying on the screen) on the other hand. Yet "typescript" and "electronic" each introduce great imprecision. Binkley's *Manual* is a typescript book presumably because Edwards Brothers typed it for reproduction. But for readers, of course, it is not the direct output of a typewriter; rather, it is a reproduction that represents — rather like a picture of — the typed pages that retain the monospace letterforms and unjustified right-hand margins of the original. Where the typescript book is concerned, typescript is weirdly more a genre than it is a format or medium. The typescript book can be a hectograph, mimeograph, or a planograph and still count as "typescript" according to the *Manual*. Indeed, it is never only a typescript, the way a printed book, in contrast, is only a printed book — that is, until it becomes or is made into something else entirely, like microfilm. In correspondence with catalogers of the American Library Association, Binkley urged them not to use "the same term to apply to all forms of reproduced typescript." A whole series of descriptors offered greater precision: typescript, carbon copy; hectograph typescript; mimeograph typescript; planograph typescript (Binkley preferred "planograph" to "photo-offset" because the latter "does not make a good participle").[48] The idea that there was any "original" typescript is certainly murky, too, since Binkley's assistants Josephine McCarter and Adeline Barry typed the *Manual* before Edwards Brothers did (and Binkley himself may have composed parts of it by typing). Likewise an electronic book always involves text on screen, but in common parlance it can take a lot of forms — in a browser window, as a Kindle, in a Kindle app, or on a Kindle, Nook, or iPad, for instance — and it has been electronic in one way or another from its author's computer or its publisher's scanner all the way through to the database from which it was downloaded. Typescript books, if you like, are typescript all the way up, while electronic books are electronic all the way down (or vice versa?). Individual printed books, however, are only printed, and they are printed only once.

I will return to the question of texts that are somehow also pictures of themselves in chapter 4 below. My point here is that the typescript book of Binkley's day was a contradiction in terms, because books were published but typescripts were internal or unpublished, even if somehow public. The internality of typescripts — if I can call it that — both resulted in and resulted from their relative informality. "Our habits of judgment have been so formed," Binkley writes, "that we always expect to see certain kinds of thought going around in their working clothes; others we expect to see parading in formal dress."[49] Typescripts are instrumental and vernacular, adapted to the "kinds of thought" that routinely circulate among employees or among the constituents of shared bureaucracy, internal to business, government, and education. This made them attractive in some contexts but problematic in others, a contrast that Binkley understood to be fraught with irony, since at the same time that the scholar was "trying to find an economical means of making small runs that look like printing rather than typescript, the business man [was] trying to make large runs . . . look like typescript rather than print."[50] Scholars typically "fetishize" the printed page (that's Binkley's term).[51] They didn't want their monographs typed instead of printed any more than scholars today want their books published exclusively online.[52] At the same time, however, the look of typescript had particular value for form letters, circulars, direct mail, and — eventually — advertising copy, since advertisers could use it to signal the confidential, insider tone that apparently sells widgets so well.

Like the look of print, the look of typescript has of course changed meanings over time: today one purveyor of digital typefaces notes that the American Typewriter face renders "an old-fashioned, personal look," when once the same face would in certain contexts have had a decidedly impersonal look.[53] By the 1930s even publishers had begun to notice the value of typescript, Binkley notes in "New Tools for Men of Letters," since specialized business publications could be sold at higher prices if reproduced from typescript than if printed conventionally.[54] Everyone wants to be an insider.

Again an analogy to electronic publication — albeit imperfect — makes some sense. As Johanna Drucker, Matthew Kirschenbaum, and Katherine Hayles have explained, electronic texts need to be seen more as processes than as anything solid-state or as anything — another great imprecision — merely virtual.[55] This is true in a number of different respects. On the simplest level, electronic texts are the results of many different layers of instructions rendered in code. And as processes, electronic texts remain dynamic, changeable at multiple levels. They can be edited and their appearance altered — for example, by changing the metadata or the display specifications. In contrast, typing fixes letters on the page. Yet the internality of typescripts did lend them their own in-process or in-progress quality, a quality that has become difficult to see in retrospect, now that familiarity with electronic texts has obscured the view. The in-progress quality of typescripts arose by virtue of their association with manuscript, where "manuscript" refers not to handwriting but to copy that an author produces for publication. Not only did many writers compose things by typing them or—in some contexts—by dictating them to a typist, but by the 1930s typescript was the only form of copy accepted for print publication.[56] Whether in business, literature, journalism, or other spheres, a writer's final manuscript was certain to be a typescript, even if corrections were later added by hand. In contexts where print production was the goal, typescript copy worked as a cleanly rendered set of instructions for the typesetter and proofreader; typescript was integral to the process of print publication. Typed copy worked as a sort of natural language code, one might even say; it was executable according to the "Follow copy" command directed to a typesetter.[57] Unlike the final printed version, however, the typed manuscript could still be edited or amended with ease, by being either scribbled on or literally cut and pasted as needed to approximate the author's or editor's intentions with greater precision.

Even in contexts not oriented toward print publication, typescripts must have implied process—secretarial processes in particular, like the transcription of dictation, the laying out of business letters, and the preparation of memoranda and reports, all tasks performed according to the norms of business communication, typically by women workers. Typescripts and reproduced typescripts looked close to the scene of office production. They were closer to the scene of writing than letterpress printing, certainly, a proximity that recommended them for works requiring immediate availability as well as works likely to be quickly superseded by revised versions, including "manuals and pricelists in business, instruction material for classes in high school and college, and any number of letters of information, reports, and memoranda for groups of consultants in government and business."[58] Such are the genres of internality, which structure "the great mass of writing that is neither scientific nor literary but exists *primarily* to transmit information."[59]

The strangely in-process quality of typescripts may help to explain how Binkley could have come so remarkably close to foreseeing forms of online communication and publication that lay sixty years into the future. "Perhaps the time may come," he muses, "when the internal documents of scholarship will circulate like the internal documents of a great business enterprise. . . . Such possibilities lie in the realm of dream and prophecy."[60] What Binkley dreamed of were not just "new tools" for men and women of letters, but whole new patterns of scholarly communication that developments like xerography — the subject of my next chapter — and networked personal computers have helped make possible in the decades since Binkley's day: e-mail, listservs, blogs, wikis, and so on. "If [people] can but accommodate themselves to the new techniques," Binkley writes, "important barriers to intellectual intercourse can be made to fall."[61] Today the term "tools" is again a watchword, as collaborative teams in the digital humanities work to understand, develop, and promote what McGann has called "a new set of scholarly tools."[62]

New tools become tenable only if the attendant social organization of labor changes in concert with the development of the tools, if adjustments are made to the ways that labor and expertise are divided and that resources and rewards are distributed. Indeed, humans, not tools, come first. As Binkley saw so clearly, scholars, for their part, were going to have to abandon their print fetish. And they would have to prepare clean copy themselves, not foist the niceties of editing and formatting off on a publisher's hirelings. Librarians would need to unbend, too; they would have to be able to catalog typescript books intelligibly, and they would have to adjust their storage protocols, since at 8½″ by 11″ books like the *Manual* would be considered "oversize" in too many collections. More important, librarians would have to broaden their roles, since new imaging techniques (that is, microphotography) meant that collecting research materials might become tantamount to publishing them.[63] Publishers might adjust, but printers would be the big losers, and it is no surprise that amid the many positive reviews Binkley's *Manual* received, it was roundly condemned in the pages of the trade's *Inland Printer*. "We cannot help but feel that those interested in the conservation of eyesight," the reviewer carps, "would find ample cause for registering a rather strong protest against the manner in which this particular study, highly important as it is, has been presented in book form." Elsewhere the same reviewer is either self-defeating or obtuse: "The material in this manual merits better treatment."[64] Material indeed.

Just as it makes no sense to think of electronic books today without the largely corporate repositories that store and serve them up to readers, or without the processing power, bandwidth, server farms, and business models and operations that all of this entails, so it makes no sense to think about the typescript book of the 1930s without the realignment of professional roles that the *Manual* suggests and all of the varied media of textual reproduction that it describes. Reimagining scholarly communication meant changes in the work of scholars, librarians, editors, and publishers, but it would also mean the canny deployment of multiple formats, different scales of reproduction and distribution, and a coordinated "hierarchy of control" over resources, along with a robust network of cooperating local, state, regional, national, and even international institutions.[65] The *Manual* may offer its readers an avalanche of niggling details, but Binkley and the Joint Committee were thinking big.

Privately and publicly Binkley worked to describe just how scholarly communication might be rationalized, streamlined, and expanded in scale and scope. An index of Cleveland newspapers, for instance, might hypothetically be "distributed in [a reproduced typescript] edition of 200," while two microfilm copies of the papers themselves might be deposited in the Library of Congress along with the film negative. Then a more generalized checklist or guide to newspapers and newspaper indexes might be distributed to libraries across the country and beyond, requiring an edition of more than a thousand.[66] Patrons could borrow a positive copy of the microfilm after examining the guide and then the index, or they could purchase their own print of selected reels. Typescript books reproduced by a variety of appropriate means would work in tandem with microfilm to deliver to the scholar materials for research. Serving is just the right metaphor, since the operation of microfilm cameras and retention of archival negatives introduced what would be called today client-server architecture. Like the web browsers (client applications) of today, microfilm reading devices were the local display mechanisms used to view images from afar, as positive prints were pushed out from centralized repositories, the Library of Congress in this example, or UMI's underground storage vault for negatives, as later became so common.[67]

Two additional cohorts would be required to make any such system work; Binkley called them "gentlemen" and "amateurs." The term "gentlemen" was apropos because copying library holdings might put students, scholars, and librarians in conflict with rightsholders, most notably publishers, who are typically quick to speak for authors' rights. As part of his work on the Joint Committee, Binkley was the instigator and one of two signatories of something called "The Gentlemen's Agreement," executed in May 1935 and published in the *Manual*. "The Gentlemen's Agreement" was an attempt to sketch the boundaries of scholarly fair use, "not as a contract relationship but rather as a mutually acceptable statement of the practical scope of the doctrine of fair use as applied to documentary reproduction."[68] In an exchange of letters, Binkley agreed with W. W. Norton, president of the National Association of Book Publishers, that scholars (or libraries acting for individual scholars) should be allowed to make "a single photographic reproduction" that would be "in lieu of loan . . . or in place of manual transcription and solely for the purposes of research." There were strings attached: no one could make a profit on this copying, the scholars in question would have to receive a notice about copyright and copyright infringement, and they would have to agree not to reproduce the copies further "without the express permission of the copyright owner."[69] Librarians would be exempt from liability. Scholars and publishers would act like gentlemen: "photocopying," as it was sometimes called, had arrived.

The American Library Association had a standing committee on re-production — Binkley was of course a member — and in 1936 it convened a meeting specifically to discuss microphotography. M. Llewellyn Raney, director of the libraries at the University of Chicago, compared the arrival of the microfilm camera to that of the printing press. "A generation familiar with carburetors, fuselage and static will now have to hob-nob with emulsions," he predicted, observing that "the subject can be no more ignored than the existence of typewriters."[70] Niceties about emulsions never became common knowledge, of course, but Raney's mistake indicates that microfilm technology was still rudimentary and its standards unsettled, while best practices for its use remained in question. The American Library Association, like the Joint Committee, would discuss and evaluate film chemistry and film formats, equipment produced by various manufacturers, and any planned or existing library initiatives that involved microfilming. The librarians even talked about what kinds of reading the cumbersome microfilm-reading devices were good for, brooding over the differences among superficial, casual, rapid, continuous, and intensive reading.[71] The Library of Congress, NYPL, and Huntington Library, as well as the libraries at Yale, Harvard, and Brown universities, were experimenting with microfilm in one way or another, and Eugene Power of Edwards Brothers — who would found UMI in 1938 — had gotten permission to place a modified movie camera in the library of the British Museum for microfilming. There a technician was already busy filming early English books to provide subscribing libraries with copies of the approximately 27,000 items listed in Alfred W. Pollard and G. R. Redgrave's *Short Title Catalogue* (STC), the reference work published in 1927 (dated 1926). Power paid the library a minimal fee per exposure, and he already had enough subscribers to break even. The STC metadata — in today's parlance—would help to identify facsimile images on the film.[72] This effort, like so many others it helped to inspire, was for profit, though Power and later UMI would voice a gentlemanly sense of obligation to scholarship, especially in the area of dissertations.[73] "The Gentlemen's Agreement" didn't apply abroad or in cases—like those thousands of British imprints from before 1640—where copyright was irrelevant. But the British Museum and very soon its peers across Europe were certainly being gentlemanly about letting the new imaging technology in the door, not a little unlike the libraries that have allowed Google to scan their collections in recent years.

If new modes of mechanical reproduction prompted the hope that actors associated with materials for research might proceed in a spirit of mutual responsibility, more according to the principles of a gift economy than to those of a market one, then the same modes of reproduction also prompted the hope that a new class of amateurs beyond the academy would associate with materials for research. Binkley imagined Americans engaged in scholarly activity "for the fun of it or for the glory," as a hobby, the leisure-time fulfillment of an improved liberal arts education and better training for teachers.[74] He was thinking big again. These amateurs might—with proper coordination—support the scholarly research done by professionals, but they would certainly strengthen the fabric of America's democratic society and encourage a sense of international community by living purposeful intellectual lives rather than succumbing to Babbittry and isolationism. (Think Wikipedia, not Facebook, but think a Wikipedia in which original research is welcome, not forbidden.) Binkley didn't want a nation of Casaubons; he wanted a nation of Benjamin Franklins, a "living culture" comprised of many "active cell[s]."[75] Local literary societies and amateur theatricals should have their counterparts in the field of local history. Amateurs could produce family and community histories that evaded both the "superficial travesty" of genealogy and the sort of narrow-minded boosterism or tedious antiquarianism of so many existing community history projects. The point was to see the local in terms of nonlocal forces that had expressed themselves so differently in different localities.[76] "Go down the table of contents of any good book on western civilization," Binkley told those assembled at the eighty-eighth meeting of the Minnesota Historical Society in an address reprinted in *Minnesota History*, "and, item by item, it will be discovered that if the thing was important in one way or another, it happened in St. Paul."[77] "The thing" didn't happen only in St. Paul, but the world's cultural, intellectual, and economic history could be read there in importantly particular detail.

Sources for this sort of local history were hard to find, Binkley knew: if one went to the Cleveland Public Library, for example, it was much easier to find out "how many goats there are in Egypt [than] how many automobiles there are in Cleveland."[78] This is where a different and temporary corps of amateurs could help — not enlightened, college-educated hobbyists but the white-collar unemployed. In advocating for and helping plan the HRS, Binkley seized the day: "We have before us an opportunity to localize, decentralize, and democratize culture" (figure 2.2).[79] The HRS began in 1936 with an inventory of county archives conducted in all forty-eight states; many of the inventories were eventually published as typescript books. Other HRS projects varied from place to place, and its goals changed over its years of operation. Binkley served as a technical advisor to the HRS in Ohio, where relief workers aimed to produce — among other material — a 200-volume digest and index of Cleveland newspapers, including foreign-language papers and the so-called Negro press. At least fifty-three volumes of the *Annals of Cleveland, 1818–1935* were eventually produced in an edition of 100, "Multigraphed by the Cleveland WPA Project 16823" and distributed by the Cleveland Public Library.[80] (HRS workers in other Ohio cities worked on annals as well, and there were similar projects in other states.) Historians wishing to study the city's cultural history would have its own citizens to thank. Robert Lynd, coauthor of the groundbreaking studies of the city he called Middletown, praised the *Annals* project in the *American Sociological Review*, noting that it offered a unique, "folk-eye view" because that was the view that had greeted the "eyes of citizens of Cleveland year after year" in the pages of their own newspapers.[81] He might also have added that it was a folk-eye view because it was prepared by folks in Cleveland.

To twenty-first-century readers this may sound like a radical vision: amateur cultural production meets progressive politics, a Wikipedia wrought in typescript, or the Open Content Alliance and Internet Archive sans Internet. But at base the HRS had a centrist or even conservative tenor, with the aim of providing a palliative for current ills rather than a remaking of the social order.[82] In comparison with the highly politicized Federal Writers Project and Federal Theater Project of the WPA — both of which had attracted the attention of the House Un-American Activities Committee, chaired at that time by Representative Martin Dies Jr.

FIGURE 2.2. Photograph taken as part of the Survey of Federal Archives. The Survey of Federal Archives began in 1936 as a pilot project for the Historical Records Survey, into which it merged in 1937. Courtesy of the Portland Art Museum, Portland, Oregon.

(D-Texas) — the HRS was tame indeed, cloaked in the studied apolitical demeanor of methods of reproducing research materials. It democratized cultural production by spreading it everywhere in the United States and involving nonprofessionals, but Binkley and other HRS architects and supporters made clear that it worked according to a Fordist logic, a factory system in which employees — like cogs in a giant machine — were organized into a local, state, and federal hierarchy. Like other WPA projects, the HRS directed its workers through a series of guidelines, instructional memoranda, and eventually manuals. There was a manual prepared about preparing inventories of public records, two manuals prepared about preparing an inventory of American imprints, another two about indexing newspapers, and so on. In the language of encoded text today, these manuals worked something like document type definitions, schema that "parameterize" authorship, effectively disempowering authors.[83] According to other lights, they worked like and in concert with elaborate fill-in-the-blank forms, specifying conditions for filling in entries that would constitute each inventory, index, or calendar of documents. The need for each manual arose in the course of work it sought to describe, and having a manual frequently led to subsequent editions or additional manuals aimed at disambiguating earlier efforts. Like Binkley's *Manual*, the HRS manuals sought to fix a moving target — methods regarding research materials — onto a reproduced typescript page.

The amateur archivists and chroniclers of the HRS were hardly the enlightened hobbyists that Binkley dreams in "New Tools for Men of Letters," though amateurs of both stripes — like the young-adult amateur printers of Oscar Harpel's day — were conceived of in relation to the media in which their works were to be reproduced and disseminated. Media do not themselves make amateur cultural producers, of course. Amateur printers of the late nineteenth century were born partly of changing constructions of childhood and adolescence, the demise of the apprentice system and increase in manufactures, as well as the saturate culture of news and newsprint that characterized the decade of the Civil War and those that followed. Adult amateurs of the 1930s were born of different cultural and socioeconomic patterns — mass unemployment was only the most immediate — and different observers explained them differently. Binkley emphasized the recent growth of white-collar labor, which he thought refuted Marxian predictions of an expanding proletariat.[84] Others did not agree.

From Benjamin's perspective, amateurs of the 1930s were really a new form of expert. They were the bearers of contemporary expertise rationalized to the point of banality, perhaps, yet ripe to be productively politicized. These amateurs were related to the ones who had written letters to the editors of newspapers in an earlier generation, but the phenomenon had grown and changed. It "has now reached a point," Benjamin writes,

> where there is hardly a European engaged in the work process who could not, in principle, find an opportunity to publish somewhere or other an account of work experience, a complaint, a report, or something of the kind. Thus, the distinction between author and public is about to lose its axiomatic character. . . . At any moment, the reader is ready to become a writer. As an expert—which he has had to become in any case in a highly specialized work process, even if only in some minor capacity—the reader gains access to authorship. Work itself is given a voice. And the ability to describe a job in words now forms part of the expertise needed to carry it out.[85]

The axiomatic distinction between author and public depended on a difference in number—few authors, large publics—that the bureaucratized work process with its internal production and circulation of documents had now collapsed. For the traditional work of art, this spelled trouble ("literary competence is no longer founded on specialized higher education but on polytechnic training, and thus is common property"[86]), but new forms—enabled by new media—might allow new actors to exact revenge on the dehumanizing apparatus of modern life. The model of mass authorship was exemplary for Benjamin. Now that "work itself is given a voice" in the domain of documents, he looked with particular hope toward a Soviet-style documentary cinema, in which the people "portray *themselves*—and primarily in their own work process." If only "film capital" could everywhere be expropriated on behalf of the proletariat.[87]

Seeing Binkley in terms of Benjamin helps clarify the conservatism of Binkley's vision, the HRS, the typescript book, and now—one may well wonder—the digital humanities, to which the Joint Committee's project in a few respects seems so similar.[88] *The Annals of Cleveland* was no *Man with a Movie Camera*, and the *Manual* was no manifesto, though such comparisons are hardly fair. Seeing Benjamin in terms of Binkley, furthermore, helps clarify the attendant conditions of technological reproducibility that helped prompt both men to such appealing idealism and helped make the 1930s such an extended and important moment for documentary expression. Benjamin's discussion of art in the age of reproducibility leaves out carbon paper, ditto, blueprint, mimeograph, and photo-offset (a lithographic process) in its thumbnail history of mechanical reproduction — which runs from woodcuts to Gutenberg through lithography to photography[89] — but they certainly haunt the idea of mass authorship. And Benjamin's hopes for cinema never mention microfilm, even though the two uses of 35 mm film stock would come to inhabit related logics, the further alignment of documents and documentary, even if both would also — in defeat of hope — come to support and embody national traditions, not international workers' politics. At least for now, national or area-specific traditions of cinema and national archives of microform still rule the day, despite the forces of globalization that may prevail in other spheres.

....

Microfilm deserves more attention than I have room to give it here. It seems clear, however, that UMI and the era of scholarly microfilm became thinkable in this moment because of the Joint Committee and the typescript book as well as the broader contexts from which both emerged. By Power's own account, he and Binkley had tinkered together at microfilming; he was consulting with Binkley and his assistant about publishing the *Manual*; and he was hearing what the Joint Committee had done and what it had learned about microfilm cameras. He had a conversion experience: "It was as if a great light had gone on in my mind; for here, before my eyes, was the long-sought answer to the problem of how to produce [even] a single copy of any printed document 'on demand'"; "'That's it!' I shouted."[90] (This is from Power's charming autobiography, *Edition of One.*) Naturally, there were many actors beyond Power and Binkley who helped make microforms — film, microfiche, and microprint — viable if widely disliked media for scholarly research. Nor, of course, is microfilm the end of this story.

Today Chadwick-Healy, an imprint of ProQuest, offers institutional subscribers a database called *Early English Books Online* (*EEBO*), which contains digital facsimiles of books and other works printed between 1470 and 1700 in England, Scotland, Ireland, Wales, and British North America, as well as English-language works printed elsewhere. As of December 2011 *EEBO* contained catalog information for approximately 128,000 items, and all but a few records are linked to page images. What most users of *EEBO* probably don't know or seldom pause to consider is that the digital facsimiles of printed works that they can click to view — if their library subscribes — have been scanned from microfilm. Deep in the heart of *EEBO* lies Power's STC microfilm, begun in 1935 at the British Museum and supplemented by multiple microfilm projects undertaken by UMI over the next fifty years as well as by efforts that continue today. (ProQuest is currently filming on four continents, working with more than 125 libraries around the world that hold works from between 1470 and 1700.[91]) Other proprietary research databases offer subscribers digital scans of other microform projects that the Joint Committee encouraged or looked forward to before it dissolved after Binkley's death. The American Periodical Series and the Digital Evans, for instance, are both Readex products owned by NewsBank. There are research databases that aren't built on scans of microforms, like EBSCO's new American Antiquarian Society Periodicals Collection, but so far many of them are. One might wonder what difference it makes — or what kinds of difference it makes — that *EEBO*'s and Readex's facsimile page images are really digital reproductions of microform reproductions of materials for research?

Analogies between the work of the Joint Committee and today's digital humanities and life online more generally have admittedly been easy to draw in the pages above, perhaps too easy. Anachronistic comparisons like that between the typescript and the electronic book — like any comparison between the economic downturn of the 1930s and the economy today — always oversimplify. One suggestive alternative to these analogical jumps presents itself in tenuous through lines like that of the STC, running as it does from bibliographical reference through microfilm series to digital collection. And there are other tendrils of connection besides the STC that merit further exploration. Despite declining in the 1930s to initiate the publication service that the Joint Committee once so urgently pressed it to, the ACLS now offers individual and institutional subscribers its Humanities E-Book database, created in 2007 and based on an earlier failure, the History E-Book Project. Today the database contains approximately 3,300 e-books and is growing at the rate of roughly 500 per year. Many are scans of printed books, but some are "near print" publications, as Binkley would have said: they are "born digital," in today's terms, and published exclusively online. Social scientists have a much more open and robust online platform for sharing preprints, abstracts, and articles, called the Social Science Research Network.[92] And for its part, Edwards Brothers still exists, "specializing in short and ultra-short runs for publishers, authors, scholarly societies, industrial firms, universities, and others."[93] So the reproduction of materials for research continues to prosper in old ways and new. Meanwhile, deaccessioned library copies of Binkley's *Manual* can sometimes be had for between $150 and $200. On the rare occasions that Oscar Harpel's works come on the market, *Poets and Poetry of Printerdom* can cost $1,000 and *Harpel's Typograph* $2,500. The ultraspecialized labor of handset letterpress printing still counts for something, or so it would seem.

Binkley's *Manual* and *Harpel's Typograph* each document an important moment in the modern media history of documents, allowing an admittedly idiosyncratic glimpse of relevant concerns. If *Harpel's Typograph* is handy as a window onto the kinds of knowledge work to which job printing once catered, it also evokes the situation of printers and of letterpress printing in the broader cultural economy of the nineteenth and early twentieth centuries. The *Manual* opens an entirely different prospect. Something like "the internal documents of a great business enterprise," the documents with which the Joint Committee was concerned were proper to the internal workings of scholarship. At the same time, they were constitutive of the cultural heritage to which they potentially offered access and enabled the production of new knowledge that is the aim of scholarship. They were created as "near print" productions rather than print both because of economic barriers to print publication and — although this is contradictory — because money isn't supposed to matter that much within the ivory tower: circulations are typically small and readerships specialized. But they were near print for other reasons as well: internal documents can reflect the cutting edge(s) and moving parts of the spheres to which they are internal, and thus it makes sense to reproduce these documents easily and quickly, to allow for updates and new versions and editions. Reproduction means timely access.

It remains to offer another word here about amateurs, to whom I return in the afterword. The many talented amateurs of Harpel's day earned that identity partly because of their distinction from commercial printers. The printers may have seen them as a threat, but the amateurs surely had other designs beside competition — goals such as self-expression, virtuosity, reputation, communication, and the consequent formation of collective identities. The amateurs that Binkley described in the 1930s were different. Though also imagined in relation to the media that would be used to reproduce their documents, these amateurs were hardly amateur in contrast to printers or any commercial producers of near print, such as Edwards Brothers or UMI. The enlightened amateurs that Binkley dreamed of in "New Tools for Men of Letters" were amateur instead as a result of their distinction from professional scholars, those with PhDs who had been successful in securing research appointments. Today they have their closest counterparts in the amateurs who are being asked online to help transcribe the papers of Jeremy Bentham, for instance, or to recover meteorological data from early twentieth-century ships' logs, or to help astronomers wade through masses of data for signs of exploding stars.[94] The amateurs of the HRS, in contrast, were amateur compared to newly professionalized archivists, but also—like Benjamin's amateurs—compared to the managerial frame in which they labored, compared to their bosses, and compared to elite tradition.

The genie of the printers' monopoly came out of its bottle in the second half of the nineteenth century, and the bottle itself was broken by the mid-1930s. It would continue to shatter into smaller pieces as newer new media were deployed and documents became ever more materially diverse. The following chapter jumps ahead in time to consider another episode in the history of documents, again by thinking through the media of documentary reproduction and their contexts. If the typescript book—reproduced by mimeograph, photo-offset, or other means—helps reveal the work of documents that is internal to a specific social sphere, then the photocopies considered next offer an opportunity to consider more particularly how insides and outsides relate to one another and how documents traverse this divide. Insiders and outsiders are not precisely professionals and amateurs, of course, but these and related designations for the actors involved do merit further attention. Compared to mimeographed or photo-offset documents, xerographic copies are relatively frictionless, at least insofar as they take less time and don't require the preparation of a master from which to make duplicates. But friction is a back-formation, existing only in retrospect. Until the widespread availability of photocopies, the media that Binkley describes were what made the reproduction of documents thinkable as such, especially when those media became more and more prevalent as cheaper models became available. In the mid-1960s a journalist visiting the headquarters of Students for a Democratic Society noticed that "taped to one of the walls was a picture of a mimeograph machine. Just beneath it someone had written the words 'Our Founder.'"[95] One must imagine that the caption was sardonic, but it was affectionately so.

Even a private xerographic copy can be a primary record if a person who used it becomes

a subject of historical inquiry—or, of course, if one's topic is the history of reproductions.

—G. Thomas Tanselle, *Literature and Artifacts*

A former researcher at Xerox's Palo Alto Research Center remembers when the concept of the photocopy began to crumble. "In the late 1980s," he writes, "Xerox Corporation began to wrestle with the consequences of the upcoming technological shift" from optical to digital copying: "Informally, it was easy to see that what had been a unitary operation of 'copying' was being broken down into a series of parts: scan, store, and print; or perhaps scan, store, modify, and print; or even scan, store, modify, retrieve, and print."[1] There was a conceptual shift taking place in conjunction with technological change. But if the ideas of xerography and xerographic documents had started to break apart in some quarters, how and when had they ever coalesced in the first place? What was the idea of the photocopy that stood to be so broken and displaced? The answers to these questions involve the invention and promotion of xerographic technology, of course, but they also involve untold millions of documents—photocopies—and the people who made them. When Haloid Xerox (as it was known then) was developing what eventually became its model 914, introduced in 1960, the company mistakenly believed that xerography would fill a very specific niche in current office practice. Thinking along the lines that Robert Binkley had in his comparative analysis of different methods of documentary reproduction, the company imagined that xerography would be good for anywhere from five to twenty copies: too many for carbon paper, but too few to be worth the time and expense involved in making a photostat, mimeo, or ditto master. Instead, Haloid customers found myriad new uses for copies, not infrequently making as many Xeroxes in a month as the machines had been designed to produce in a year.[2] An engineer named Chester Carlson invented xerographic reproduction, one might say, and the corporation that helped develop his ideas invented Xerox machines, but the photocopy itself was invented by users and on the fly.

The concept of xerography came together unexpectedly, emerging in the 1960s according to the varied uses of Xerox machines. Although it is impossible to chase down all the ordinary people who — to the initial amazement of Haloid salesmen — helped make that happen, this chapter seeks to retrieve the idea of the photocopy as it existed then. That said, xerography — unlike either letterpress printing or the near print technologies of the 1930s — can be hard to see and grapple with today, both because xerographic reproduction remains so ubiquitous and because, thanks to digital copying and scanning, it has become so entangled with digital processes. Today the idea of the photocopy has been corrupted by our intuitive knowledge of things digital, as well as muddied by the confusing proliferation and convergence of digital technologies: the copier down the hall now also prints, scans, faxes, sorts, and staples. As a methodological workaround, then, and as a way of getting a clearer look at the early xerographic era, this chapter address itself to famous photocopies: the Pentagon Papers, copied in 1969 by Daniel Ellsberg and leaked to the *New York Times* in 1971; and a few less widely known examples from the 1970s, among them John Lions's "Commentary on the Sixth Edition UNIX Operating System," called by programmers "the most photocopied document in computer science."[3] Though hardly typical Xeroxes, these examples are nonetheless suggestive. Together they help reveal the idea of the photocopy in some complexity, framed, for instance, by a politics that is seldom remembered today and was rarely acknowledged then, at least outside of Russia and its sphere of influence. Xerographic reproduction remained effectively illegal in the Soviet Union until its collapse, and, according to George Soros, the project he initiated to promote an open society in Hungary began in 1984 by making photocopiers available for purchase by cultural and scientific institutions.[4]

The title of this chapter, "Xerographers of the Mind," alludes to and acknowledges a 1969 essay by the great bibliographer D. F. McKenzie called

"Printers of the Mind." In that essay, McKenzie is concerned with early printed books and with a number of speculative assumptions regarding their production that he saw creeping into textual studies. Once iterated by lions like Fredson Bowers or Charlton Hinman, these speculations had begun to function as received wisdom, populating early modern Europe with imaginary "printers of the mind." McKenzie wanted to test imagination against the surviving archival record. He argued that twentieth-century scholars had been "too readily imputing" their own ideas about labor, efficiency, and throughput to the printing houses of the seventeenth and early eighteenth centuries.[5] They wrote as if early modern printers punched a clock. His essay offers an elegant redress of anachronism. My hope in appealing to McKenzie is that the necessary figments of my project—xerographers of the mind—can at least be birthed without anachronism. Documentary reproduction is a labor and a knowledge practice both dynamic and diverse. Even as we bustle off today to make digital copies before class and unthinkingly call them "Xeroxes" and "photocopies," we need to understand xerography on its own terms and according to the double xerographic subject of its day: the self who pushes the button and the self-concerning document that lies face down on the glass. As the case of Ellsberg and the Pentagon Papers suggests, xerography must be understood specifically within the cultural politics of the Cold War. And as the case of Lions and his commentary on UNIX demonstrates, the idea of the photocopy would ultimately help shape the digital knowledge practices that would eventually render it paradoxically so ubiquitous, transparent, and naturalized and at the same time so complicated and obscure.

....

The copying, leaking, and publication of the Pentagon Papers occurred as part of the groundswell of popular resistance to the Vietnam War in the United States. The government invoked national security concerns and moved to bar publication of the papers by the *New York Times*. A federal court in New York enjoined the *Times* from publishing them, but before the Supreme Court could hear the case on appeal, other newspapers began to publish the papers. The Supreme Court ultimately ruled in favor of the *Times*, making this an important First Amendment case. But the whole episode had a much more tawdry side too: government improprieties in pursuit of Ellsberg, the xerographer, included ransacking his psychiatrist's office, an operation carried out by a covert group known as "the Plumbers," who worked to plug leaks for the administration of President Richard M. Nixon. Not only was the government's case against Ellsberg eventually dismissed on the grounds of prosecutorial misconduct, but further covert operations by the Plumbers would include the infamous Watergate break-in, a key link in the twisted chain of events that led to Nixon's resignation in 1974.

The whole affair started in October 1969, when Ellsberg began to copy in installments a multivolume work with the ungainly title "History of U.S. Decision-Making Process on Vietnam Policy," also known as the "Report of the Office of the Secretary of Defense Vietnam Task Force." He took sections of the history home from his office at the RAND Corporation, returning each section after secretly photocopying it at night on a machine in the office of a sympathetic friend. The history was bound in cardboard covers with metal tapes, which could be removed for copying. There were forty-seven volumes in all, and Ellsberg started in the middle. He was Xeroxing one of fifteen extant duplicates, produced in house at the Pentagon at the behest of Robert McNamara. McNamara had commissioned the history in 1967, when he was secretary of defense, and a team of thirty-six authors had worked on it for a year and a half, compiling some four thousand pages of documents from Pentagon and State Department files and writing an additional three thousand pages of original narrative in order to frame, connect, and analyze the documents. The thirty-six authors were—by design—anonymous, so they could be critical without risking their reputations. Their secretaries were anonymous by custom: the history employed an unknown number of Pentagon clerks and typists. Even though it included some public, unclassified material, the whole study was classified, and the words "TOP SECRET—Sensitive" appeared on every cardboard cover and at the top of almost every page.[6]

If the authors and typists had managed to turn many documents into a single history—edition of fifteen—Ellsberg was now turning one history back into multiple papers. Xeroxing was only the first step in what became a lengthy disaggregation and multiplication process. Ellsberg made two copies that fall, but it wasn't until the *New York Times* began to publish from and about the history on June 13, 1971, that it became public and—inconsistently at first—plural, acquiring the name the Pentagon papers and, ultimately, the Pentagon Papers. As Ellsberg recalled in an interview the following year, he "took out the Pentagon Papers from Rand and began to Xerox them. . . . My hope was that I could get it to the—to the Senate Foreign Relations Committee for hearings, somehow."[7] Seen from the vantage point of 1972 they were plural — "Xerox them" — yet as the intentional subject of 1969 it was singular — "get it to the Senate." Them and it, the Pentagon Papers and the history: this schizophrenia only gradually resolved itself.

The phrase "the Pentagon papers" cropped up on page 38 of the *Times* when the story broke, but not in either of the stories on page 1, where the papers were called a "Vietnam Archive" in one headline and a "Vast Review of War" in the other. They/it was typically referred to as "a Pentagon study" and "the study," as well as "documents" and "papers." Nixon and his administration vainly tried to reframe them as the "Kennedy/Johnson papers on the war," but that name never stuck.[8] Though capitalized in headlines,[9] in news articles, columns, and editorials the Pentagon Papers remained "Pentagon papers," at least until that fall, after the Supreme Court decision in *New York Times v. United States* and the publication of *The Pentagon Papers as Published by the New York Times*, a wildly successful Bantam paperback edition selling for $2.25.[10] Only then did journalists begin to appeal to what "is now known as 'the Pentagon Papers,'" with two capital *P*s.[11] Common parlance emerging from public controversy and headline news had completed the multiplication process that Ellsberg began when he undid the bindings, Xeroxed the history, and collated it into two loose sets of pages. Additional multiplications followed, as Beacon Press and the Government Printing Office published different editions, so that soon the term "Pentagon Papers" referred indistinctly to a whole muddle of versions, contents, ancillary drafts, selections, secrets, and disclosures.[12]

McNamara and others at the Pentagon had tried to ensure that the history lacked an identifiable author. Like *Harpel's Typograph* and Robert Binkley's *Manual*, the history emerged as the result of collaborative labors altogether too recondite to reconstruct in hindsight; yet unlike the earlier works, it emerged from the processes of its composition and reproduction without an author's name attached to it. It was government work, classified as a state secret and thereby without recourse to the more general classificatory operations that Michel Foucault calls "the author function."[13] Only public discourse spurred by controversy attached the "Pentagon" and then cemented it to "Papers." It was as if the papers, instead of having an author or authors, had sprung from a giant five-sided filing cabinet. And the filing function, unlike the author function, organizes documents rather than classifies discourse. For that reason the definite article "the" ended up doing as much work as the two capital *P*s, as "the Pentagon Papers" became the imprecise designation for an overlapping cluster of anthologies and potential anthologies of government documents about the Vietnam War, *the* documents—whichever ones they were exactly—that had so suddenly become controversial. It became, in short, a convenient moniker for a giant bone of contention.

Despite their keen and conflicting interest in the Pentagon Papers, neither the newspapers nor the state had much explicit interest in the papers as Xeroxes. They cared about the papers' linguistic meanings, that is, to the virtual exclusion of their bibliographical meanings.[14] When the *Times* was pressed by a judge to explain why it wouldn't and shouldn't hand over "the huge document," it insisted that giving up "the documents" might somehow reveal the identity of its anonymous source.[15] Yet nowhere in its publication of the papers did the newspaper go out of its way to report that the documents were xerographic copies. The copies were assumed to be identical to the documents, and—or rather, because—the documents were assumed to be self-identical with their linguistic content. Similarly, when the government finally did learn Ellsberg's role, it obtained a fifteen-count indictment against him and his associate, Anthony Russo, but only the first count of the lengthy indictment contains the word "copy" (used twice) or "Xerox" (once). Instead, Ellsberg and Russo were charged with embezzlement, theft, and "conversion to their own use" of government property. They were accused of communicating, delivering, transmitting, and retaining classified documents. And they were charged with conspiring to do all of these things. Copying was mentioned only as an incidental component of conspiracy.[16] Their real offenses, according to the state, were theft (six counts) and espionage (eight counts). Xerography was by implication merely a modus operandi.

Xerographic interests are thus dramatically asymmetrical: if the newspapers and the state lacked explicit interest in the papers as Xeroxes, the same cannot be said of Ellsberg or his supposed coconspirators. Although it must be self-evident that Ellsberg cared about the papers as Xeroxes—because he Xeroxed them—what is less patent is the nature of this bibliographical investment in these documents. He had a certain political interest in the history and in leaking it, of course, but his interest in the photocopies *as* photocopies was additionally complex and depended on xerography as an unacknowledged form of cultural production, a form of making, remaking, and self-making that was framed in part by the always emergent bureaucratic norms of statecraft and citizenship. Ellsberg's bibliographical interest was at once editorial, mimetic, and variously egoistic.

....

First, xerographic reproduction offered a way to edit or remake the "History of U.S. Decision-Making Process on Vietnam Policy" as well as to expropriate it.[17] Ellsberg edited out some of the history when he decided (though accounts vary on this point) not to copy the four volumes on diplomacy, but more important, when he edited out the words "TOP SECRET — Sensitive" wherever he could. To begin with, Ellsberg and his companions — working after hours in the advertising agency of Russo's ex-girlfriend — cut the words off the bottom and top margins of the photocopies, first with scissors and later with a paper cutter. Then Russo suggested that they photocopy the words off. He contrived a cardboard mask for the Xerox machine, so that every page of the history was copied without its margins, producing new, empty margins: the history was literally reframed for public access. At least in theory: in practice a lot of page numbers and top or bottom lines of text were also edited out this way, and plenty of "top secret" markings remained. In Ellsberg's retrospective account of this xerographic "declassification" process, the words "top secret" crop up like dragon's teeth. No matter how careful Ellsberg and Russo were at the photocopier, a few of the markings still seemed to be there whenever Ellsberg ruffled through his piles of copies. Particularly when he later took his copies to be recopied at commercial Xerox shops, Ellsberg had to check his editing, resorting to scissors again and again to remove "top secret," so the clerks wouldn't be suspicious as the pages in question got copied and, in effect, grew back into 8½" × 11" pages of the history.[18]

In a certain respect Ellsberg's editorial interest in xerography can be seen as both a response to and a continuation of McNamara's and the Pentagon's editorial interests. Textual reproduction and compilation have always been close allies. Leslie Gelb had directed the preparation of the history, which involved the location and duplication of documents in the files of the Department of Defense, the Department of State, and the Central Intelligence Agency (figure 3.1). The history was made with and out of photocopies, it seems — and photocopies of photocopies, photocopies of transcripts of cables, photocopies of mimeograph copies, and so on — while the heterogeneity of the final version reflected that process when it was typed and reproduced in house.[19] Ellsberg himself had been recruited

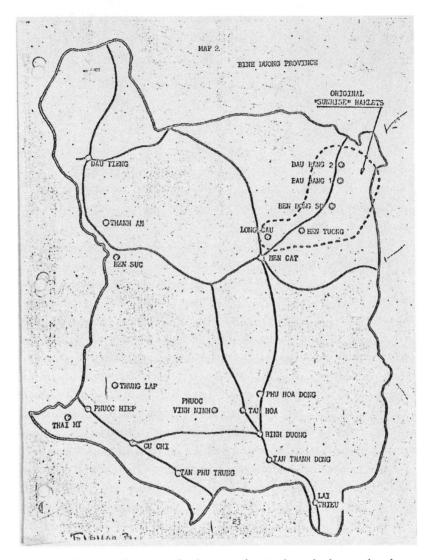

FIGURE 3.1. Map 2, a photocopy of a photocopy (notice the multiply reproduced loose-leaf holes), reproduced as part of the Pentagon Papers Part IV-B-2 (1969) to document the beginning of the U.S.-backed "Strategic Hamlet Program" in South Vietnam (1962), digitized by the National Archives and Records Administration in 2011.

as an author for the history while he was an employee of the RAND Corporation. He worked for several months during 1967 compiling material and drafting a section on the policy of President John F. Kennedy's administration — although, according to Gelb, little of Ellsberg's draft survived in the final version.[20] Ellsberg was now effectively reediting the edit to which he and his subject had been subject.

While part of Ellsberg's investment in the photocopies as photocopies was editorial, another part of it was mimetic, concerning reproduction itself. Once he began copying, he didn't (or perhaps he couldn't) stop. Some of the choicest documents seemed to beg for duplication: Ellsberg "sometimes [made] as many as forty or fifty copies of a particular document."[21] However, he started with two copies of the whole, because making more than that would take too long — the Xerox 914 machine he and Russo used took at least six seconds to make each copy[22] — and because he was "obsessed" with the thought that if he were discovered the copies would be confiscated and all of his efforts wasted.[23] Better to make two copies and store them separately. The same logic led to a giant but partial third copy, and then the additional logic of having one's copy and giving it away too took hold. Ellsberg eventually gave a whole set of copies to Senator J. William Fulbright (D-Arkansas) of the Senate Foreign Relations Committee, in whose hands it languished, and then he felt he wanted to replace those copies with more copies of the copies he had retained. This led Ellsberg to commercial Xerox shops in New York City and Cambridge, Massachusetts, where Massachusetts Avenue near Harvard University had just become what one observer called the "Sunset Strip of copying."[24] Retailers — even clothing stores — had rushed to add coin-operated machines, as a single generation of Harvard students began effectively to download the Harvard libraries.

According to its redevelopment planners, the Harvard Square neighborhood in Cambridge had three copy shops in 1956, but by 1971 there were eight.[25] Meanwhile on campus, the medical school library was the first Harvard library to introduce a Xerox machine in 1960, "available on the honor system" for five cents a copy. A year later there were two machines in operation, yet they "prove[d] scarcely sufficient to keep up with the demand." Widener Library and the other Harvard libraries added machines, too, making some immediate changes in the way that engineering literature — for one — circulated, since article copies, instead of bound journals or unbound issues, became the new unit of transaction. Demand was high everywhere: when Baker Library installed its Xerox 914 in 1964, it made 25,000 copies in the first three months, "twice as many as had been expected."[26] America's great circulating libraries had long promoted the secular "devotions of self-realization that embody freedom in liberal democracy,"[27] in the form of selecting, borrowing, and reading books, and now those devotions were being joined by the practice of xerographically excerpting books. Anyone can "make his own book," Marshall McLuhan pronounced, and make it out of other books.[28] Copying—as few scholars have admitted publicly—would become a surrogate for reading, displacing knowledge: you can read something and have it in mind, or you can Xerox something and have it at hand.[29]

Ultimately Ellsberg had copies or partial copies of the history squirreled away with different friends. Xerography was an "addiction," according to one contemporary account, and Ellsberg came close to proving this point. One of the things you did with photocopies was photocopy them; you could also, as Ellsberg also did, loan them to others—like Neil Sheehan of the *New York Times*—who might photocopy them. The result might be "the insidious growth of a negative attitude toward originals—a feeling that nothing can be of importance *unless* it is copied, or is a copy itself."[30] By this token, perhaps Ellsberg was unconsciously trying to make his copies more important—or more clearly important—by recopying them. In this he would hardly have been alone. It seems clear in hindsight that copying copies was effectively the so-called killer app that Haloid Xerox had initially overlooked in developing and marketing the 914.

The year 1971 seems to have been when American observers of bureaucrats and bureaucracy detected with certainty the new, bureaucratic norm. "Before the Xerox era," noted an official at the National Archives, government agencies had central files, and "when anyone needed information he went to that central file." By 1971, however, the government had acquired some 60,000 copy machines with predictable results: "Many a government executive prefers to maintain files in his own office. . . . The result is that where we used to have a limited number of central filing places we now have thousands, with endless duplication of papers."[31] Keeping something meant photocopying it. In the 1930s documentary reproduction had meant access; now it meant archive.[32] The techniques of mechanical reproduction in the 1930s—with the exception of carbon paper—were typically framed as techniques of distribution, of circulation. Photocopying shared this same logic, but it was also used as a technique of preservation, an embrace of plenitude and redundancy. So a new crisis in information management loomed. Lucky, then, that the Pentagon's production of its history happened after the "Xerox Revolution" but before the crisis, gloated the historian Richard Ullman, another of the authors who worked on the Vietnam study for Gelb: "Not only is there unauthorized reproduction and circulation (within the government usually) of even the most restricted formal documents; but also informal [ones, such as drafts, memos, and notes] . . . the like of which in a prior era would have been confined to the personal files of their writer are now reproduced and circulated to his colleagues and friends — and, in turn, are retained in their files. These informal materials . . . were among the most valuable sources at the disposal of the authors of the Pentagon study." [33] Though according to Max Weber modern bureaucracy assiduously separates home from office, and business from private correspondence, [34] the xerographic medium was helping to personalize files. Filing, like reading, was become a means of self-possession. [35]

In addition to his editorial and mimetic investments in the Xeroxes as Xeroxes, Ellsberg had other, more nebulous ego investments, which can only be guessed at in relation to peculiar circumstances both personal and professional. One of the oddest details of his Xeroxing is personal: Ellsberg had his two children — then ten and thirteen years old — help with the copying and collation on several occasions, which struck at least his ex-wife, their mother, as appallingly irresponsible. Retrospectively Ellsberg explains that he wanted his kids to be a part of things, to see that he was acting "normally" and "calmly" rather than "weird" or "crazy." [36] (It is tempting to read normality in this instance as masculine and weirdness as hysterical or feminine, if only because Xerox machine operators of the day were "almost invariably" women. [37] Ellsberg was in one sense performing his masculinity.) Whatever his motivating impulse, the incident suggests that xerography — whatever else it offered — here enabled, enacted, or expressed his ego-identity at some basic, even primal, level.

Xerographic interests soon structured Ellsberg's professional identity as well. At the September 1970 meeting of the American Political Science Association, Ellsberg, who was by then working at the Center for International Studies at the Massachusetts Institute of Technology, delivered a paper about the war titled "Escalating in a Quagmire." He drew, of necessity, on his secret, personal archive of Xeroxes, but he couldn't cite them. In a lengthy footnote he explains his perspective as a *view from inside* and warns suggestively that "until more materials are made public," his conclusions "must be regarded as hypotheses whose implications can at least be analyzed, and which can be tested against the honest judgments of others who have had access to official sources."[38] At both a personal and a professional level, Ellsberg's investment in the photocopies as photocopies helped him position himself as an insider outside: inside his family although outside his marriage; outside the government yet in on its workings.

This was a position interestingly in keeping with the outsider-inside role that Ellsberg had previously cultivated as a government employee and consultant. In a 1966 letter to McNamara, for instance, he noted that "official reporting (including Nodis and Eyes Only, back-channel and what-have-you) is grossly inadequate to the job of educating high-level decisionmakers." To really be informed, he suggested in a letter to Walter Rostow, the national security advisor, it was important to get "out, beyond the end of the chain of paper and electric signals, [and maybe even] out from Saigon, into a world of red dirt, green rice fields, burned schoolrooms and little, three-sided mud forts." "There is simply no substitute," he wrote to McNamara, "for long, unhurried, *private* conversation with the regrettably small number of people [that is, Americans] with prolonged and broad experience" out there and (as he put it to Rostow) "*inside* South Vietnam."[39] You could get so far outside that you were in. Sometimes the best insider was out. The inside-outside rhetoric is unstable, inconsistent in all but its binarism, and thoroughly opportunistic. Most importantly, it parrots the self-authorizing inside-outside by which the executive branch routinely if cynically produces its own distinction from the rest of the world.

As Sheehan saw with such clarity when he framed the Pentagon Papers for publication in the *New York Times*, the leaked material handily reveals the ways in which the postwar executive branch functions as a "different world," with "a set of values, a dynamic, a language and a perspective quite distinct from the public world of the ordinary citizen":

> The segments of the public world — Congress, the news media, the citizenry, even international opinion as a whole — are regarded from within the world of the government insider as elements to be influenced. The policy memorandums repeatedly discuss ways to move these outside "audiences" in the desired direction, through such techniques as the controlled release of information and appeals to patriotic stereotypes.
>
> The papers also make clear the deep-felt need of the government

insider for secrecy in order to keep the machinery of state functioning smoothly and to maintain a maximum ability to affect the public world.[40]

In such a context, a leaked copy has the potential not only to transgress or leak across the inside-outside boundary but also, importantly, to mirror — one might say technologically to reproduce — its iteration as a form of critique. The leak speaks inside-outside rhetoric in the arena that reverses its presumptions. When the leaked document is published, the sheer "incommensurability of the *locus* of enunciation and the enunciated *text*" serves as a "mockery" of the executive branch — the machinery of state — in precisely its own terms, in literally its own voice.[41] The leak thus draws lavishly on one tradition of parody: Tina Fey repeats Sarah Palin verbatim on television, while the modern security state must create tone-deaf zones where parody can't exist. No joking at airport checkpoints: "Your safety is our priority," says the Transportation Security Administration's website, adding: "Think before you speak."[42]

If the executive branch under Presidents George W. Bush and Barack Obama has managed to bring the term "gulag" back into circulation,[43] Ellsberg and the Pentagon Papers, like Nixon and the Watergate tapes, in retrospect lend the term "glasnost" a certain appeal. Glasnost — openness, transparency, availability to public speech — did not become a familiar term in the West until the era of Soviet president Mikhail Gorbachev in the late 1980s, although it was long used by authors and producers of samizdat, self-made publications — typed carbon paper duplicates, triplicates, quadruplicates, etc. — which circulated semi-privately in the Soviet Union as a medium of dissent.[44] It can be applied in a narrow sense to the exposing of the Pentagon's machinations and Nixonian malfeasance. When Western authors took stock of xerography, they typically did appeal to the idea of self-publication, like samizdat, but without any explicit attention to openness, Ellsberg notwithstanding. (Why appeal to openness in an already open society?) Slow to invoke glasnost, observers were quick to see the implications for copyright holders: Congress began to hold hearings on reprography as early as 1965 and soon after that contemplated the first major revisions to the Copyright Act of 1909, partly to protect publishers from Xeroxes.[45] Librarians and libraries were already worried about their own liability.[46] In one sense the Xeroxed Pentagon Papers were entirely beside the point of this debate, because they were government documents and therefore not subject to copyright protection. In another sense, however, Ellsberg and the Pentagon Papers demonstrate the value of openness, to which librarians and libraries and civil libertarians are dedicated and that the law seeks to maintain and constrain in diverse, intricate ways. The public domain in the United States has been structured in relation to copyright—a form of private ownership conceived in the public interest—but Ellsberg provides a nice reminder of the additional motivations that attend copying. Xerography, in short, is a way of making, not always or only of owning or taking.

I will return to the question of xerography and copyright below, but first I want to follow openness a little further, both in relation to the bureaucratic norms of statecraft and citizenship and in relation to computer science and software development in the same period. While the so-called Xerox revolution helped make filing more certainly a form of self-possession and documentary reproduction a potential element of self-making, it also helped to alter the subjectivities of bureaucratic labor within a broader climate that was characterized by increasing attention to disclosing files and releasing information, sometimes in the breach. The Nixon administration in general and the Watergate hearings in particular became a stage on which multiple dramas of documentary destruction and its disclosure were played. Most famously there was the erasure of eighteen and a half minutes discovered on one of the secret White House tapes, a long hiss in place of what should or could have been a discussion about the Watergate break-in between Nixon and his chief of staff. (In testimony that strained credulity, Nixon's secretary, Rose Mary Woods, claimed to have erased the tape by mistake.) Paper documents also disappeared. For example, L. Patrick Gray III, acting director of the Federal Bureau of Investigation, resigned after it was reported that he had destroyed documents given to him by John W. Dean III, the White House counsel. Dean's testimony later suggested that Nixon's advisor John D. Ehrlichman had wanted the documents shredded. This was before paper shredders were widely available, so there was both exoticism and intrigue to the story. Ehrlichman would testify before the U.S. Senate that "shredding is just not something that I have ever resorted to under any circumstances nor proposed to anybody under any circumstances." Infelicitously, he continued: "We have a great disposal system at the White House. If you really want to get rid of a document, you put it in a burn bag and seal it up and it's never opened again, and it goes into a furnace and that is the end of it."[47]

Scandal led to pressure for greater openness, and in 1974 Congress passed a toothsome amendment to the 1966 Freedom of Information Act, overriding President Gerald Ford's veto. (Ford vetoed the bill at the urging of his chief of staff, Donald Rumsfeld, and his deputy, Richard Cheney, who had consulted with Antonin Scalia, then a government lawyer.)[48] In the face of growing anxiety about computer databases, Congress also passed the Privacy Act of 1974, which requires federal agencies to inform the public about the systems of records they use at the same time that it establishes rules for the protection of personally identifiable information. Both gestures by Congress helped initiate the information regime in which Americans have continued to live, a regime additionally structured by an extended sequence of laws of fluctuating strictness and enforcement and, in some cases, evasion, if one thinks of the Patriot Act of 2001 and the expanded powers of the Bush presidency, with its national security letters and avoidance of the Foreign Intelligence Surveillance Court, or if one thinks of questions raised under the Obama administration about electronic surveillance by the National Security Agency. Privacy and the retention or destruction of paperwork in the private sector are governed by a related body of law that includes everything from rules about privacy in the Health Insurance Portability and Accountability Act of 1996 to laws like the Public Company Accounting Reform and Investor Protection Act of 2002 (popularly known as Sarbanes-Oxley), which strengthened corporate accounting standards after the collapse of Enron. In general, the law reflects a growing concern to protect not just documents but also data.

....

My second example in this chapter, John Lions's "Commentary on the Sixth Edition UNIX Operating System," offers a way to think about xerography and the digital together, to begin to see how the one helped to make sense of the other and vice versa. Lions's commentary was a self-published textbook for computer science students at the University of New South Wales. UNIX was an operating system written in 1969 by Ken Thompson, Dennis Ritchie, and members of the computer science research group at Bell Labs, the research arm of AT&T. Rather than distribute UNIX commercially, AT&T licensed the software to researchers worldwide for a nominal sum, sending both machine code and source code out to its licensees. The software was proprietary, though, so Lions could not legally distribute the commentary (which included the source code) in any but his immediate, licensed, context. Throughout the 1970s and into the 1980s, researchers everywhere "ported" UNIX to different makes of computer, tweaking, debugging, "forking," and extending the software, which was then issued in new versions in installments by Bell Labs: a storied chapter in the prehistory of free and open-source software familiar to geeks and hackers everywhere.[49] While this early instance of "sharing" software to develop it depended upon the emerging research community, that community likewise depended upon the communicative means of its association. Lions's commentary, for example, started as part of the gray-market economy of coursepacks but soon escaped its immediate context to become "the most photocopied document in computer science" and "the most famous suppressed manuscript in computer history," according to hacker lore.[50]

The significance of UNIX and the lessons of Lions's commentary are both detailed in Christopher Kelty's important book, *Two Bits*.[51] Rather than rehearsing Kelty's argument, I want to point instead to another coincidence of UNIX and Xerox—besides Lions's commentary—and then briefly consider software documentation—including the commentary—as the quintessential xerographic subject of its day. The coincidence I have in mind is a pure one: when the inventor Chester Carlson (briefly a Bell Labs employee himself in the 1930s) began his dogged pursuit of xerography, he was moonlighting from his day job in the patent department of an electronics firm. That work impressed him with the need for more efficient means of documentary reproduction.[52] Coincidentally, when Thompson, Ritchie, and their colleagues at Bell Labs started writing UNIX, they got approval to purchase the necessary hardware (a new microcomputer, the PDP-11) only because they promised to work on document preparation techniques for the patent department at Bell Labs. The patent department was the first user of UNIX.[53] So both xerography and UNIX emerged against and amid similar bureaucratic pressures, the immense shuffling of paper involved in making inventions public—disclosure—in order to claim limited-term monopolies on them: letters patent.

Thompson and Ritchie's in-house commitment to paperwork meant that whatever else the UNIX operating system was able to accomplish— it remains in many ways the inspiration for all of today's operating systems—it could be used as what had just been dubbed a word processor, or a system to create, edit, save, retrieve, format, and run off documents.[54] If documents were newly xerographic subjects, then they were also very recently digital ones. Because specifications and manuals were authored in association with the software they detail, they were early and important digital documents, produced with and about digital systems. It was obvious to programmers that "among all tools" required to produce software documentation, "the one that saves the most labor may well be a computerized text-editing system, operating on a dependable vehicle."[55] In 1971 Thompson and Ritchie used their system to produce a hard copy, printed manual for the first version of UNIX. On its cover page, they warn: "The rate of change of the system is so great that a dismayingly large number of early sections [of this manual] had to be modified while the rest were being written. The unbounded effort required to stay up-to-date is best indicated by the fact that several of the programs described were written specifically to aid in preparation of this manual."[56] Documentation and its digital subject are inextricable: programmers must document in order to program, and program in order to document. Any effort "to stay up-to-date" is "unbounded," as Thompson and Ritchie put it, because the operating system and its documentation (like digital networks and their specifications, as it happens, or — as Kelty explains — online "recursive publics" and the communicative means of their existence as such) develop together through a process of "bootstrapping," an ongoing "contest" to keep the technology and its self-description mutually and exactingly germane.[57] "Round and round goes the preparation" of any manual, "as feedback from users and implementers" drives changes to the subject documented and its documentation.[58]

In the context of UNIX versions, manual revisions, and "man page" additions (man pages are man[ual] pages, explanations — help — that exist within the program itself), John Lions's commentary offers a snapshot, freeze-frame, a view in and of an impressively fluid landscape. Every additional Xerox of the commentary, and every Xerox of that Xerox, further stabilized its object on the page. In this respect Xeroxes, like printouts and other outputs, are supremely inertial as cultural forms. Yet Lions too knew something of the contrasting accelerative pressures that came from running UNIX while explaining it. As he put it in his acknowledgments, "The co-operation of the 'nroff' program must also be mentioned. Without it, these notes could never have been produced in this form. However it has yielded some of its more enigmatic secrets so reluctantly, that the author's gratitude is indeed mixed. Certainly 'nroff' itself must provide a fertile field for future practitioners of the program documenter's art."[59] Lions's documentation efforts, like Thompson and Ritchie's, were "unbounded" and ongoing: he admitted freely that he was unable to "publish through more usual channels" for legal reasons, and he urged his readers to forward "corrections, criticism and suggestions" to improve the commentary in future versions.[60] The very means of creating documentation ("nroff" is from "run off") would need further documentation.

Both UNIX manuals — one corporate and the other samizdat — offer early instances of documents as doubly invitation and subject to change. Machine output was frozen on the page, while shared labors were "unbounded" or ongoing, and documentation therefore remained in flux. The paint was never dry. The manual and the operating system were each the mutual result of inertial and accelerative pressures, at the same time stuck (and restuck, like so many nth-generation photocopies) in versions while also sputtering forward in annotations, patches, and revisions. Xerographic reproduction and the versioning of digital objects thus offered contexts for one another, even apart from the idea of digital copying. In this early era of minimal networking, digital copying remained encumbered by the necessity of transporting programs and data on magnetic tape or other hard media. Even the networked contexts of the day prove this point. In 1967 Douglas Engelbart and his team at the Stanford Research Institute were challenged to provide documentation for the Advanced Research Projects Agency Network (better known as ARPANET) as it came online. There were a few things they knew for sure: they wanted users to be able to access documentation remotely across the network; they were certain that the distribution of hardcopy documents was also necessary, possibly in the form of microfiche; and they would obviously need a system of documentation that would allow frequent updating. They wanted a category of "changeable" documents that were "computer-sensible."[61] So documentation depended on fixed documents and dynamic ones, where the necessary proliferation and dissemination of fixed copies both enabled and ennobled digital ones, making their advantages clear.

Today changeable, computer-sensible documents are sometimes called "functional," "evergreen," or "living" documents. Wikipedia uses itself as an example of a living document.[62] This terminology is a little misleading, because digital documents are not all "living" in the same ways, and analog documents are not necessarily "dead." The next chapter will consider the PDF format, a file type frequently used today for coursepacks (of varying degrees of legality) and documentation — think of your cell phone manual—precisely because it is experienced as less living than other formats, less subject to change by users yet still easily produced in updated versions by corporations. In the analog realm, the U.S. Constitution is the nation's most important "living document." The Constitution lives at least because it has been and can be amended, though for everyone who rejects a purely "originalist" judicial philosophy, it lives as well because it remains interpretable as circumstances that its framers could not have anticipated present themselves to the judiciary. That's "living" in a very different sense than a Wikipedia article "lives." In the early era of xerography, the Port Huron Statement—a manifesto that the Students for a Democratic Society issued in 1962—described itself as "a living document subject to change with our times and experiences," because its authors invited dialogue. "Living" for a document, then, is not a technological condition as much as a social one. Like open-source software, living documents exist as shared objects of revision, though they can just as easily be shared via corporate management systems as by an open democratic process. Software documentation—like software itself—has lived and lives in many settings.

Observers in the mid-1960s noted that xerography was producing "a discernible change" in "the attitude of educators toward printed textbooks,"[63] and by the mid-1970s the attitudes of educators and their students in computer science seem to have experienced discernible change from two directions at once. Coursepacks and manuals helped suggest the potential fluidity of print publication—its fixity melted by selection, excerption, collection, versioning, and reproduction—while UNIX, time sharing, networking, and similar endeavors helped affirm the fluidity of digital documents, their fixity melted in the ongoing and the online. Documents—always a sprawling, diverse genre—became more noticeably distinct from questions of format when they were apprehended as digital objects amid and among other digital objects.[64] Indeed, the bibliographical standing of digital documents remains something of a puzzle, and a productive one.[65] Xerography, though itself a specific bibliographical form (and meaningful to Ellsberg, among others, as such, as I have been at pains to argue), ironically helped to gesture toward bibliography in eclipse. The typescript book had embraced multiple formats and media in its way, and now the Xerox machine worked a similar trick in spades. You could photocopy almost anything, observers noted with enthusiasm: a Xerox machine can make "copies of almost any page—printed, handwritten, typed, or drawn," including "a flat page, two pages of an open book, or even a small

FIGURE 3.2. 1960s advertisement for the Xerox 914. The 914 was named for the dimensions of the documents it could copy (9" × 14"), yet variety became more of a selling point than width and breadth.

three-dimensional object like a watch" (figure 3.2).[66] Whatever it was—no matter what medium, format, or genre—it became a document.

Documents have a long history, of course. What is so important here is that in addition to reproducing documents, xerography both identifies and creates them. Xeroxing became a way—part of a whole repertoire of ways, really—of seeing documents as documents. That is, it was and remains a way of reading. Xeroxing is reading not in the sense that machines such as scanners are said to read, but rather in the way that people are variously trained to read, first by becoming literate and later within additional disciplinary frames. This is not to say that Xerox machines read, in other words, but that people who Xerox read with the machines, under the particular conditions by which the document is the genre being read. To Xerox something, in short, is to read it as a document. The medium and the genre are fully entangled. Computers do not work in the same way, since to encounter a document online is to discern it amid a heterogeneous assortment of other electronic objects. Anything Xeroxed — like anything scanned — is a document, but only some things digital count as documents.

Virginia Jackson has worked out a helpful analogy in her study of the ways that literary critics over the last 125 years have read the manuscripts of Emily Dickinson. The Dickinson archive contains letters, envelopes, so-called fascicles, and repurposed scraps, some of which have been read to contain lyrics by the poet and others of which have not. Poems have been found within one letter and not another, written across this envelope and not in the words across that one. Jackson's point is that what counts as lyric depends at least as much on how Dickinson's words are read as on what they say or even what they look like, handwritten on the page. And the way that Dickinson's words are read depends in turn on time, on the extended historical moment of "the emergence of the lyric genre as a modern mode of literary interpretation," coincident with critical practices that are self-consciously literary.[67] Lyric reading — if I can rob Jackson's argument of considerable nuance — is a way of reading that helps to produce lyrics as such. In comparison, xerography offers a way of reading that helps produce documents as such, where the way in question depends not upon the discipline of literary study but rather on the disciplinary structures of modern bureaucracy, including its media of documentary reproduction. Of course there are plenty of distinctions to be drawn between the ways literary genres work and the ways bureaucratic ones do, but each domain has (that is, produces) its generic subjects.

If you ever Xeroxed your hand or your buttocks — not something I recommend — it was funny because of the incongruity of reading your hand or butt as a document. Although Xeroxing body parts effectively repudiates the document genre that is being read, there have been plenty of other xerographic practices that rely on incongruity yet stop short of outright repudiation. Artists have turned to xerography as a medium,[68] while office workers have adopted and adapted photocopies variously according to editorial, mimetic, and egoistic meanings just as Ellsberg did. Indeed, any sort of selection — any filing — depends on noticing differences or incongruities among documents, and there are many ways in which documents and selves might be aligned as xerographic subjects. Office workers (I used to be one) select, Xerox, and preserve documents in personal "just in case" files valued for their potential openness and filled with documents kept in order to prove that we know better than — or have some dirt on — our supervisors, even if we hesitate to act outright as whistle-blowers, lacking the occasion or lacking Ellsberg's courage. Equally, office workers select, Xerox, and preserve documents in "accidental research" files, noticing incongruities in the everyday stream that might come in handy on another day, in a different context, or to some other end. It wasn't — it isn't — as funny as Xeroxing your butt, perhaps, but (like your butt) these files can sometimes be handily disclosed to make a point to those in power.

Office workers have also used xerography as a means of anonymous and semi-anonymous in-office publication, posting waggish reproductions above the copier or at the proverbial water cooler. With the help of students and colleagues at the University of California, Berkeley, the folklorist Alan Dundes and his associate Carl Pagter spent the late 1960s and early 1970s collecting examples of office humor that were being reproduced and circulated on paper in the United States, publishing them in 1975 as *Urban Folklore from the Paperwork Empire*. What Dundes called "urban folklore," others have variously called "Xerox-lore" and "photocopy-lore."[69] Though Dundes and Pagter initially had trouble finding and then keeping a publisher because of the raunchy nature of some of their accumulated lore, they continued to extend and publish their collection of photocopied photocopies, putting out additional volumes in 1978, 1987, 1991, 1992, 1996, and 2000, by which time additional denominations like "folklore by fax" and e-mail had suggested themselves.[70]

These books apparently sold well — the first going through three editions — but Dundes and Pagter were after something like respect, not financial reward.[71] They wanted to persuade folklorists that these items of office ephemera were indeed folklore, which meant correcting the long-held definition of "lore" as an exclusively oral phenomenon that arrives on paper only through the professional offices of the trained folklorist or through some other, often regrettable, expedient. The materials that Dundes and Pagter collected could never have existed orally, since they consisted of cartoons and other forms that necessarily inhabit paper: mock memos, lists of rules, tests, and applications. These were documents (figure 3.3). Oral transmission had been replaced in this instance by xerographic reproduction and other inscriptive forms of business communication, yet just like more traditional lore, the same content showed up repeatedly in multiple, variant forms, testifying — according to Dundes and Pagter — to the existence of the "folk" that produced it.[72] In their introduc-

FIGURE 3.3. Photocopy lore, an example in two variations, Alan Dundes and Carl R. Pagter, *Work Hard and You Shall Be Rewarded: Urban Folklore from the Paperwork Empire*; reproduced by permission of the American Folklore Society.

tion to the 1975 volume, Dundes and Pagter claim that the folk in question are "bound together by the mutuality of [their] unhappy experiences in battling 'the system.'"[73]

The variously waggish, snarky, raunchy, and tongue-in-cheek humor of the lore suggested to Dundes and Pagter that it worked partly as a safety valve and partly as a defensive response, the ironic co-option of machinery (literally the Xerox machine, metaphorically the office) in the face of "the ills," "problems," "plight," and "strain" of living as modern bureaucratic subjects.[74] With the benefit of hindsight—and feminism—others have supplemented his interpretation, noting that "diversionary practices" offer a "tactic for contesting extant power-relations between employers and workers, [but] also simultaneously provide a means for workers to negotiate" social constructions of power more broadly. "On this level," Cathy Lynn Preston notes, the "dominant culture's constructions are just as frequently [re]produced as they are challenged."[75] *Urban Folklore from the Paperwork Empire* and its successor volumes constitute something of a shrine to office politics, circa 1970, evidence of inertial pressures that attend the structural conditions of bureaucratic labor. No matter how "bound together" its workers may be supposed to be, the American office was and remains fractured according to a host of inequalities — perhaps most notably gender inequality, but certainly class, racial, and ethnic divisions as well.

Alan Liu elaborates the postwar history of alienated white-collar labor and its affect, noting the "weekday anesthesia" of the workplace, a barren landscape of "human resources" and of identities subsumed within "corporate culture," where authoring is reduced to the selection of templates: "Whether one was a higher manager, middle manager, professional in the specific sense (e.g., lawyer, engineer), office supervisor, or even secretary, the rules were the same: one family picture on the desk (at most two), the occasional cartoon or satire tacked on the wall, a few office parties per year on well-defined occasions. These and other now-familiar markers of affect in the white-collar office define an emotional landscape as pure and as clean as a desert."[76] The persistence of office ephemera, like an allotment of "personal days," may represent the ultimate, rationalized diminution of the carnivalesque.

Nowhere is it clearer than on the level of genre that Xerox-lore contests the bureaucratic relations of power that it simultaneously helps solidify: every item mocks the document genre that it reproduces. It's an interesting twist: Ellsberg had taken documents out of bureaucracy (the leak), while these office workers were taking documents in (an infiltration). Their documents were incongruous, testimony to the document as a peculiarly "distressed genre," in Susan Stewart's terms, but nonetheless a genre — *the* genre — of modern bureaucracy.[77] Where the leak offers a mockery of state power by reproducing its words verbatim in the public arena, the lore offers something like the self-mockery of bureaucracy by ventriloquizing its officious tone of voice. *The Office* — both the British television series, which first aired in 2001, and the American remake, which first aired in 2005 — works (to the extent that it does) in part by transposing just such a ventriloquism onto its mock-documentary or "mockumentary" frame. Its office workers — employees of a failing paper company — bumble about parodying contemporary office politics according to its own clichés, which the camera's documentary mode of address helps to paint as all the more ridiculous and retrograde.

It remains to note that as the Pentagon Papers, John Lions's commentary, and Dundes's lore became part of and party to early ideas of the photocopy — now so obscure — more explicit if yet faltering attempts at discernment were afoot: Congress held hearings, and the courts heard cases. The first major xerography case in North America was *Williams & Wilkins Co. v. United States* (487 F.2d 1345), decided by a federal court in November 1973. Rather than coursepacks (which would be adjudicated later in the so-called Kinko's case and which continue to be at issue today in different ways), the matter in question was the copying of scientific articles by the National Library of Medicine (NLM). The court was asked to consider whether the NLM's practice of photocopying journal articles on request violated the copyright of the journal's publisher, who was losing money on subscriptions. Like the Harvard engineering library, the National Institutes of Health and the NLM were using copies of articles as their unit of scholarly transaction, preferring to keep original, complete issues out of broad circulation. Both the verdict — in favor of the NLM — and the hearing are particularly suggestive in light of recent discussions of open access publishing in the sciences, while the majority decision written by Judge John Davis offers a revealing puzzlement over the idea of the photocopy.

Since the Copyright Act of 1909, U.S. law had explicitly forbidden anyone but a copyright holder to "print, reprint, publish, copy, and vend" a copyrighted work. "Read with blinders," the court now declared, "this language might seem on its surface to be all-comprehensive — especially the term 'copy.'"[78] But the court was convinced that the term "copy" in this instance did not mean copy, when the copyrighted work in question was a book or periodical. Copying a photograph, a painting, or an engraving was one thing — patently illegal — but copying a book or article was enshrined in practice as "fair use." Scholars could always make copies by hand or have them made. And even mechanically reproduced copies were "fair." Librarian of Congress Herbert Putnam, who supported the Copyright Act of 1909, had proved as much when he issued guidelines for use of the Library of Congress's collections: "photography is freely permitted" (said the rules of 1908), and photostats of items in the collection were offered for nominal sums (after 1913). "The Gentlemen's Agreement" instigated by Robert Binkley had publicly taken the same view in 1935. Judge Davis was left to discard "the dictionary or 'normal' definition of 'copy.'"[79] Copying articles has long been legal and remains so, but now the "proliferation of inexpensive and improved copying machines" and the resulting "surge in such duplication" somehow pressed the question. Wasn't it still just copying, even if photocopying had newly made copying quick, cheap, easy, and ubiquitous?

In short, the court turned, as McKenzie had in "Printers of the Mind" several years before, to questions of labor, efficiency, and throughput. McKenzie had scolded his contemporaries to locate early modern print within early modern labor conditions and practices. Judge Davis decided, contra McKenzie, to locate 1970s photocopies within pre-1970s conditions, back in Binkley's day, when making copies was slower, more cumbersome, and more expensive. Copying then was allowed; so copying now must be permissible too. Part of the judiciary's chronic vagueness concerning the doctrine of fair use, certainly, but the *Williams & Wilkins* decision suggests further that the idea of the photocopy remained emergent. The U.S. Supreme Court heard the case on appeal but effectively affirmed Judge Davis's decision by splitting four to four (one justice was absent). The courts would wait for new legislation, and the "'normal' definition of 'copy'" would continue to change. For the moment, fair use was in the ascendant; Congress codified the doctrine for the first time in the Copyright Act of 1976, acting in light of *Williams & Wilkins* while drawing in part on "The Gentlemen's Agreement."[80]

Despite its role in legislative history, *Williams & Wilkins* has long been overshadowed in histories of copying and fair use by a related case, *Sony Corp. of America v. Universal City Studios* (464 U.S. 417), decided by the U.S. Supreme Court in 1984. *Williams & Wilkins* was widely cited in the course of *Sony*'s adjudication, though the latter case concerned videotapes rather than photocopies. In *Sony* the Supreme Court decided that selling videocassette recorders (VCRs) was legal because it was fair use when individuals taped television shows for their own later viewing. Even if a bit of copyright infringement did take place, the "substantial non-infringing uses" of VCRs by the general public actually served the interests of television producers, whose programs and commercials could be time-shifted and thereby gain a larger audience.[81]

The fortunes of fair use would soon turn,[82] but the analogy to VCRs and videotapes suggested by the Supreme Court in *Sony* offers an apt comparison. Like the lost idea of the photocopy, there are ideas of videotape that have been similarly lost. They were ideas produced in part by unnamed, un-knowable thousands of videotapers beginning in the mid-1970s and later reshaped and ultimately obscured by experiences of additional formats and contexts for video, particularly digital video. (Think if you will of DVDs, QuickTime, Blu-ray, YouTube, TiVo, and video-enabled cell phones.) The lost ideas of videotape have recently been described by Joshua Greenberg and Lucas Hilderbrand, and though there are important differences be-tween videos and photocopies, both accounts help locate some striking resemblances. For example, the first generation of videophiles caught the makers of VCRs and videocassettes by surprise: "Initial studies claiming that VCR owners would want to purchase between one and five blank tapes proved to underestimate early adopters' desire to archive, rather than simply time shift television, and chronic shortages plagued the indus-try."[83] Here again reproduction had come to mean archive, not just access. Furthermore, just as Ellsberg had edited out "top secret," Greenberg notes that early videophiles wanted clean copies of television shows, so "editing out commercials was an oft-discussed topic, and tips for doing so were in high demand."[84] And if the bibliographical meanings of VHS appear to have been partly editorial in the hands of early users, those meanings were certainly mimetic and egoistic as well, if difficult to recover in retrospect. Like nth-generation photocopies, nth-generation videotapes have a dis-tinctive, degraded look to which those who used them have in retrospect attached nostalgia; Hilderbrand profitably explains it as an aesthetics of bootleg.[85]

Though admittedly imperfect, the analogy between photocopies and videotapes may be carried one small step further. Like copy shops, video stores occupy a specific retail niche whose fortunes have faltered in recent years. Taking again the examples of New York City and Cambridge, Massa-chusetts, dedicated copy shops and video stores still exist, though in notice-ably fewer numbers than was the case a decade ago. The ascent and descent of both kinds of stores help mark something about the cultural logic of the copy, about the situation of reproduction in the broader social and eco-nomic order—something that has changed of late with the availability of new digital tools, networks, and the related structures of commerce. One of the things still being lost about the idea of the photocopy is the retail counter at which customers present their jobs. One of the things already lost about video is the feel and sense of the cassette tape itself, as stores have devoted themselves exclusively to DVDs and have deaccessioned VHS tapes. That said, there are of course important differences between the two kinds of retail. Unlike copy shops, video stores are repositories; they are warehouses that share the logic of the database at the same time that they have had profound effects on the weight and substance of cinema as shared culture as well as on cinema as an industrial product.[86] Simply in terms of urban geography, there was a period of fifteen or twenty years when every neighborhood had a video store in the same way that every neighborhood still has a dry cleaner, though of course the circulation of videos (owned by the store, a repository of cinema) differs dramatically from that of clothes (owned by customers, a scattered repository of style). The urban geography of copy shops is different; they often cluster around college and university campuses, forming gray zones where a combination of illegal and legal copying helps support the intertwined aims of pedagogy and research.[87]

The idea of the photocopy that emerged in the 1960s and 1970s was structured partly in relation to the question of copyright without being nailed fully to that cross. Concerns about intellectual property arose in selected contexts, while photocopies helped broach questions of openness, possession, and self-possession more broadly. At the same time that xerographic reproduction helped shift the meanings of reproduction from access to archive—toward personal files and other redundancies as bureaucratic norms—the examples of Ellsberg, Lions, and Dundes and Pagter demonstrate ways in which access remained at issue. The transit and potential transit of documents, leaked in or leaked out, worked to mark the organizational structures within which documents were created—were read—as such. The genre of the document grew more capacious, according to the tolerance and agnosticism of the Xerox machine: all documents are not photocopies, but all photocopies are documents. If the relative ease of photocopying aided in the unprecedented proliferation of documents, that proliferation itself aided in and called attention to versioning, helping emphasize and enable documents as potentially "living" sites for continued and collective interpretation and revision, both fluid and fixed, on and as paper. Though typing and typescripts remained ubiquitous, episodes from the early history of xerography show how entwined photocopies and digital documents were from the very first.

What do files mean to the future of human expression? This is a harder question to answer than the question "How does the English language influence the thoughts of native English speakers?" At least you can compare English speakers to Chinese speakers, but files are universal. The idea of the file has become so big that we are unable to conceive of a frame large enough to fit around it in order to assess it empirically.

—Jaron Lanier, *You Are Not a Gadget*

Today, rather than print and distribute, we distribute and then print. In other words, we send the file electronically to the recipient, who then prints it out. This is underlined by the fact that between 1988 and 1993, the worldwide installed base of copiers increased by only 5 percent, whereas the worldwide installed base of printers increased by 600 percent.

—Abigail J. Sellen and Richard H. R. Harper, *The Myth of the Paperless Office*

Brightly colored advertising inserts spill out of Sunday newspapers these days, touting the latest and greatest, the largest and flattest high-definition television sets. These circulars share certain conventions. The TVs they advertise are typically pictured as if they were all tuned to the same channel. They are arrayed side by side and vary only slightly in size, as if to represent their respective merits through an obscure scalar logic: "Look at this big beauty," they seem to urge, "and get a load of this one." Of course news-print and color process printing are woefully inept at the job they have been given. Nothing even close to a high-definition television image can be pictured this way, yet every image is pictured, as if picturing were at once essential and completely beside the point. In short, the reason for these illustrations seems to be the very thing they cannot illustrate. We might chalk this paradox up to consumerism, with all of its conflicts, intricacies, and blind spots, but the same sort of problem crops up in other, less commercial settings too. Histories of photography, for instance, often illustrate early photographic processes. You can picture a daguerreotype, but a scan of a daguerreotype reproduced as a halftone in a book can never picture it with the process you are illustrating. Captions are almost universally silent on this point: they label halftones of daguerreotypes as daguerreotypes without qualm, since no one really expects an illustration to *be* the thing it illustrates. Except, of course, when they do.

The most spectacular example I have ever encountered along these lines is in Bamber Gascoigne's invaluable reference *How to Identify Prints*. Gascoigne alerts his readers at the outset "that there is no point in looking through a glass" or studying the illustrations too closely, since all that doing so would "reveal is the very recognizable characteristic of halftone offset lithography, the process by which the book is printed." The illustrations have been carefully "devised" to suggest printing processes they cannot in fact be, and they should simply be held and looked at from a "reading distance" for the plan to work.[1] A reminder like this in a field guide to birds would be nonsensical ("These illustrations are not birds," etc.), yet the combined subject and function of Gascoigne's manual—prints identifying prints, not birds—confuses the point. In this instance, as in the TV advertisements, the framing contexts of illustration belie expectation. Those framing contexts are crucially epideictic[2]—that is, relying on rhetoric of praise that singles out specific visual technologies, technologies that cannot be fully represented by other means but are instead conjured for the eye of the beholder.

In one sense this is a familiar sort of conjuring, based on the indexicality of photographs and the iconicity of figurative images. As Roland Barthes writes, "a photograph is always invisible: it is not it that we see."[3] We tend to look through an image to whatever it represents, at the same time that an intuitive check—some sort of unconscious guardian—typically helps us hold the line between reality and representation. Even a crude picture of a pipe "is a pipe," we say, even as we understand that it can't be picked up and smoked. The language of mimesis wears thin somehow, especially where the language of the real, of what is, rubs against the pursuits of realism. In another sense, however, the conjured televisions and daguerreotypes arise more subtly. There are some pictures, after all, that *are* self-identical with the subjects they picture: An illustration of redness is red, a picture of a triangle is triangular, an image of the letter Q is that letter itself, and an illustration of pornography is — arguably, at least — still pornographic.[4] The image and its subject are self-identical in cases like these because of the distinctive symbolic characteristics of the subjects at issue, however difficult it may be to describe what those are or what they have in common. (What *do* color, shape, decency, and indecency have in common?) Advertising circulars and histories of photography and printing seem to thread the needle: We're looking at an image of a bird or a pipe, in effect, but encountering it as (an image of) a triangle or a Q. It's not that anyone is fooled, of course; that's not the point. It is just that we seem so lulled — that is, conditioned — by norms and expectations that attend the different uses of printed illustrations. This is partly about images, then, and partly about print.[5]

Printing, too, has enjoyed a long and complex association with what is. Even when the printed matter in question is fiction, its bibliographical identity is factual or fixed: we trust that any printed matter at hand was published by the publisher indicated, authored by the author named, and addresses a reading public in an edition of like copies. When two people read "the same" book, they can each read different copies and be sure — even unthinkingly so — that they can compare notes. People are "on the same page," we say, with confident approbation. Certainties like these help make modern texts self-evident, giving them that "air of intrinsic reliability" that today frames print media. It wasn't always so, as Adrian Johns explains in *The Nature of the Book*.[6] "Printed texts were not intrinsically trustworthy," according to Johns, who observes that "fixity exists only inasmuch as it is recognized and acted upon by people — and not otherwise."[7] The defining fixity of print emerged, he argues, according in part to the circulation of natural knowledge (what would become science) in the sixteenth and seventeenth centuries. The self-evidence of letterpress and the universality of science were mutual constructions, as it were, both based on the actions and attitudes of the authors, printers, booksellers, and readers involved. High-definition TVs may be a far cry from early modern science, but printed advertising circulars today partake of the self-same logic of fixity. We understand them as circulars by understanding print publication as it attends the marketplace, so that the little TVs they so crudely picture are meaningful partly because of the self-evidence accorded to printed texts and the related commonsensicality of advertising wares in print and on paper to a consumer public.

This chapter tackles a related instance: not illustrations that conjure visual media, but rather documents that may be said to conjure themselves. I am interested particularly in cases where the self-evidence or facticity of modern texts becomes variously if often surreptitiously self-conscious, when documents are experienced as pictures of themselves. This is where the media of documentary reproduction come into play, framing and framed by the know-show function. Oscar Harpel's specimens, Robert Binkley's typescript books, and Daniel Ellsberg's Xeroxes have offered earlier instances in curiously different ways, but the most commonplace examples today are without question the digital documents that appear as images on screens, transient and legible forms that are perceived in luminous windows. Whatever else they are, digital and (even more so) digitized documents appear as pictures of themselves. There is nothing simple here. "The computer screen," Anne Friedberg notes, "is both a 'page' and a 'window,' at once opaque and transparent," a flat surface that nonetheless enables "deep virtual reach to archives and databases," to local disk storage and the cloud.[8] Both screen environments and digital documents already have a long history, of course, so one challenge of what follows is to define a selective domain. This chapter focuses specifically on the portable document format, on PDF files. When computer users click to open a PDF, they experience a brief, theatrical moment as their PDF reader opens — the Adobe Acrobat application, for example — and then they likely have a keen sense that they are looking at an image and/of a text, a text that is somehow also an image of itself.

Digital documents take many different forms, of course. They can be *.txt, *.doc, or *.html files, for example, but the *.pdf format differs in a few important ways that make it a particularly apposite and instructive sequel to the documents handled by Harpel, Binkley, Ellsberg, and their contemporaries. PDFs variously partake of the form and fixity of print that other digital text formats frequently do not. PDFs aren't print in the absolute sense that they aren't printed onto the screen, of course, but they look like print when they are open in a PDF-reader application. Better, they look as if they work like print. And, in a way, they do: "today, PDF, which also can serve as a platform for multimedia production, is the basis of the most widely used workflows for professional publishing," that is, for traditional book publishing.[9] The "look of printedness," as I have called it, has been separated from paper and mobilized online, even in the process of producing printed books. Whether they render digitized text or text that has been born digital, as it were, PDFs present what are called page images; they look something like pictures of pages produced by one printing process or another, or by word processing. Viewed within a PDF-reader application, they are emphatically not "living" documents of the sort discussed in the last chapter. They aren't ongoing or "evergreen": like print artifacts, they are open for reading but closed for any in-text, in-kind revision. (Some PDFs are specifically designed to be fill-able forms, a feature introduced in 1996 that mobilizes an obvious resemblance to job-printed blanks.) The portable document format thus represents a specific "remedial" point of contact between old media and new, one that is particularly important to consider because — at least for the present — PDFs are so widely deployed.[10] They have become "normal."[11] The portable document format is today "the de facto standard for printable documents on the web" and thus part of and party to the knowledge work we do with documents, whether that means the research we conduct, the readings we assign, the manuals we consult, the reports we submit, the forms we fill out, or the tickets we present.[12] PDFs offer a challenge for designers and users of today's handheld devices with their smaller screens, but they nonetheless remain ubiquitous. Consulting a PDF on your smartphone can be a giant headache, but there is no question that the manual for your phone exists somewhere as a PDF, one you can probably download from the websites of both its manufacturer and your service provider.

E-books today remain framed in large measure by the genre of the novel (not only is the market for fiction e-books stronger than that for nonfiction e-books, but the design, advertisement, and discussion of e-book readers remain tilted toward novels), but it seems clear that PDFs in contrast are and have been framed by the genre of the document. Though it is hardly their exclusive domain or their domain exclusively, PDFs have a special association with the category of so-called gray literature, which includes items like technical manuals, government documents, college coursepacks, reports, and — ironically — white papers. These are familiar genres of internality, at least since Binkley's day, more recently called gray in the field of library and information science because they are typically produced and circulate outside more formal publishing channels, often in small editions that can be hard to locate, prove problematic for cataloguers, and quickly become obsolete. In the previous chapter, we saw how documents like these can leak out of institutions (like the Pentagon Papers) and how they can — at least mockingly — sneak back in (like the photocopy lore), but the ins and outs of PDFs are significantly less clear, at least because the eventfulness of online publication remains so contested and confused across platforms, formats, and applications.[13] In what sense is posting — to Facebook, for example — publishing or making public? Can a web page unnoticed by Google or other search engines be said to exist in public? How are the documents on my laptop privately mine if my document-creation software is subject to automatic updates and versioning by the company I license it from? Where does spam come from? Questions like these dramatize the diversity of digital texts at the same time that they underscore the fact that the potential grayness of documents may be more intense (grayer?) in the digital realm. Because of the vagaries of online publication, the digital medium may itself turn communications variously gray, in other words, in ways that compound gray subgenres of the document. (In the same way that it creates headaches for cataloguers, gray literature can be tricky to cite: Readers will find electronic sources and amateur publications detailed in my endnotes, along with archival sources, but the works cited list that follows them contains far less gray.)

The examples of Harpel, Binkley, and Ellsberg each offer helpful points of comparison, yet this chapter cannot proceed in the same manner as those that precede it, at least because I have not been able to imagine any exemplary PDF, in the way that *Harpel's Typograph*, Binkley's *Manual*, or the Pentagon Papers seem so illustrative — if not entirely typical — of the media of documentary production and reproduction that each exploits. Famous documents still crop up — one thinks of President Barack Obama's birth certificate, for example, or the so-called Killian documents about President George W. Bush's National Guard service, which fooled Dan Rather's team at CBS — but no famous PDFs as such, as far as I can recall. Why not? Chalk it up to a failure of imagination on my part or an accident of history if you like, or consider that PDFs are digitally processural entities and so in some sense break the mold of earlier, analog forms.[14] They may require that we think differently. Or maybe, as Jaron Lanier observes (see the epigraph to this chapter), the idea of the file in general has simply gotten too big to reckon with.[15] Like xerography or photo-offset, PDF is certainly a "near print" technology of the sort that Binkley celebrated in the 1930s for internal or specialized contexts, yet PDF is also different because it is constituent of putatively paperless work practices that Binkley and his contemporaries could hardly have imagined.[16] PDF represents a "format" in a context where that term refers more to dense layers of technical specifications — the result of "decisions that affect the look, feel, experience and workings of a medium"[17] — than it does to specific bibliographical codes, such as the size and weight of paper onto which Harpel might have printed his jobs. And as much as the lack of an exemplary PDF may stem from contrasts between analog and digital, it must follow, as well, from the fact that documents in the era of PDF technology have become the objects of relational databases. One of the tasks of this chapter, then, is to broach the question of how or whether documents are somehow different when aggregated and served up by databases rather than collected and fished out of filing cabinets. Consider the size and complexity of Wikileaks, for example, beside the Pentagon Papers. This is of course only partly a question of scale.

At the same time that I have failed to identify an exemplary PDF, I have also resisted as much as possible focusing on PDFs solely through the lens of Adobe Systems or the entrepreneurs and engineers who developed the format. The pages that follow touch on the work of John Warnock — a founder of Adobe — and other figures familiarly hailed as founding fathers of digital work processes and the networked personal computers that support them, yet I think it is important to go further than that. If the bubble of attention that surrounded the passing of Steve Jobs has taught us anything, it is that the supposed "rebel hero story" has a seductive appeal to which the previous chapters, it seems, have to some degree succumbed.[18] Instead of heroes, this chapter offers a brief account of PDF technology, both by describing some of the contexts of its development, promotion, and widespread utility as well as by offering a partial, speculative reading of the format itself, the uses and users that it appears to imagine. My interest here is not in the technical specifics of how PDF technology actually works, how it has been versioned and capitalized by its developers, or even what a PDF or the document it renders on screen ontologically is — instead, it is in the experiences that everyday users may have of PDF files and the portable document format as such. I am proposing, in short, that PDF technology imagines its users — that certain uses and conditions have been built in to the technology — at the same time that actual users continue to imagine and reimagine what PDF files are for, how and where they work, and thus what they mean. Only by taking account of these intersecting imaginaries can we understand the specificities of this digitally mediated format or, indeed, of any technology. As Darren Wershler puts it, "we need to spend more time considering not only how" different formats are developed, "circulated, incorporated into various software packages, and eventually abandoned, but also how they manifest and reciprocally help to shape cultural values."[19] The values at stake in the case of PDF, I argue, are crucially those that attend the genre of the document in its digital incarnation.

....

PDF is a file format, a technical specification, created by Adobe Systems in 1991 and refined and enhanced in conjunction with the subsequent commercial release and versioning of Adobe's own PDF-oriented software.[20] Though proprietary to begin with, elements of the specification have been released by Adobe to encourage the development of PDF-oriented software by others. Finally, and at Adobe's instigation, PDF 1.7 was adopted as an open standard by the International Standards Organization in 2008, so it will continue to be developed by relevant communities of practice and remain open to all. As noted above, the acronym stands for portable document format because PDFs (here the acronym stands for the files in that format) make the visual elements of documents — layout, letterforms, figures, and so on — portable across platforms and devices.[21] The website of the U.S. Bureau of the Census, notably, makes the same point in plain English: a PDF "is a file that will look the same on the screen and in print, regardless of what kind of computer or printer someone is using and regardless of what software package was originally used to create it."[22] (Since January 1996 all new Census publications have been available as PDFs.) "Looking the same" in this context appeals to the fixity of print — since undamaged instances from the same print edition all look the same wherever you encounter them — at the same time that it depends upon what Matthew Kirschenbaum has called "formal materiality," a property of digital objects that arises as the result of "procedural friction, or torque" produced "by different software environments" as they are encountered in contrast with one another.[23] In this enlarged sense, "looking the same" or "looking as if" happens as digital documents are used in different applications and operating systems, as well as across modes of what gets generalized as output (screen images and printed versions). In general, then, the documents rendered by PDFs achieve a measure of fixity because of the ways they simultaneously compare to printed documents and contrast with other kinds of digital documents that seem less fixed — less print-like — as they are used.

The fixed or stable page image — quite often encountered amid multiple page images in a sequence — is the basic formal component of the PDF interface, but it is hardly unique to PDFs or native to computer screens. The arc of the previous chapters offers one context for considering PDFs and the documents they render, yet media history also suggests many others. Taking a long view, for instance, one might trace page images all the way back to antiquity, to the parallel columns of text called *paginae* that were arranged along papyrus scrolls, which were designed to be unfurled horizontally for reading. Or one might trace them back to the multiple units of typographical matter that were composed and then arranged by letterpress printers ("imposed") in order to print large sheets on both front and back. These sheets would then be folded into folio, quarto, or octavo signatures. As Bonnie Mak explains, the page in cases like these is emphatically not a page in the sense that it is not a discrete leaf, "a thin sheet of material in three dimensions." Papyrus scrolls and printers' sheets instead contain multiple visual chunks or graphical units called "pages," only in a different sense of the term. These pages are not tangible, three-dimensional objects; rather, they are the formal, visual conventions of one "standard interface" or another, according to the ways that interface displays graphical design features: text and image, layout and letterforms.[24] These pages can be read, then, but they can't be turned. It is in this sense that computer screens contain pages — think of web pages and Word files — of which page images form a special class and PDFs a specific variety.

Taking a more proximal view, the history of screens might also offer contexts for the PDF page image. Twentieth-century documentalists and other visionaries long dreamed of attaching bibliographical records to the items that they described, and microfilm, microfiche, and microprint page images figured prominently in those dreams. Vannevar Bush's famous "As We May Think" (1945), with its multiple desktop screens, exemplifies this strand of thought in its futurological mode, while Eugene Power's earlier microfilm edition of items listed in Alfred W. Pollard and G. R. Redgrave's *Short Title Catalogue* — with items identified by their number in that reference work on the film (see chapter 2) — inhabited its aspirational verge. Along these same lines, the subsequent era of mainframe computing included a number of experimental reference retrieval systems within which university- and industry-based researchers incorporated the retrieval document page images. The Intrex (short for Information Transfer Experiments) system at the Massachusetts Institute of Technology (MIT), for instance, focused on journal articles in materials science and engineering that were held in the MIT libraries. Intrex provided a catalog of 20,000 items, and in 1970 it was "the first online search system in which a terminal could display on the same viewing screen [both] input-output communication and microform images of source documents." Microfiche was retrieved mechanically on demand, and "a flying-spot scanner generated video signals" that were displayed remotely on screen along with catalog information.[25] Two years later, the *New York Times* Information Bank — another fascinating, short-lived experiment — tried the same kind of thing, but fiche retrieval proved so unreliable that eventually "a person wearing white gloves pulled fiche on demand" and positioned it in front of a video camera.[26] More typical than these experiments were reference systems that stopped short of serving up page images, providing instead catalog entries, search results, and extracts or synopses of documents, as if to insist that it is the content and not the look of a page that matters. In contrast, Intrex and the *Times* Information Bank put a premium on documents, not just information, appropriating the logic of microform (and the logic of direct quotation) and delivering it to the electronic screen.

Almost a decade before systems like these paired reference metadata and microfiche images on the same screen, another effort had arrived at screen-based pages by an entirely different route. Instead of reference retrieval, Ivan Sutherland's Sketchpad (created in 1963) aimed at what he called "man-machine graphical communication."[27] A doctoral project created at MIT, Sketchpad has been described as "the most important ancestor of today's Computer Aided Design (CAD)" as well as a key breakthrough in the history of computer graphics and the first — or at least an early — step on the path to object-oriented programming and the graphical user interface.[28] It ran on the TX-2 computer with an oscilloscope cathode ray tube (CRT) display, and users interacted with graphics on the screen by means of a light pen, which they pointed at the screen while manipulating a set of buttons and switches on a keyboard and knobs on the monitor. Users drew points on the screen to suggest lines on a page, and then the system smoothed and rendered ("inked") the resulting figures computationally, making them available for further manipulation and, if desired, as objects ("masters") for future designs. As Sutherland explains in his thesis, the display system allowed users to view "any portion of the page desired, at any degree of magnification," which gave the screen display itself the feel of a portal onto the document or a "window-into-the-page." Stable or "fixed" page coordinates described a virtual drawing plain "about ¼ mile" square, which could be magnified on screen so that users effectively zoomed in as needed to work on any detail, down to the level of a segment that was seven inches square.[29] It was like looking at a massive sheet of paper through a tiny moving porthole. Users could include brief snippets of text, "to put legends on a drawing," but Sutherland's great innovation was an interface that depended not on typing instructions but on drawing lines. Even his text was drawn, in the sense that the text display program used to put legends on drawings built characters "by means of special tables which indicate the locations of line and circle segments to make up the letters and numbers"—a process that, in a sense, looked forward to PostScript, TrueType, and PDF.[30] Characters were typed in, but then they were generated graphically by the system for display on screen.

Both microform databanks and Sutherland's Sketchpad gesture selectively toward a prehistory for the PDF page image because both—though differently—mobilized pages and images of pages for a screen-based interface. The databanks retrieved televisual reproductions of existing source pages, modeling not just information retrieval but also encouraging certain citation norms (since users could indicate that, for example, "the information appears on page 10"). Meanwhile, Sketchpad established a page as a fixed computational field, a visible ground on which further computational objects might be rendered. The portable document format is related more tenuously to mainframes and microform, even though today's reference databases—the majority of which of course include and serve up PDF—clearly descend in some measure from experiments like Intrex and the *Times* Information Bank. A much more direct line of descent—though across a longer span of time—might be drawn between Sketchpad and PDF, in the very least since John Warnock studied at the University of Utah after Sutherland joined the faculty there. What happened between these early page images and the development of PDF was the storied development of personal computers, and there is no need to rehearse that story here, since so many of its features are by now familiar: Douglas Engelbart and the demo; Xerox's Palo Alto Research Center and the Alto; Microbrew, Macintosh, and Microsoft.[31]

PDF technology would become both thinkable and desirable in the context of personal computing in the 1980s, and its conception would stem in particular from the emergence of desktop publishing as an application for personal computers toward the middle of that decade. In 1983 *Time* magazine named the personal computer its "machine of the year," with a cover story announcing: "The Computer Moves In."[32] Two years later, desktop publishing effectively joined word processing and spreadsheets as a killer application for personal computers. Like word processing and spreadsheets, that is, desktop publishing seemed to offer a perfect answer — quickly and intuitively grasped by a wide audience — to the question of what personal computers were actually for. Desktop publishing involved both tools to produce pages and tools to reproduce them: at first, there were Aldus's PageMaker software and the Apple LaserWriter printer (both released in 1985). Like the specialized, small platen job presses of Harpel's day or the relatively cheap, paper-plate offset presses of the 1960s, the desktop publishing technology of the 1980s offered new, less expensive tools to those already involved in page design, printing, and publishing while it also significantly opened the field to newcomers — including amateurs — as personal computers "moved in" to homes and to offices. "I think everyone at Apple publishes some kind of newsletter," one employee noted at the time. "Come back from vacation and your desk is covered with four pages on the use of Macintoshes in Lithuanian pear farms — in Times Roman and Helvetica."[33] Copy shops became copy and "instant print" shops, while corporations and other institutions internalized increasing amounts of their own print production.[34]

Much of the popular mythology surrounding the development of the personal computer has tended to focus attention on questions of who, what, when, and — of course — how much money, but the success of desktop publishing requires focusing briefly on questions of where, questions that cannot be answered with "California" or "the garage." The success of desktop publishing required both "what you see is what you get" (WYSIWYG) composition tools and laser printers. For WYSIWYG to work, there had to be continuity across screens (WYS) and the pages printed out (WYG). But the fruitful combination of computers and printers had long been haunted by "questions of where printing software lived — whether it was part of an operating system or part of applications or [part of] the software associated with particular printers."[35] Answers to these questions depended as much on market structure and competition as on technology, since if you made operating systems, then they were going to be your answer (recall John Lions's early struggles with nroff, described in the previous chapter).[36] John Warnock and Charles Geschke, the founders of Adobe, offered their own elegant solution by moving as far from the operating system as possible: they developed the PostScript language for describing page images at the laser printer. The Apple LaserWriter — like hundreds of subsequent models — relied on PostScript, which was built into the device and ran page descriptions locally when print jobs arrived from the computer: "PostScript made printers smart."[37] And as early as 1986, Warnock was looking ahead to uses for PostScript outside of printers, "in the screen world" somehow. That was the general idea behind PDF.[38]

Planet PDF, an independent (that is, non-Adobe) electronic newsletter, has published Warnock's six-page description of "The Camelot Project" of 1991, which developed into PDF.[39] The document describes the thinking behind PDF, noting "a fundamental problem" confronting companies: people were still carrying paper around to surrogate networking.[40] The problem was, Warnock writes, that "most programs print to a wide range of printers, but there is no universal way to communicate and view this printed information electronically."[41] "Printed information" in this sentence is a curious concoction, since it must include all of the meanings that appear on the surface of a page or pages, whether linguistic or graphical, designed or accidental, the result of traces or absences. (Harpel's specimens are "printed information" in this sense, printed onto the pages of *Harpel's Typograph* rather than the formats — such as cards and envelopes — of their utility.) So Warnock imagines "printed information" to be removed from paper and visible on screen. Moving linguistic information around electronically was easy enough, using the American Standard Code for Information Interchange (ASCII) and ASCII-based applications. But moving page images from one setting to another in 1991 was most commonly and reliably done with facsimile machines, not computers. This was the long-awaited heyday of the fax machine, initially analog and ultimately digital, printing on rolls of specialized, slimy paper and later on what fax marketers vaunted as "plain paper."[42] Faxes transmitted formatting as well as content, handwriting as well as typescript, signatures as well as letterhead. It was like photocopying something to a different locale, if you think about it, or like beaming (à la *Star Trek*) documents from place to place. What if computers and computer networks could do that instead? (Fax machines weren't particularly good at transmitting images beyond simple line art, so in metropolitan publishing circles this extended moment from the mid-1980s to the early 1990s was also the heyday of the bicycle messenger.)

Warnock wanted to design software tools "so that a corporation [could] effectively capture documents from any application, send electronic versions of these documents anywhere, and view and print these documents on any machines." His ambitions were prescient: "imagine," he writes, if you were "able to send full text and graphics documents (newspapers, magazine articles, technical manuals etc.)" via e-mail. Not only would "full" documents persist across networks, but "large centrally maintained databases of documents [indeed, entire libraries] could be accessed remotely and selectively" displayed and printed.[43] Techniques of documentary production and reproduction thus led back to the idea of systems for document reference retrieval, but the values most explicitly informing PDF technology had to do not with reference or research but with the work processes of corporate authorship and the careers that documents have in and for the corporate sector.[44] An orientation toward the author rather than the reader emerged out of the work of desktop publishing, the in-house production of manuals, specifications, proposals, reports, and brochures. Corporate authorship of this sort is often and importantly authorship without ownership: intellectual property is moot, because corporate bodies own what their hirelings write. The author of your cell phone manual is not the technical writer who composed it but the phone's manufacturer. Corporate authorship is less about property than it is about liability and responsibility. Liability and responsibility must be negotiated across the structured hierarchy of any bureaucracy, and one instrument of that negotiation today is the file format.

In short, the Camelot Project was an expression of corporate liberalism that addressed the problem of interoperability for programs, platforms, peripheral devices, and networks, and it emerged at precisely what Thomas Streeter has called "the moment of *Wired*."[45] Warnock mentions newspaper and magazine articles, but the animating interest behind the development of PDF was corporate speech. Adobe's supporters and promoters note that PDF "freed [electronic] documents from the constraints of vendor-specific applications and file formats," yet it was a freedom — justly celebrated — that had initially been imagined as a corporate benefit.[46] The first corporation to benefit, of course, was Adobe Systems itself. Adobe's solution to the problem of sharing printed information electronically involved a "family" of applications to create, edit, and view page images that were described in seven-bit ASCII files, the PDF. Acrobat Exchange cost $195 in 1993 and was used to create PDFs. The Acrobat Reader initially cost $50 and was just a viewer. Acrobat Distiller cost $695 and converted PostScript files—generated by desktop publishing programs like Quark-XPress and Adobe's PageMaker—into PDFs. (Confusingly, Adobe Acrobat is today's name for Acrobat Reader; the family has grown and changed significantly, but that will not be my concern here.)

Portable document files resemble faxes, yet unlike facsimile transmissions of the early 1990s, PDFs aren't "dumb"—they contain so-called content streams that can be searched. Then again, unlike PostScript language programs, PDFs don't get too bulky, or they shouldn't. The format is designed to be compact and efficient, supporting multiple data compression filters, and each PDF contains a "cross-reference table" and other features that help "optimize" it for random access and speedy display.[47] PDFs are "smart" about their own internal building blocks, or objects, and the order those are in.[48] The technology works by compression, giving ingredients and instructions, data and directions for the PDF reader and the printer to follow in rendering the visual elements and alphanumeric values: the document in question. This means smaller file sizes for quicker delivery and easy storage. All of this makes PDFs perfect for transmission across networks, even in low-bandwidth environments like that of 1993. One implication is that, like the MP3 format, PDF technology has succeeded in some measure by dint of its transmissiveness.[49] PDFs are easy to send, quick to download, cheap to store, and—particularly after Adobe started giving the Acrobat reader away for free in 1994—a snap to open. Unlike "lossy" MP3s, though, and more like microfilm, PDF technology is also being promoted as an archival standard.[50]

Adobe described the way PDF worked in a technical manual, *Portable Document Format Reference Manual*, as well as in a promotional booklet titled *Beyond Paper: The Official Guide to Adobe Acrobat* (figure 4.1).[51] The former is an example of a familiar—if gray—genre, addressed to specialists, while the latter represents something a little more unusual and a little more ironic, since *Beyond Paper* is made of paper. Published by Adobe Press in conjunction with a division of Prentice Hall, *Beyond Paper* is a diminutive 5″ × 8″ consisting of 127 pages, and it listed for a whopping $16.95. *Beyond Paper* begins with a foreword by Warnock, who describes "Adobe™ Acrobat™" as a way to save paper and reduce the environmental burden of transporting it, while allowing corporations the flexibility to use

FIGURE 4.1. Front cover, Patrick Ames, *Beyond Paper* (1993).

diverse platforms and applications. What follows in the book is an hour-by-hour account of a day in the life of two imaginary corporations, one a packaged-food multinational with 15,000 employees around the world, and the other a smaller manufacturing firm with 350 workers making office partitions, the cubicles that so decisively divide and relegate white-collar workers to what Shoshana Zuboff terms "the realm of the machine."[52]

Corporate managers figure prominently in the story that *Beyond Paper* tells, but so do the underlings on whom they make extraordinary demands. The copier jams repeatedly as an executive secretary tries to use it, and then her boss vanishes before she can protest how long it will take to fax 100 pages across the country; a mail boy with a cart already full of deliveries to make is hijacked by a marketing director who wants him to rush to deliver an important interoffice envelope; and a four-person team struggles to prepare a new sales proposal needed immediately by their persnickety boss, only to come up with four separate files and two different handouts: all problems solved, of course, by Adobe™ Acrobat™, which aimed at reducing but not replacing the uses of paper and the uses of copiers, fax machines, express mail, interoffice mail, airplanes, envelopes, binders, staples, and paper clips.[53] Reducing labor costs remains an unspoken benefit. The workplace described in *Beyond Paper* is one of "squabbles, fights, wars, feuds, power plays, reorganizations, [and] positioning," to which workers respond not with the sardonic photocopy "lore" described in the last chapter but rather with self-destructive "memo grenades." Here, *Beyond Paper* offers a brief "look at the lighter side" of office life: "Everyone has either launched their own memo grenade at one time or another or has sighted one lobbed over office partitions and across org[anizational] charts." These are the memos sent up the chain of command—to complain, criticize, or aggrandize the writer—that fall flat, "explode," and embarrass him or her instead, with potentially career-damaging results. And "unfortunately, memo grenades will exist as long as there is office communication," even if Adobe™ Acrobat™ exists to deliver them.[54] Employees in this world don't so much bond together at the water cooler and the photocopy machine as they delight in deriding each other's foibles and ambitions.

Although *Beyond Paper* renders with great clarity the materiel and the stresses of office work circa 1993, it also offers a reminder that the moment of *Wired* was an extended one, in which new tools and the expertise associated with them were the objects of uneven penetration inside as well as outside large-scale institutions—whether corporations, government and nongovernmental agencies, or universities. Just as "online access came first among those who *did their own word processing*" rather than the top-level executives who didn't,[55] it was the workers who knew how to change the paper in the fax machine and who collated documents and delivered them by hand whose labors were eased and ultimately erased by technology like PDFs and local area networks. And it was the corporate "team" and other mid-level "content producers" who were likely to grow adept at paperless work processes before the top-level executives to whom they reported. By 1996 it seemed clear to even the most casual observers that "structurally, the secretary is no more."[56] If xerography in the 1960s had finally allowed office workers to keep their own files, then office technology in the 1990s helped make many of them into their own secretaries, for good and ill.[57]

Particularly revealing of the emerging work processes were the ways in which their promoters struggled to describe them, even at an incidental level. From the first, there was uncertainty. In *Beyond Paper*, users of the Acrobat software are said to "print electronically," when the PDF Writer (a program—a printer driver, really—that formed part of Acrobat Exchange) "'prints' an electronic file" as a PDF on screen.[58] The scare quotes around "print" in this second instance signal the discomfort of calling something paperless the result of printing, as the author of *Beyond Paper* grapples with the novelty of printing to the screen instead of onto paper. This language of printing did not survive for long—in some contexts today's users have adopted the verb "to PDF" as a replacement—yet clarity remains elusive. As Adobe explained the situation more recently, a "PDF represents not only the data contained in the document but also the exact form the document took."[59] Putting it this way suggests that form and content are all too separable, even as keeping them together is being praised. It implies that representation (of data) and exactness (of form) are both straightforward projects. (We're back to something very like pipes and triangles.) In promotional formulations such as these, Adobe strategically overlooks the ontological complexity of electronic objects in general and electronic texts in particular. That complexity—on which Adobe's considerable success rests—has inspired some enormously interesting debates about the character of textuality among scholars in media studies as well as a good deal of delirium and denial in the commercial sector. For instance, Webopedia .com (a self-described dictionary of computer and Internet terms that claims to contain "everything you need to know") alleges that "essentially, anything that can be done with a sheet of paper can be done with a PDF."[60] "Anything" in this case must refer to a tiny range of activities: *Beyond Paper* mentions printing, sharing, reading, filing, copying, and archiving.[61] These are the gerunds that animate the myth of the paperless office. Forget all of the other things that you can do with paper, like folding, smelling, tearing, crumpling, shuffling, and wiping.

As Abigail Sellen and Richard Harper explain in *The Myth of the Paperless Office*, we use paper literally to "[get] *to grips with* information," "to fully grasp the meaning of the text in question," and no amount of wishful thinking will make PDFs into an equivalent, even if the cursor in many PDF readers sometimes takes the form of a tiny, grasping white hand.[62] No miniature cartoon hand can get to grips with something the way a human hand can. What the cartoon hand does instead, according to Michele White, is "[act] as a kind of avatar or extension of the [user's] body," at the same time that it offers an example of the myriad little ways that "race is rendered through the interface."[63] Although the white cartoon hand in one sense works to "downplay the interface, because the user seems to have slipped inside the screen,"[64] its limited range of functions—compared to actual hands as well as to cursors in other software environments—emphatically calls attention to the interface as such, as well as to the downsizing and displacement of labor in the work practices it supports. As if echoing the person wearing white gloves and adjusting microfiche in front of a camera for the *Times* Information Bank in the 1970s, the hand-shaped cursor within the Acrobat Reader can be used to adjust the placement of page images within the program window. And that's all it can do. Perhaps the most critical thing the miniature cartoon hand can't do is hold and manipulate a miniature cartoon pair of scissors or a cartoon pen: it can only grip or grab the fixed page image—the cartoon paper—not edit or excerpt.

The Acrobat Reader's hand-shaped cursor works as a foil for both the disciplined writing hand and the more mechanized typing one. Called the "hand tool" for "navigation" by Adobe, the hand-shaped cursor represents a reader's hand, in effect, not an author or editor's hand. As such it is part of a long tradition in which reading has been considered hand-oriented, although also certainly involving other organs, faculties, and sensations: the keen eye, the knowing brain, the feeling heart, and—at least metaphorically—the digesting stomach.[65] Hands have always figured within the readerly imaginary. They have also long been figured graphically on the page. Unlike the eye, brain, heart, or stomach (which wouldn't make much sense as cursors), hands are common in marginalia across the centuries. William Sherman notes that the small pointing hand, or "manicule," is "a visually striking version of the most common marginal notation of all— *nota* or *nota bene*."[66] Thousands of manicules were drawn into the margins of early modern books, where, unlike the Acrobat hand cursor, they point, they index—literally, with an index finger—and they select, all in the "expanded sense" of "showing and teaching."[67] The Acrobat hand cursor, in contrast, doesn't point. It shows (*docer*) only as it positions selected regions of the page image for view within the active program window, working the contrast between screen coordinates and page coordinates in the way that Sketchpad's interface first exemplified. Gripping and moving a PDF with its hand cursor makes the window interface of the PDF-reader application seem more obviously in front of—windowing, it's sometimes called—the page image that it contains.

Limited in its movements across the plane of the window (that is, in the pane plane), the hand-shaped cursor abets what Walter Benjamin calls the "dictatorial perpendicular" of modern reading.[68] The newspaper column, billboard, cinema screen, and now computer screens offer reading surfaces that are more vertical than horizontal and thus are at odds, so Benjamin thought, with the kind of penetrating or absorptive reading that a book might inspire or enable as it lies open on the table or is held at a slant in a reader's lap. The office walls contain cubicles, the cubicles contain screens, the screens contain windows, and the windows contain page images. These vertical surfaces nest within each other, interfacing like a sequence of Russian dolls, waiting to funnel attention toward documents as if their very perpendicular sequence could ward off distraction. As if the dictatorial perpendicular could ever fully refute "the frightening anesthetic power of company papers," as Primo Levi once put it.[69] The hand-shaped cursor is ultimately a messenger (*cursor* means *messenger*) who carries only the implied message "Look here!" as it gestures crudely to address the user's attentiveness to his or her field of vision, assuming in the process the complex dynamics of human-computer interaction. Those dynamics depend of course on the user's actual hand — unwatched and forgotten, if the human-computer interaction is working well — as it manipulates a mouse, track pad, or some other pointing device.[70] The Acrobat Reader interface, like any interface, works to manage a user's attention — here focus, there neglect — in dynamic distribution across cognitive and bodily functions that are at once perceptual, haptic, ergonomic, and — at least metaphorically — digestive.

Because PDF technology was designed with the practices of corporate authorship in mind, it works partly by imagining hierarchical labor relations in which readers above, below, or beyond the authoring process passively receive its fruits. This is a pretty simplistic model of reading.[71] Though Sellen and Harper have found that reading in the modern office workplace "occurs with writing more often than it occurs without," PDF technology works to enforce or at least encourage reading without writing.[72] "Most documents are created for basic informational purposes," Warnock avers knowingly, "not for someone else to edit." By separating the software used to create and (especially) modify PDFs from the software used merely to open and read them, it is as if Adobe reimagined the monopoly lost by printers in the nineteenth century and then effectively reinstalled it in miniature within the everyday channels of business communication: "When I get financial reports for my CFO [chief financial officer] in the form of spreadsheets, I don't edit those spreadsheets; I look at the information. When I get *Business Week* in the mail, I'm not tempted to edit it, and I'm not interested in editing the majority of memos and proposals I receive."[73] Whether published, like *Business Week*, or internal, like memos and spreadsheets, these documents are circulated simply for reading, not for more writing. Whether circulated up a chain of command, down a chain of command, or across or even beyond an organization, these documents are launched on their career as fixed expressions. Authoring is cut off. The pages have "congealed" into page images.[74] Plenty of other digital text technologies work this way too — HyperText Markup Language (HTML) editors are distinct from browsers, for instance — and textual production and reproduction within the modern office has long involved a hierarchical division of labor. PDF technology merely offers a particularly good example of the basic ways in which bureaucratic relations of power are increasingly managed as "usage rights," which the creators of digital objects build into them.[75]

PDFs and PDF-reader applications are designed to insulate reading from authoring. Nor is product design the only factor involved in this project: the costs of reading — whether measured in dollars, time, or technical sophistication — have long been significantly less than the costs of revising PDFs. When Adobe started giving away its PDF reader for free, it stimulated the market for PDF-oriented applications and at the same time added inertial weight — in terms of market share and so-called mind share — to its reader-author distinction. "Work itself" may have been "given a voice" by the bureaucratized work processes of the twentieth century (see chapter 2),[76] but PDF technology has a reactionary, not a revolutionary, feel. It looks back toward the fixity of analog print artifacts and the division of labor between print publishers and their reading customers at the same time that it participates in the mystification of digital tools for an average user trapped in a "friendly" environment where uses are parameterized, constrained to menu-identified tasks, and divided among discrete "tools" and "views."[77] No wonder, then, that geeks and hackers are leery of PDF. The crews who collaborate to publish unauthorized scans of comic books on bit torrent sites, for instance, have adopted open-source formats instead — the *.cbz and *.cbr, which can be made without specialized software. "From the point of the scanners," Wershler writes, "the PDF, the usual choice for professional publishers circulating licensed discrete digital copies of their comics, is the file-format equivalent of bottled water: corporate, proprietary, and bloated with unnecessary features." One newsgroup frequently answered questions (FAQ) section includes the question of whether alt.binaries.pictures.comics.dcp participants make PDFs. "Ugh.

F* no," is the answer, which continues: "Sharing PDF comics will get you ridiculed, ignored, etc."[78]

Nor are all of the enemies of PDF piratical or anticorporate geeks. A prominent web usability expert complained in 2003 about their "big, linear text blobs that are optimized for print and unpleasant to read and navigate online": Jakob Neilsen itemizes the drawbacks of PDFs encountered on the web, mentioning everything from how "jarring" they can be to use — because the browser has to kick open the separate PDF-reader application — to how bloblike they typically are, with limited features for internal navigation. He surveyed users who were trying to use investor-relations pages on corporate websites, and found that they complained bitterly: "I hate Adobe Acrobat. If I bring up PDF, I can't take a section and copy it and move it to Word"; and "It's a pain that I have to download each PDF. Pain in the ass." In 2003 at least, paper was still the preferred medium for reading documents like these, while as an emerging de facto standard for such documents online, PDFs were compared to "the monster from the Black Lagoon" because they had become so tenacious, trapping users in their clammy grip.[79] A few years later another expert in computing asked similarly, "What is the PDF format good for?" There's a long answer to this question and a short one. The short one is simply that the PDF format is good for "nothing. Use HTML and/or (compressed) PostScript instead."[80]

Although complaints about the portable document format have to do partly with how clunky the files are "to read and navigate," they also have to do with how clunky navigating the web itself is, now that it has gotten so peppered with PDFs. (In short, it's a "pain in the ass.") Google's web crawlers have been indexing PDFs since 2001, yet since at least November of that year, Google has also been telling its users how to avoid them. As one of its FAQ pages explains, if you want to get search results without any PDFs in them: "Simply type '-filetype:pdf' within the search box along with your search term(s)."[81] Among those who do publish PDFs online, one gets the sense of grudging acceptance rather than enthusiastic embrace, now in the context of enhancements to the format and the way it is deployed or in the context of alternatives that extend beyond HTML and PostScript files to include more dynamic formats or more proprietary ones.[82] Like microform storage media before it — though not quite to such an extreme — the PDF is an unloved documentary form. Eugene Power and Robert Binkley may have loved microfilm, but no one who ever cranked through reels and frames on a microfilm reader does. John Willinsky, Alex

Garnett, and Angela Pan Wong, who argue for improving the portable document format and the way it is used in scholarly communication, joke in an aside that one of them "keeps a fax machine in his closet, and every so often takes it out to hug it," but the faxlike PDF simply can't be loved that way.[83]

....

Unloved or not, the portable document format has succeeded by dint of the ways in which it imagines and inhabits the genre of the document mobilized within the digital environment. The format prospers both because of its transmissiveness and because of the ways that it supports structured hierarchies of authors and readers ("workflow") that depend on documents. One might generalize that PDFs make sense partly according to a logic of attachment and enclosure. That is, like the digital objects we "attach" to and send along with e-mail messages, or the nondigital objects we still enclose in envelopes or boxes and send by snail mail, PDFs are individually bounded and distinct. Just as an e-mail attachment must exist before the e-mail message that makes it one ("Attached please find . . ."), so PDFs are already authored entities, understood as distinct from the written systems in and by which they are individually named and potentially manipulated or downloaded. The written system in question might be the web itself, a document management system created for a special purpose, a database, or any repository for storing digital files that has a query language and an interface for retrieving them. Using a file manager application to look on your own hard drive for a PDF is something like rooting through a filing cabinet, if you could ever root through files paying attention only to file names and locations, and not to things like thickness or signs of wear. And if you can let go of the idea that the document you call to the screen is actually entirely the same (rather than just looking the same) each time you call it up.[84] Searching computationally for PDFs is different, though, both because searching can rely on data and metadata that go beyond file names and because of the ways that today's searchable databases, at least, render location as relation.

I have been suggesting in part that PDFs and the page images they render make sense according to a set of broad distinctions, like that between analog documents and digital or digitized ones, or among different digital file formats for text. One last such distinction remains to be considered, since the very notion of a page image—of a document that is experienced as a picture of itself online—draws attention to the distinction between electronic texts and electronic images. If it is a commonplace today that words and images and sounds are closer together than they have ever been before—now that all of them come as data strings, in bits and bytes—nonetheless there are important ways that "as computational data structures, images differ radically and fundamentally from electronic text."[85] The big difference, as Kirschenbaum explains, is that unlike digital text, "images remain largely opaque to the algorithmic eyes of the machine."[86] Images cannot be searched internally as text files can. Search Google Images or Flickr all you like: you are effectively searching associated tags—textual metadata—rather than actual images. PDF page images inhabit the text-image distinction as texts, not as images, because all PDFs are potentially searchable. That said, there are plenty of PDFs—called "image-only"—that cannot be searched within a PDF-reader application until or unless they have been manipulated computationally to identify the alphanumeric characters they contain through optical character recognition (OCR), which produces machine-encoded text. Before being scanned, these image-only PDFs do function as images, and very "poor" ones at that.[87] "To OCR" a document has become a verb at least as handy in some situations as "to PDF" one.

Optical character recognition points precisely to the line that separates electronic texts from images. It is a line that disappears at the level of the alphanumeric character since "the algorithmic eyes of" scanning technology effectively identify the shapes of characters, "seeing" them as patterns of yes/no variables that can together be "recognized" (that is, processed) as alphanumeric characters. Image searching is an intensely hot area for research—think of facial recognition technology, fingerprint analysis, or Google Goggles—but for everyday users, OCR is as close and as necessary as it gets. Except for the images of alphanumeric characters, that is, word and image remain distinct in the ways they function and feel online, despite the apparent pictorial qualities of page images as they appear on screen and the ubiquity of digital images that include pictured text, text that has not been "seen" computationally (that is, encoded) as such. Notably, this fundamental difference between electronic texts and electronic images is confirmed on human terms whenever users encounter CAPTCHA technology (the acronym stands for Completely Automated Public Turing test to tell Computers and Humans Apart): Servers generate a selection of distorted alphanumeric characters and ask users to retype them into a blank. This works as a security measure against bots because "algorithmic eyes" can't "read" anything but patterns of yes or no values within a specified, normative range. When you retype the warped letters and numbers that you see, you prove to the server that you are human, because — however rule-based literacy is in fact — real reading is more flexible and more capacious than character recognition can ever be. CAPTCHA is often called a reverse Turing test. In a traditional Turing test human subjects are challenged to identify whether they are interacting with a computer or a human; here a computer has been programmed to screen for interactions with humans. A little like the nominal blanks pervasive in eighteenth-century letters (see chapter 1), CAPTCHA works as an "I know you know" game, where a computer and a reader both "know" which alphanumeric characters need to be filled in. Shared knowledge in this case is not the common currency of the public sphere; instead, it is the interface of unequal functions (machine) and abilities (human) in the zone of alphanumeric code.

Universal product codes (UPC), often referred to as barcodes, and quick response (QR) codes (matrix or two-dimensional barcodes) work as a sort of inverse in alignment with CAPTCHA, since barcodes are specifically designed for "the algorithmic eyes" of a machine and not for human eyes, while they additionally position users as the subjects of databases as well as of systems, institutions, and bureaucracies.[88] Indeed, pattern codes like these represent an endgame of sorts for the genre of the document, a displacement of *docer* into the realm of the machine: not the end, but rather *an* end imagined within the repertoire of the so-called posthuman. Scan the barcode on a product label or the QR code on an airline boarding pass, and the know-show function of the document in question is in a sense self-allegorized by numerical processing within the relevant system architecture.[89] Not quite text (from a reader's standpoint) and not entirely image (at the scanner), barcodes like these require a fixity that makes them perfect content for PDFs as well as for paper. So the document persists. Like Harpel's specimens of ink shaped by specimens of labor, barcodes must inhabit or adhere to a page or page image, like the product label stuck on a tangerine or the boarding pass held open on a smartphone. They recall the sort of global positioning already hinted at by job printing, as they help triangulate the self in relation to authority: the authority of documents, on the one hand, and the authority of specific systems and bureaucracies, on the other hand.

Amateurs Rush In

The 1930s sci-fi zine, the dada art zine, the chapbook created by beat writers in the 1950s, small-scale radical magazines of the 1960s, punk zines of the 1970s, the zine explosion of the 1990s, online blogs and guerrilla news reporting of today all started with individuals sharing a similar DIY ethos.

—Amy Spencer, *DIY: The Rise of Lo-Fi Culture*

Zine producers have historically embraced new technology. They quickly adopted small hand presses in the 1930s, mimeograph machines in the 1950s, photocopy machines in the 1980s, and desktop publishing in the 1990s.

—Stephen Duncombe, *Notes from Underground*

The future presented by the Internet is the mass amateurization of publishing and a switch from "Why publish this?" to "Why not?"

—Clay Shirky, *Here Comes Everybody*

Try writing a book that is partly about photocopies and mimeographs, and everywhere you go someone is bound to ask, "Are you going to write about zines?" It started to bother me. Although the pressing relevance of amateur cultural production online seems clear—whether elaborated enthusiastically by Henry Jenkins in *Convergence Culture*, for instance, or excoriated by Andrew Keen in *The Cult of the Amateur*—the question about zines that kept coming up wasn't about the Internet at all, at least not explicitly.[1] Asking about self-published, homemade, small-run amateur publications sounded like pure nostalgia to me, or worse. I detected pie-eyed cultural studies, trapped in celebrations of subcultural resistance as cultural critique. And I detected some sloppy media history, too, rushing to connect while forgetting to distinguish. Yet in fact amateurs have kept coming up while I have been thinking about documents, whether in the subtitle to *Harpel's Typograph*, variously in Robert Binkley's "New Tools for Men of Letters," or in pondering the tactical uses of photocopies and the desktop-publishing origins of PDF files.[2] Technological developments that have helped enable the expansion of the scriptural economy have arisen largely according to the interests of officialdom, but their benefits—thank goodness—devolve to outsiders as well. The meanings of media are not prescribed, we know, but rather evolve amid the conditions of use. Amateurs can certainly play roles as users, but they also inhere within, and help structure conditions of, use in general.

The previous chapters have gestured "toward a media history of documents" without completing one: many are the paths not taken, and much is left to do. New questions must arise. Rather than conclude too neatly, then, this afterword finally responds to the persistent question of zines. After being prompted so often, I started to wonder, what would—what should—a history of amateur publication look like? How do zines have history?[3] More particularly, is—or how is—that history relevant to the media history of documents upon which this project dwells?

Returning to Oscar Harpel makes some sense here, both because the subtitle of *Harpel's Typograph* addresses "master printers, amateurs, apprentices and others," and because of his anthology, *Poets and Poetry of Printerdom*.[4] Taken together these titles testify, as I have suggested, to an important moment largely overlooked by media history: the moment when the printers' monopoly was finally broken. Before the Civil War letterpress, printers had a lock on the look of printedness; afterward and increasingly they did not. (This happened so long ago that we have forgotten what it was like to be—even forgotten that we ever were—limited to writing by hand. Few elementary schools even teach cursive these days.) So although Harpel's *Poets and Poetry of Printerdom* sounds like a quaint assertion of printers as poets, one must be aware of its darker undertone, a complaint that by contrast poets really should not be printers. Yet just a few years before, *Harpel's Typograph* had addressed itself to amateur printers inter alia.

It seems likely that Harpel's use of the term "printerdom" was a reaction to that other coinage, "amateurdom."[5] The *Oxford English Dictionary* is no help here, saying only that -*dom* as a suffix was first noticed by its compilers in an 1880 publication. It is easy to antedate the *OED* now that there are searchable databases, of course, but there is something more interesting here: according to the first edition of the dictionary, the suffix -*dom* is "freely employed to form nonce-derivatives." ("Nonce-derivative," like the related "nonce-word" and "nonce-form," was invented by James Murray, the dictionary's editor, to refer to words "used only 'for the nonce.'") Ironically, a quick search of relevant databases shows that "nonce-derivative" is itself a nonce-form, used only once or twice and only by or under Murray. And searching databases likewise reveals that "printerdom" was also a nonce-derivative, but "amateurdom" was not. It had legs: by the mid-1870s it was standard American usage. And by the early 1880s it was familiar enough to be shortened as second-order slang, with increasing numbers of amateur printers, editors, and writers participating in the domain that some of them sometimes called "the dom."

The character of amateurdom may be gleaned from the American Antiquarian Society's collection of more than 50,000 amateur newspapers. Early examples are "pen-printed" (that is, written by hand) or job printed (by hired printers), but the collection suggests that the production of amateur papers increased tenfold after 1869 when a small platen press, called the Novelty Job Printing Press, came on the market aimed at amateurs — including merchants and druggists — as well as at boys (figure After.1).[6] Amateurdom organized as such soon followed.[7] A cursory survey of "the dom" is available from contemporary sources. The children's magazine *St. Nicholas*, for instance, published an account of "Amateur Newspapers" in 1882, and the following year Thomas Harrison published a 330-page book, *The Career and Reminiscences of an Amateur Journalist and a History of Amateur Journalism*, the bulk of which narrates his life as an amateur from 1875 all the way to 1878 — that is, from the age of fifteen to the age of eighteen.[8] (A second volume was promised but does not seem to have been published.) Accounts like these agree in most of their particulars. Indeed, the features of amateurdom seem quickly to have achieved a potted quality, rehearsed again and again as core themes that consumed

FIGURE AFTER.1. Advertisement for the Novelty Job Printing Press, advertisers' addenda to Oscar H. Harpel, *Harpel's Typograph* (1870), courtesy of the American Antiquarian Society.

the geographically "vast literary society" of this "little literary world," as Harrison puts it.[9] Amateurdom was intensely self-referential, forever consolidating itself as itself. Motivations were clear. Although "the anticipated pleasure of seeing articles from [his] own pen in print, was an entrancing one" (88), amateurs like Harrison did what they did out of a keen ambition to become known to—even to become storied among—other amateurs through the circulation of their publications via the mails. The U.S. Post Office allowed free exchanges of newspapers until 1878, when it cracked down on those that lacked significant subscriber lists and only exchanged copies. Two offending categories of publication were singled out: printer's trade circulars dressed up as periodicals and amateur newspapers.[10] The so-called "postal troubles" briefly put a damper on things, but amateurdom continued, with its active contributors estimated by Harrison at eight or nine hundred (69, 14). That was likely a zenith.

In what sense was amateurdom amateur? This is a more complicated question than it may at first appear. Harrison indicates when a publication he refers to is "(prof.)," but it would be a mistake to define "amateur" in contrast to "professional" and leave it at that. For one thing, taken together these terms too easily invite anachronism: any profession against which these amateurs might have been defined was still emerging. Professional journalism did not yet exist — there were no journalism schools, no professional associations for journalists, and no avowed ideal of objectivity — and we know that the roles of author, editor, and publisher were professionalized primarily insofar as individuals made and were known to make a living writing, editing, or publishing, or doing some combination of the same.[11] Printing, of course, was not a profession; it was a trade dressing itself as an art ("the art preservative"), and one that had for decades experienced wrenching structural changes — loosely put, "industrialization" — as the apprenticeship and journeyman system broke down, while some labors (like presswork) were deskilled and others (like typesetting) were not, or at least not yet. Print production in general experienced explosive growth, yet talented printers like Harpel struggled. Job printing grew more specialized (in its distinction from periodical and book work), inspiring still further innovations in printing technology, among them smaller iron hand presses that after 1850 included myriad versions of the platen press, or "jobber."[12] It was this press that was eventually miniaturized for and pitched to amateurs. As one purveyor of printing outfits urged, "Every man his own printer. Every boy a Ben Franklin."[13]

According to Harrison, "the real history" of amateurdom didn't begin until the Novelty press (26); *St. Nicholas* magazine agreed. The figure cut by Benjamin Woods and his little press in these accounts — like those that have followed — suggests that the amateurs of "the dom" might be reckoned in purely technological terms, but that too would be a mistake. New media do not themselves make amateur cultural producers, even though each of the two is regularly cast in terms of the other. Access to new tools was key, it's true, but access to consumer culture is much more to the point. Following Karen Sánchez-Eppler, we need to see amateurdom as a specific and specifically gendered class formation, part of "enormous and extremely swift shifts in the cultural understanding of childhood, work, and play" then under way in American culture.[14] Childhood leisure — especially boyhood leisure — was a class privilege, increasingly enshrined in compulsory schooling laws and epitomized in the merchandising of goods specifically for children. By this light, the amateurs of amateurdom — mostly but not entirely male — can't be defined against "(prof.)" as much as they can against the figure of a working-class child. Harrison's corresponding "other" wasn't Harpel, it was the newsboy, the bootblack, and—already a little bit of a throwback—the trade apprentice and printer's devil.[15] If the figure of the working child was associated in the popular imagination with play, as Sánchez-Eppler indicates, then it made perfect sense that middle-class play got associated with work.[16] Again and again amateurs insist to their readers how hard they work, how much time and effort their papers require, while they also stress that their labors are self-improving yet money losing, not profit making.

In so adamantly describing itself as a realm of hard work and money losing, amateurdom was able at once to participate in consumer culture and to reject its logic. This wasn't just consumption, in other words; they didn't say they were buying the same things, only that they lost money and spent time and energy. The repeated lip service paid to nonprofit production locates amateur newspapers (as Miranda Joseph writes of nonprofit organizations generally) within "the absent center of capitalism," a place where the very subjects of capitalism have gone missing, revealing their discontents. These subjects abscond by dint of energies expended compensatorily toward a communal cause. Today we'd call the result "community"; by 1872 or 1873 North Americans at least said "amateurdom."[17] The amateurs were individually ambitious and unstintingly critical of one another, prone both to empire building and to fractiousness: they were capitalists in training, dressed in a classically liberal discourse of the educable self, yet they zealously participated in and cherished their printed-and-postal community and the corresponding gaggle of amateur press associations that they organized to represent and support it. Amateurdom arose not in the commonality of choosing and buying, but rather in the collective imagination of itself as a sphere of productive communication, an imaginary domain for what observers of later zines have called "cooperative individuality" and healthy "intersubjectivity."[18]

The tensions involved in training for capitalism by abandoning its putative object of desire (that is, profit) made perfect sense within the ongoing construction of young adulthood as a liminal stage, between and yet neither. We might consider, too, that these tensions emerged partly as an outgrowth of readerly subjectivities that evolved amid the postbellum explosion of secular magazines for young readers.[19] Harrison himself acknowledges amateurdom's debt to *Oliver Optic's Magazine* (26),[20] which chirpily editorialized in July 1867, during its first year of publication: "We suppose Lowe's press is the best for boys; if they don't like it, try Hoe's twelve-cylinder press!"[21] (The Lowe press was a portable field press used during the Civil War.) By 1873 "Oliver Optic"—the intensely prolific William Taylor Adams—was offering both coverage of and encouragement to amateur printers, editors, and journalists in the pages of his magazine. Children's periodicals had long sought active readerships, but the new magazines perfected them. In November 1865 *Our Young Folks* chidingly instructed children how to write to the editors; *Oliver Optic's* included one regular column called "Our Letter Bag" and soon included another called "Wish Correspondents," where readers named the subjects they were interested in to solicit correspondence from other readers with the same interests; and *St. Nicholas* reinvented the letters column so that it more readily promoted "community and connection among all of [its] readers and contributors."[22] Like the shared "fantasy" of a "textual commons," which Jared Gardner suspects cut against the success of so many of the earliest American magazines (by encouraging feelings of shared ownership that may actually have inhibited people from paying their subscriptions),[23] these new magazines for children carried mixed messages. Yes, they were crucial agents in the interpellation of children as subjects of consumer culture, yet they also spun the accessory magic of a less—even a non-commercial—communal domain.

The fin de siècle psychologists who eventually described adolescence as a developmental stage noted a "reading craze" among their subjects.[24] Had they noticed amateurdom, they might have seen it as a peculiarly acute form of that craze. Amateur youngsters read so crazily that they wrote, edited, printed, and published. One example is chronicled in amateur lore. Following the model of earlier magazines, *Golden Days for Boys and Girls* (founded in 1882), cultivated correspondence among readers and "clubs" of readers. At some point, "a member of one of its clubs suggested the idea of issuing a small paper to serve as the organ of his particular club. The idea caught fire, and hundreds of these club papers were issued" until 2 September 1895, when a fourteen-year-old named William H. Greenfield started the United Amateur Press Association to organize them.[25] That same trajectory—from the readership of commercially published magazines with letters columns, to clubs of readers, to amateur publications that comment on each other, and finally to a self-organizing sphere of postal communication and exchange—would also describe the 1930s evolution of fanzines and fandom, as it was eventually called, but that may be jumping ahead too quickly. It's a pattern, except when it's not.[26]

I should emphasize that money-losing amateurs like Harrison and Greenfield didn't say they were jumping off the good ship *Kapital* or steering it clear of the rocks of adulthood; they said the opposite. It was feeling that gave them away: amateurdom was an affective state as well as a textual commons. Young Harrison became "possessed," he says, by the desire to join amateurdom (88). A "'printing fever'" seized another amateur, David Bethune, and elsewhere it was a "mania for editorship" that prevailed.[27] The writer H. P. Lovecraft suffered a short-lived "poetical delusion" when he first encountered amateurdom in 1914, at the ripe age of twenty-three.[28] As he explains in a brief reflection titled "What Amateurdom and I Have Done for Each Other," he was introduced to the United Amateur Press Association when he was "as close to the state of vegetation as any animal well can be — perhaps I might best have been compared to the lowly potato in its secluded and subterranean quiescence." The United — in which Lovecraft quickly became chairman of the Department of Public Criticism — gave him at once "a renewed will to live," the "very world in which" to live, and also "life itself."[29] That figure of the lowly, secluded, and quiescent potato — known to us today as the couch potato — probably alludes to Samuel Butler's *Erewhon* (1872), a novel that includes a humorous bit on the emotions and sentience of a potato. Lovecraft remained a denizen in and exponent of amateurdom throughout his career, even while enjoying success as a professional writer of fiction in the *Erewhonian* vein.

But can the amateurdom that Lovecraft joined and described in the 1910s and 1920s be the same amateurdom of Harrison and the others from the 1870s and 1880s? Better questions: Are the amateurs of one era the amateurs of another? Is do-it-yourself (DIY) publishing the same thing, whenever and however you happen to do it? So much of what Lovecraft describes about "the United" rings familiar. He acknowledges its origins around 1870, notes a common "yearning" to have "thoughts and ideals permanently crystallized in the magic medium of type," and celebrates those who labor "purely for love," "without the stultifying influence of commercialism."[30] The amateur press associations — the United and the National, founded in 1876 — had persisted and matured, each holding annual meetings, publishing an official organ, serving as clearinghouses, and awarding annual "laureates" in the different genres of amateurdom: poetry, sketch, history, and essay (65), as well as eventually a laureate "for the best home-printed paper," which suggests a decline in the number of amateurs who were printing their own.[31] Yet according to Lovecraft's telling, amateurdom was open to all comers, "boys and girls of twelve and men and women of sixty, parents and their sons and daughters, college professors and grammar-school pupils." Being open to all was now part of the reigning ethos, important to the encouragement of a "genial" forum for "instruction and fraternal cheer."[32]

Amateurdom, it seems, had gradually become less of a liminal stage in life — a mixture of training for and unspoken deferral of — and more of a clubhouse or hideaway geared toward self-improving self-expression, tenanted by successive waves (well, actually trickles) of far-flung amateurs warmed partly by the accumulated lore of years gone by. (The annual laureate for history generally meant the history of amateurdom.) Along the way, one might speculate that amateurdom had also become less of a formative assertion of middle-class identity and more of a formative assertion within it. The same distinction between amateur and commercial publications held sway, in other words, but no longer were the contrastive "others" of amateurdom working-class, urban youths or the long-gone trade apprentice. More likely the "others" of amateurdom were either sorry couch potatoes — isolate and quiescent subjects of the emerging mass culture — or else they were other amateurs finding their own alternatives, some comfortable with the label "amateur" and others not. Those alternatives might be organized amateur athletics, the high-school yearbook, or the college newspaper. One must wonder in particular about amateur radio, which had exploded onto the scene with the 1906 crystal set and boy operator playing the role of the 1869 Novelty press and boy Benjamin Franklin. The far-flung amateur radio operators didn't need to imagine a realm called "amateurdom": they had one called the ether, though perhaps it was a little diffuse. Amateur radio operators didn't need to publish on paper or communicate by post, though the eventual practice of exchanging QSL cards by mail to confirm radio contact does make interesting food for thought. ("QSL" was telegraph and radio code for "I confirm receipt of your transmission.") In less than a decade amateur radio in the United States had probably exceeded amateur journalism by three orders of magnitude (several hundred thousand amateurs, instead of several hundred), as wireless captured the popular imagination.[33]

Meanwhile the amateur writers, editors, printers, and publishers of amateurdom's long maturity—a small group of them called The Fossils, acting in the mode of alumni, still exists—shared a history that tended to be chronicled year by year with elections, schisms, and intrigues, as well as an occasional and fleeting golden age, all studded with the names of predecessors and their typically short-lived publications. Harrison had approvingly discerned a shift from "sensational" to "pure literature" during his brilliant if brief career (47); 1886 brought turmoil surrounding an amateur Literary Lyceum, dead in 1888;[34] 1891 saw the publication of a 500-page retrospective literary anthology or "cyclopedia";[35] and Lovecraft eventually likened amateurdom to a "university, stripped of every artificiality and conventionality, and thrown open to all without distinction," its membership seeking mutually "to draw their minds from the commonplace to the beautiful."[36] As a putative "*revival* of the uncommercial spirit,"[37] amateurdom had become an antimodern gesture toward authenticity, evolving in contrast to the slick magazines that heralded mass culture and during the same extended moment in which literary critical authority was ceasing to be a matter of individual taste or editorial selection on the part of commercial publishing and was instead becoming a matter of academic consensus.[38] Lovecraft and his compatriots soldiered on as junior elementary aesthetes, exerting individual discernment toward their own common cause. The fact that amateurdom was in general "more newsy than literary"—that is, more about itself than about literature or anything else—only made it more fun.[39]

The answer then is no, amateurs of one era are not the amateurs of another, even when a continuous tradition exists to connect them. H. P. Lovecraft was no Thomas Harrison, in more ways than one. What changed and continues to change across time is not the DIY ethos or even what the amateur happens to do, but rather the ways that doing and its do-ability are situated within the broader cultural economy and the lives that cultural economy helps to shape. Self-publishing is culturally situated according in part to ongoing constructions of class, race, gender, stage of life, and *Bildung*, as well as the ongoing articulation of domesticity, the disciplines, vocations, and professions. We know too—as I have been hinting—that amateur doings and do-ability would come to be situated in relation to the structure and content of mass culture. Richard Ohmann starts the clock on mass culture with the major monthly magazines of the late 1890s, while it was the model of commercial broadcasting—radio again—developed in the late 1920s and 1930s, that would come to epitomize mass culture for its later and most influential critics.[40] But mass culture is less to the point here than managerial culture. The so-called managerial revolution of the late nineteenth century produced the modern corporation and with it the modern office, replete with new genres of and new tools for communication, new bureaucratic imperatives, and new labor cohorts and configurations. The printers' monopoly on the look of printedness, broken with the advent of amateur printing, collapsed with the proliferation of typewriters and the ensuing century of innovation directed at reproducing typescript without setting type: the technologies of the mimeograph, hectograph (ditto), photo-offset, and eventually Xerox. Journalism (like English-professordom) had become a profession, yes, but office work — its patterns and practices — had undergone an even bigger and more salient change.

Of course it will take a lot more than generalizations like these to explain the specific forms that amateur publishing has taken in the extended era of managerial capital, and I can offer only the briefest gesture in that regard. Amateurdom eventually did connect to the fandom of the 1930s through figures like Lovecraft, who participated in both domains. And amateur radio connected to fandom, too, through the figure of Hugo Gernsback, who promoted amateur radio and published magazines that eventually included and explored what he called "scientifiction."[41] In other ways, however, fanzine fandom was substantially its own animal.

To the extent that there was one, the Thomas Harrison of fandom was Sam Moskowitz, a prolific chronicler and devoted collector who had become a fan at age fourteen and then stuck around for life, even working professionally for a time as an editor for one of Gernsback's magazines. Moskowitz published a multipart history of science fiction fandom, which was republished as a typescript book in 1954.[42] Entitled *The Immortal Storm*, its 250 pages cover only the 1930s, though Moskowitz hoped that someone would publish a sequel that would be appropriately "bibliographical" and "detailed," complete with the "individual personalities, aims, ambitions, [and] emotional motivations" that make his chronicle of associations, rivalries, and upsets the very obsessive work that it is.[43] Reading *The Immortal Storm* along with a selection of fanzines from the 1950s offers a snapshot of fandom at this juncture.[44] By 1953, to give some idea, the accumulated corpus of fanzine titles was roughly 9 percent printed, 17 percent reproduced by ditto, 60 percent reproduced by mimeograph, and 14 percent in another category or in a category unknown to indexers.[45]

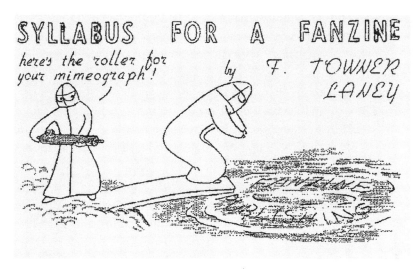

SYLLABUS FOR A FANZINE

here's the roller for
your mimeograph!

by F. TOWNER LANEY

FIGURE AFTER.2. Bill Rotsler, illustration for Francis Towner Laney's mimeographed "Syllabus for a Fanzine" (1950); digitized by the FANAC Fan History Project (www.fanac.org) and reproduced here by permission.

In general — but only in general — the earliest fanzines were small and printed — 6″ × 4½″ (in an era when most of the commercial "pulp" magazines were 7″ × 10″). Then came the brief day of the hectograph, or ditto (when fanzines grew to 8½″ × 11″ and turned purple, but could be reproduced in batches no bigger than about fifty copies). Next came the mimeograph, which became fandom's most popular and consistent medium of publication, at least into the mid-1960s (figure After.2).[46] Fanzine archives and collections are full of mimeographs, easily recognizable by their soft, absorbent paper, which took mimeograph ink so well.

As late as 1986 one astute fan noted wryly, "mimeography recapitulates hagiography."[47] Earlier fans write not of hagiography but of "ego boo," short for ego boosting. Like amateurdom before it, fanzine fandom was intensely self-referential, forever consolidating itself as itself by means of chronicles, conventions, published comments, correspondence, and collecting, as well as reviews, digests, indexes, insider jokes, and jargon. Like amateurdom, fandom put a premium on originality and authenticity, yet it largely escaped an antimodern tinge by focusing on what one fan called "the literature of tomorrow": science fiction.[48] I think I can safely generalize that fandom to this point remained more engaged than amateurdom was with the for-profit sphere from which it distinguished itself, because of consistent if modest crossover by figures like Lovecraft and Moskowitz as well as a certain amount of rubbing shoulders at conventions and for the purposes of collecting. One might speculate that fandom differed from amateurdom in this respect partly because science fiction — the catalyzing object of fandom's self-imagination — evolved and persisted as a low-brow form, so that literary critical authority over it was never relegated to the academy but instead remained in negotiation across fandom and commercial — primarily "pulp" — publishing and (at a remove, of course) Hollywood.[49] The late nineteenth-century evolution of "the literary" as an object of academic inquiry made no difference to fandom, though the evolution of psychology as an object of inquiry may have mattered. The amateurs of early amateurdom had been all about building character; now the no-less-passionate fans of fandom had personalities. As Francis Laney puts it in "Syllabus for a Fanzine," a good fanzine has an "editorial persona" or some "extensionalisation" of the editor.[50] It's not that amateur newspapers of the nineteenth century lacked editorial personae; it's just that having them didn't figure this explicitly or grandiloquently into the self-consciousness of amateurdom. The denizens of fanzine fandom — almost universally white and male into the 1960s — saw themselves as selves, and selves of a special sort. It wasn't membership that made them unique; it was more that a prior uniqueness made them sensible as members.[51]

Fandom persists, of course, radically diversified, expanded, and online. Now we have scholarly fan studies, too, a "dom" of sorts if there ever was one, relying not on amateur self-publishing but rather on the not exactly profit-driven publishing of the contemporary academy.[52] But I'm going to break off my story of "doms" — amateurdom and fandom — here, before the language of underground or subculture versus mainstream takes hold, in order to reflect briefly if speculatively on the history of amateurs, DIY publishing, and only by extension the character of zines. The more recent efflorescence of zines, the recurrent rhythms of that efflorescence, and the scope and character of the relevant zine scenes all deserve further attention. My interest finally is in proposing a connection to the media history of documents with which I have been concerned in these pages.

Rather than take the self-chronicling of amateurs and fans entirely at face value, I have tried instead to gesture more broadly toward the scriptural economy, its trajectory of engagement with consumer culture, and, in particular, its late nineteenth-century expansion in the service of managerial capital. That framing I hope helps reveal some of the selectivity, if not the shortcomings, of any dichotomy like mainstream versus subculture — or, better put, any schematic that might simply contrast public and counterpublic. In one sense amateurdom and fandom are classic counterpublics in Michael Warner's terms: they are self-imagined realms of belonging evolved both by and for communication and in opposition to the larger public sphere.[53] Yet it would be well to remember that the Habermasian public sphere, with its sharp line between private and public — between the home and the coffeehouse, the manuscript letter and the printed news sheet — depends upon a very idealized notion of print publication, the event of issuing into public, that may more accurately refer to eighteenth- and early nineteenth-century life in Western Europe than to later periods or other locales. Certainly today the eventfulness of publication is complicated by the scale and temporalities of the web: the entanglement of publication with search technology, for instance; the prevalence of dead links and dynamic content; uneven and obscure calendars of updates and subscriptions; and so on.[54] But even before the web, in the extended era of amateurdom and fanzine fandom, the enormous pressures of social differentiation and the growth of institutions — of which the modern corporation only looms the largest in my ken — worked increasingly to complicate the eventfulness of publication.

In short, amateur newspapers, fanzines, and their successors have always been imagined in contrast to commercially published periodicals, but that imagination itself has become increasingly incumbent on other, unacknowledged contrasts, such as that between the zine and the less-published or the semipublished documents that issue forth amid our increasingly institutionalized existence. Think here of the reports and proposals of the corporate workplace, the newsletters and programs of the voluntary association and congregation, the pamphlets of the public-health agency, the course packs once ubiquitous on college campuses, and even the much-maligned annual Christmas letters proper to that most "important institution of control," the middle-class nuclear family. (Susan Sontag notes of the amateurization of photography that it became "enrolled in the service of important institutions of control, notably the family and the police."[55]) Amateurdom and fandom by these lights are less counterpublics than they are counterinstitutions, loosely self-organizing assemblages — of members, mail, media, and lore — that defy institutionalization partly by reproducing it cacophonously in an adolescent key. Later zine scenes and "alt" arenas differ from the "doms" of amateurdom and fandom, no doubt, yet they too might be studied not just for how they contrast with commercial publication but also for the ways in which that contrast tends to obscure other things, including the forever expanding and baroquely structured dominion of the document.

We have gotten particularly good at noticing the ways that amateur cultural production has emerged and thrived online and to what effects, but we may not be as good yet — even in our fondness for DIY publishing — at seeing from all angles the contexts that have helped to configure DIY. Are recent zines and the recently pressing question of zines ("Are you going to write about zines?") variously nostalgic reactions to digital communications media? To some extent that is certainly the case, though saying so too easily neglects the massive diversity of digital communications, which include everything from blogs and vlogs with the tenor of zines to backward-looking, paper-imagining forms like the PDF, now used to e-publish so that others may print out. In addition, DIY publishing needs to be located within and against DIY more generally. The futurologist Alvin Toffler, who was already using the term "prosumer" in 1980 — alas not "prosumer-dom" — came pretty close to predicting today's independent video, home offices, and distributed computing, but his description of 1980s-style DIY may come as more of a surprise. His futurological extrapolations take as their point of departure the then-new DIY home pregnancy test kits; direct long-distance telephone dialing; self-service gasoline pumps; and automated teller machines (ATMs).[56] Add the then-familiar mix tapes, copy shops, and film-processing kiosks, and I think it makes a wonderfully evocative context for — among other things — the imminent availability of desktop publishing, which arrived courtesy of Aldus and Apple to the embrace of amateurs and others.

PREFACE

1. Michel de Certeau, *The Practice of Everyday Life*, trans. Steven F. Rendall (Berkeley: University of California Press, 1981), 131, 132.
2. De Certeau's *The Practice of Everyday Life* is dedicated "to the ordinary man" (v).

INTRODUCTION. PAPER KNOWLEDGE

1. See Annelise Riles, "Introduction: In Response," in *Documents: Artifacts of Modern Knowledge*, ed. Annelise Riles (Ann Arbor: University of Michigan Press, 2006), 6–7. See also Carlo Ginzburg, *Clues, Myths, and the Historical Method*, trans. John Tedeschi and Anne C. Tedeschi (Baltimore, MD: Johns Hopkins University Press, 1989), 96–155; Anthony Grafton, *The Footnote: A Curious History* (Cambridge, MA: Harvard University Press, 1997).
2. John Guillory, "The Memo and Modernity," *Critical Inquiry* 31, no. 1 (2004): 120.
3. Lauren Berlant, *The Female Complaint: The Unfinished Business of Sentimentality in American Culture* (Durham, NC: Duke University Press, 2008), 314.
4. I've been influenced here by Virginia Jackson, *Dickinson's Misery: A Theory of Lyric Reading* (Princeton, NJ: Princeton University Press, 2005); Ralph Cohen, "History and Genre," *New Literary History* 17, no. 2 (1986): 203–18; Carolyn R. Miller, "Genre as Social Action," *Quarterly Journal of Speech* 70 (1984): 151–67; and conversations with Jennie Jackson, Rachael S. King, Clifford Siskin, and Anna Poletti.
5. Briet was a proponent of the European bibliographical movement called Documentation. See Suzanne Briet, *What Is Documentation? English Translation of the Classic French Text*, trans. Ronald E. Day, Laurent Martinet, and Hermina G. B. Anghelescu (Lanham, MD: Scarecrow, 2006). See also Bernd Frohmann, "The Documentality of Mme. Briet's Antelope," in *Communication Matters: Materialist Approaches to Media, Mobility, and Networks*, ed. Jeremy Packer and Stephen B. Crofts Wiley (New York: Routledge, 2012), 173–82.

6. Michael Buckland, "What Is a Digital Document?," 1998, http://people.ischool .berkeley.edu/~buckland/digdoc.html, accessed 25 June 2013.

7. "Mobilized" is a Bruno Latourism (see below). For the recent interest in "things," see Bill Brown, "Thing Theory," *Critical Inquiry* 28 (Autumn 2001): 1–22. See also, Lorraine Daston, ed., *Things That Talk: Object Lessons from Art and Science* (New York: Zone, 2004); Lorraine Daston, ed., *Biographies of Scientific Objects* (Chicago: University of Chicago Press, 2000); Hans-Jörg Rheinberger, *Toward a History of Epistemic Things: Synthesizing Proteins in the Test Tube* (Stanford, CA: Stanford University Press, 1997).

8. This observation is one subject of Leah Price's *How to Do Things with Books in Victorian Britain* (Princeton, NJ: Princeton University Press, 2012). Price notes the ways in which the distinction of work and text is an artifact of class as much as of culture (9), and she points to the work of Carlo Ginzburg to align the origins of that distinction with the history of printing (32).

9. The useful idea of "affordances" has crept into media studies from Abigail J. Sellen and Richard H. R. Harper's *The Myth of the Paperless Office* (Cambridge, MA: MIT Press, 2002), 16–18. For a more expansive view of the salience of paper in an aesthetic register, or "the logic of substrate," see Craig Dworkin, *No Medium* (Cambridge, MA: MIT Press, 2013), chapter 1.

10. See Jacques Derrida, *Paper Machine*, trans. Rachel Bowlby (Stanford, CA: Stanford University Press, 2005), 44.

11. See Andrew Warwick, *Masters of Theory: Cambridge and the Rise of Mathematical Physics* (Chicago: University of Chicago Press, 2003), chapter 3.

12. Wendy Hui Kyong Chun notes that the current scholarly interest in things or "thing theory" needs to be seen in the context of digital media, within which things "always seem to be disappearing" in such crucial ways (*Programmed Visions: Software and Memory* [Cambridge, MA: MIT Press, 2011], 11).

13. See Sellen and Harper, *The Myth of the Paperless Office*; David M. Levy, *Scrolling Forward: Making Sense of Documents in the Digital Age* (New York: Arcade, 2001).

14. Geoffrey Nunberg, "Farewell to the Information Age," in *The Future of the Book*, ed. Geoffrey Nunberg (Berkeley: University of California Press, 1996), 120.

15. See Ellen Gruber Garvey, "'<u>facts</u> and FACTS': Abolitionists' Database Innovations," in *"Raw Data" Is an Oxymoron*, ed. Lisa Gitelman (Cambridge, MA: MIT Press, 2013), 89–102; Trish Loughran, *The Republic in Print: Print Culture in the Age of U.S. Nation Building, 1770–1870* (New York: Columbia University Press, 2007).

16. On the power-control distinction, Guillory is succinct ("The Memo and Modernity," 122).

17. Ibid., 113.

18. See M. T. Clanchy, *From Memory to Written Record: England 1066–1307*, 2nd ed. (Oxford: Blackwell, 1993), 6, 46.

19. The first quotation is from Isabel Hofmeyr, *The Portable Bunyan: A Transnational History of "The Pilgrim's Progress"* (Princeton, NJ: Princeton University Press, 2004), 143 (see also 147); the second quotation is Jane I. Guyer, *Marginal Gains:*

Monetary Transactions in Atlantic Africa (Chicago: University of Chicago Press, 2004, 159). After the quotations here, I'm drawing on Matthew S. Hull, *Government of Paper: The Materiality of Bureaucracy in Urban Pakistan* (Berkeley: University of California Press, 2012), 10. Hull notes the use of "Kaghazi Raj" described below (7).

20. Bruno Latour, "Drawing Things Together," in *Representation and Scientific Practice*, ed. Michael Lynch and Steve Woolgar [1988] (Cambridge: MIT Press, 1990), 19, 21–22. This essay exists in multiple versions, frequently under the title "Visualization and Cognition: Drawing Things Together."

21. The literary in this sense is a Romantic construct entwined with "the bibliographic imagination." See Andrew Piper, who asks us to remember F. W. Bateson's challenge: "'If the *Mona Lisa* is in [Paris], where is *Hamlet?*'" (*Dreaming in Books: The Making of the Bibliographic Imagination in the Romantic Age* [Chicago: University of Chicago Press, 2009] 9).

22. Annelise Riles, *The Network Inside Out* (Ann Arbor: University of Michigan Press, 2000); see also D. F. McKenzie, *Bibliography and the Sociology of Texts* (London: British Library, 1986).

23. On the scriptural economy, see Michel de Certeau, *The Practice of Everyday Life*, trans. Steven F. Rendall (Berkeley: University of California Press, 1981), 131–35.

24. Jonathan Sterne, *MP3: The Meaning of a Format* (Durham, NC: Duke University Press, 2012); and Bonnie Mak, *How the Page Matters* (Toronto: University of Toronto Press, 2011). "Media concept" is John Guillory's useful term, which he elaborates in "Genesis of the Media Concept," *Critical Inquiry* 36, no. 2 (2010): 321–63.

25. Derrida, *Paper Machine*, 47.

26. See Matthew G. Kirschenbaum, *Mechanisms: New Media and the Forensic Imagination* (Cambridge, MA: MIT Press, 2008); Richard H. R. Harper, *Inside the IMF: An Ethnography of Documents, Technology, and Organisational Action* (San Diego, CA: Academic, 1998); Levy, *Scrolling Forward*.

27. The rearview mirror is a figure from Marshall McLuhan and Quentin Fiore, *The Medium Is the Massage: An Inventory of Effects* (New York: Bantam, 1967). "Objects in the mirror . . ." is a more recent catchphrase.

28. The argument is advanced as well, incidentally, to correct myself for using such categories in the past. Michael Winship first disparaged "print culture" to me, and I remain grateful that, on reflection, I have accepted his irritation as my own. "Hazardous" is from Leo Marx, "Technology: The Emergence of a Hazardous Concept," *Social Research* 64 (Fall 1997): 965–88.

29. Indeed, manuscript is a back formation that likely took a good deal of time to evolve; see Peter Stallybrass, "Printing and the Manuscript Revolution," in *Explorations in Communication and History*, ed. Barbie Zelizer (New York: Routledge, 2008), 115. For at least two centuries after Johannes Gutenberg, libraries in Europe made no distinction between their manuscript codices and their printed ones; see David McKitterick, *Print, Manuscript and the Search for Order, 1450–1830* (Cambridge: Cambridge University Press, 2003), 13.

30. Michael Warner, *The Letters of the Republic: Publication and the Public Sphere in Eighteenth-Century America* (Cambridge, MA: Harvard University Press, 1990), 7.

31. Paula McDowell, "Mediating Media Past and Present: Toward a Genealogy of 'Print Culture' and 'Oral Tradition,'" in *This Is Enlightenment*, ed. Clifford Siskin and William Warner (Chicago: University of Chicago Press, 2010), 231–32. "Soft" determinism is explored in Merritt Roe Smith and Leo Marx, eds., *Does Technology Drive History? The Dilemma of Technological Determinism* (Cambridge, MA: MIT Press, 1994).

32. Adrian Johns, *The Nature of the Book: Print and Knowledge in the Making* (Chicago: University of Chicago Press, 1998), 35.

33. Warner, *The Letters of the Republic*, 31, xiv.

34. Raymond Williams, *Keywords: A Vocabulary of Culture and Society*, rev. ed. (New York: Oxford University Press, 1985), 92.

35. Warner, *The Letters of the Republic*, xi.

36. Jonathan Crary, *Techniques of the Observer: On Vision and Modernity in the Nineteenth Century* (Cambridge, MA: MIT Press, 1990), 9. See also Arjun Appadurai, *Modernity at Large: Cultural Dimensions of Globalization* (Minneapolis: University of Minnesota Press, 1996), 1.

37. The apparent self-fulfillment of modernity is of course one legacy of—as it was once a driver of—colonialism and the project of empire. Scholars beyond the confines of Western Europe and North America have been alert to the limitations of "print culture" and the related "print capitalism" of Benedict Anderson; see Isabel Hofmeyr, *Gandhi's Printing Press: Experiments in Slow Reading* (Cambridge, MA: Harvard University Press, 2013), 15–16, 32–33.

38. For a recent and specific history covering some of the same chronological terrain as these pages, see Carl F. Kaestle and Janice A. Radway, eds., *Print in Motion: The Expansion of Publishing and Reading in the United States, 1880–1940* (Chapel Hill: published in association with the American Antiquarian Society by the University of North Carolina Press, 2009).

39. N. Katherine Hayles, *How We Think: Digital Media and Contemporary Technogenesis* (Chicago: University of Chicago Press, 2012), 2, 249.

40. *MLA Handbook for Writers of Research Papers*, 7th ed. (New York: Modern Language Association of America, 2009), xvii.

41. See Lisa Gitelman, "Ages, Epochs, Media," in *On Periodization: Selected Essays from the English Institute*, ed. Virginia Jackson (Cambridge, MA: English Institute in collaboration with the American Council of Learned Societies, 2010), http://www.humanitiesebook.org.

42. The phrase "emergent, dominant, and residual" refers to Raymond Williams on cultural forms, as discussed in Charles R. Acland, "Introduction: Residual Media," in *Residual Media*, ed. Charles R. Acland (Minneapolis: University of Minnesota Press, 2007), xiii–xxvii.

43. See Guillory, "The Memo and Modernity"; Craig Robertson, *The Passport in America: The History of a Document* (New York: Oxford University Press, 2010).

44. Mary Poovey, *Genres of the Credit Economy: Mediating Value in Eighteenth- and Nineteenth-Century Britain* (Chicago: University of Chicago Press, 2008).

45. John Durham Peters, "Technology and Ideology: The Case of the Telegraph Revisited," in *Thinking with James Carey: Essays on Communications, Transportation, History*, ed. Jeremy Packer and Craig Robertson (New York: Peter Lang, 2006), 143–44.

46. For example, badges and identity in early modern Europe; the persistent and diverse uses of handwritten catechetical documents in Bolivia after the expulsion of the Jesuits in 1767; or the formal division (at least by modern Assyriologists) of ancient cuneiform inscriptions into a large category called "administrative" and a smaller one called "literary." See Valentin Groebner, *Who Are You? Identification, Deception, and Surveillance in Early Modern Europe*, trans. Mark Kyburz and John Peck (New York: Zone, 2007); Akira Saito, "The Mission and the Administration of Documents: The Case of Mojos from the 18th to the 20th Century," Senri Ethnological Studies 68, *Usos del documento y cambios socials en la historia de Bolivia* (Osaka: National Museum of Ethnology, 2005), 27–72; Dominique Charpin, *Reading and Writing in Babylon*, trans. Jane Marie Todd (Cambridge: Harvard University Press, 2010).

47. On formatting as part of what memos say, see Guillory, "The Memo and Modernity," 126–27.

48. Apologies for the ugly "and/as"; see Lisa Gitelman, *Always Already New: Media, History, and the Data of Culture* (Cambridge, MA: MIT Press, 2006), 91. On materiality, see especially Johanna Drucker, "Entity to Event: From Literal, Mechanistic Materiality to Probabilistic Materiality," *Paralax* 15, no. 4 (2009): 7–17.

49. JoAnne Yates, *Control through Communication: The Rise of System in American Management* (Baltimore, MD: Johns Hopkins University Press, 1989).

50. James Beniger, *The Control Revolution: Technological and Economic Origins of the Information Society* (Cambridge, MA: Harvard University Press, 1989). See also Cornelia Vissman, *Files: Law and Media Technology* (Stanford, CA: Stanford University Press, 2008).

51. See, for example, Ben Kafka, *The Demon of Writing: Powers and Failures of Paperwork* (New York: Zone, 2012); Riles, *Documents*; Harper, *Inside the IMF*; JoAnne Yates, *Structuring the Information Age: Life Insurance and Technology in the Twentieth Century* (Baltimore, MD: Johns Hopkins University Press, 2005).

52. William Stott, *Documentary Expression and Thirties America* (New York: Oxford University Press, 1974). See also Warren I. Susman, *Culture as History: The Transformation of American Society in the Twentieth Century* (New York: Pantheon, 1984), 150–83.

53. Michael Denning, *The Cultural Front: The Laboring of American Culture in the Twentieth Century* (London: Verso, 1996), 117.

54. Jonathan Kahana, *Intelligence Work: The Politics of American Documentary* (New York: Columbia University Press, 2008), 68. On the documentary tradition in photography and film, I rely on Robert Hariman and John Louis Lucaites, *No*

Caption Needed: Iconic Photographs, Public Culture, and Liberal Democracy (Chicago: University of Chicago Press, 2007); Erik Barnouw, *Documentary: A History of the Non-Fiction Film* (Oxford: Oxford University Press, 1974); Bill Nichols, *Introduction to Documentary*, 2nd ed. (Bloomington: Indiana University Press, 2010); Paula Rabinowitz, *They Must Be Represented: The Politics of Documentary* (New York: Verso, 1994); Michael Renov, ed., *Theorizing Documentary* (New York: Routledge, 1993).

55. See Leah Price and Pamela Thurschwell, eds., *Literary Secretaries/Secretarial Culture* (Aldershot, UK: Ashgate, 2005). Secretaries and clerks are among the oldest "hidden workers" of this sort; see Greg Downey, "Virtual Webs, Physical Technologies, and Hidden Workers," *Technology and Culture* 42 (April 2001): 209–35. See also Greg Downey, "Commentary: The Place of Labor in the History of Information-Technology Revolutions," *International Review of Social History* 48, no. S11 (2003): 225–61.

56. For the worries of the historical profession, see Kahana, *Intelligence Work*, 64–69; Carl Becker's "Everyman His Own Historian," *American Historical Review* 37 (January 1932): 221–36. See also Kenneth Carpenter, "Toward a New Cultural Design: The American Council of Learned Societies, the Social Science Research Council, and Libraries in the 1930s," in *Institutions of Reading: The Social Life of Libraries in the United States*, ed. Thomas Augst and Kenneth Carpenter (Amherst: University of Massachusetts Press, 2007), 283–309.

57. Henry Jenkins, *Convergence Culture: Where Old and New Media Collide* (New York: New York University Press, 2006), 136. See also Stephen Duncombe, *Notes from Underground: Zines and the Politics of Alternative Culture*, 2nd ed. (Bloomington, IN: Microcosm, 2008); Janice Radway, "Zines, Half-Lives, and Afterlives: On the Temporalities of Social and Political Change," *PMLA* 126, no. 1 (2011): 140–50.

58. De Certeau, *The Practice of Everyday Life*, 29, xvii (emphasis in the original).

59. B. Kafka, *The Demon of Writing*, chapter 2.

60. Levy, *Scrolling Forward*, 143 (emphasis in the original).

61. On "gray literature," see C. P. Auger, *Information Sources in Grey Literature*, 2nd ed. (London: Bowker-Saur, 1989), vii. This edition revises a 1975 publication on "reports literature."

62. Buckland, "What Is a 1 Document?" 1997, http://people.ischool.berkeley.edu /~buckland/whatdoc.html, accessed 19 June 2013.

63. Geoffrey Nunberg, "The Places of Books in the Age of the Electronic Publication," quoted in Harper, *Inside the IMF*, 23. On the edgelessness of digital objects generally, see Craig Mod, "The Digital-Physical: On Building Flipboard for iPhone & Finding the Edges of Our Digital Narratives," March 2012, accessed 25 May 2013, http://craigmod.com/journal/digital_physical/.

64. For an extended inquiry into this point, see Alexander R. Galloway, *The Interface Effect* (Cambridge: Polity, 2012), chapter 1.

65. "Portable Document Format," http://en.wikipedia.org/wiki/PDF, accessed 31 July 2012.

66. The executability of code is discussed in detail in Alexander R. Galloway, *Protocol: How Control Exists after Decentralization* (Cambridge, MA: MIT Press, 2006), e.g., 165; Anne Eisenberg, "Hot off the Presses, Conductive Ink," *New York Times*, 30 June 2012.

67. See M. Mitchell Waldrop, *The Dream Machine: J. C. R. Licklider and the Revolution That Made Computing Personal* (New York: Viking, 2001), 449.

68. See Jussi Parikka, *What Is Media Archaeology?* (Cambridge: Polity, 2012); Erkki Huhtamo and Jussi Parikka, eds., *Media Archaeology: Approaches, Applications, and Implications* (Berkeley: University of California Press, 2011).

69. W. J. T. Mitchell, *What Do Pictures Want? The Lives and Loves of Images* (Chicago: University of Chicago Press, 2005), 215.

70. Piper, *Dreaming in Books*.

71. See Peter Becker and William Clark, eds., *Little Tools of Knowledge: Historical Essays on Academic and Bureaucratic Practices* (Ann Arbor: University of Michigan Press, 2001), 12; the authors are here discussing Michel Foucault's attention to what they term "the regime of diagrams, charts, lists, and above all tables."

72. In pointing out a Carlylean, hero-oriented stripe within recent media archaeology, Erkki Huhtamo and Jussi Parikka have made me sensitive to it here. See Huhtamo and Parikka, "Introduction: An Archaeology of Media Archaeology," in Huhtamo and Parikka, *Media Archaeology*, 1–24.

73. Siegfried Zielinski, *Deep Time of Media: Toward an Archaeology of Hearing and Seeing by Technical Means*, trans. Gloria Custance (Cambridge, MA: MIT Press, 2006); Guillory, "The Memo and Modernity," 114.

74. Michel Foucault, "What Is an Author?" in Michel Foucault, *The Foucault Reader*, ed. Paul Rabinow (New York: Pantheon, 1984), 101–20. See also Franz Kafka, *Franz Kafka: The Office Writings*, ed. Stanley Corngold, Jack Greenberg, and Benno Wagner and trans. Eric Patton with Ruth Hein (Princeton, NJ: Princeton University Press, 2008).

75. Marshall McLuhan, *The Gutenberg Galaxy: The Making of Typographic Man* (Toronto: University of Toronto Press, 1962), 30, 152.

76. Clay Shirky, *Here Comes Everybody: The Power of Organizing without Organizations* (New York: Penguin, 2008), 79.

CHAPTER ONE. A SHORT HISTORY OF _____

1. W. W. Pasko, *American Dictionary of Printing and Bookmaking, Containing a History of These Arts in Europe and America, with Definitions of Technical Terms and Biographical Sketches* (New York: Howard Lockwood, 1894), 47–48.

2. On moral economies, see Thomas Augst, *The Clerk's Tale: Young Men and Moral Life in Nineteenth-Century America* (Chicago: University of Chicago Press, 2003), especially the introduction and chapter 1. On cash, see Charles Sellers, *The Market Revolution: Jacksonian America, 1815–1846* (New York: Oxford University Press, 1991).

3. In this account of circulation, mobility, and inertia, I have been influenced by

the work of Will Straw (see, for example, "Embedded Memories," in *Residual Media*, ed. Charles R. Acland [Minneapolis: University of Minnesota Press, 2007], 3–31). Conversations with Michael Winship helped clarify this account of repetition.

4. Charles Babbage, *On the Economy of Machinery and Manufactures*, 4th ed. (London: Charles Knight, 1835), 191; see Martin Campbell-Kelly, "Informational Technology and Organizational Change in the British Census, 1801–1911," *Information Systems Research* 7 (March 1996): 22–36. In chapter 2 of *The Demon of Writing: Powers and Failures of Paperwork* (New York: Zone, 2012), Ben Kafka explains how Emmanuel Joseph Sieyès worked this principle out in advance of Babbage as a theory of government.

5. See Peter Stallybrass, "Printing and the Manuscript Revolution," in *Explorations in Communication and History*, ed. Barbie Zelizer (New York: Routledge, 2008), 112.

6. Patricia Crain, "New Histories of Literacy," in *A Companion to the History of the Book*, ed. Simon Eliot and Jonathan Rose (Malden, MA: Blackwell, 2007), 467–79. See also Patricia Crain, *The Story of A: The Alphabetization of America from The New England Primer to The Scarlet Letter* (Stanford, CA: Stanford University Press, 2002). On literacy, see also M. T. Clanchy, *From Memory to Written Record: England 1066–1307*, 2nd ed. (Oxford: Blackwell, 1993), 7–11.

7. On the platen press, see Harold E. Sterne, *A Catalogue of Nineteenth Century Printing Presses* (New Castle, DE: Oak Knoll, 2001), 119–20; Ralph Green, "A History of the Platen Jobber," reprinted in Ralph Green, *Works of Ralph Green* (Cincinnati, OH: Ye Olde Printery, 1981). On the job case, see Richard-Gabriel Rummonds, *Nineteenth-Century Printing Practices and the Iron Handpress, with Selected Readings* (New Castle, DE: Oak Knoll, 2004), 1:224. Job printing in this period has been considered most recently in Doug Clouse and Angela Voulangas, *The Handy Book of Artistic Printing: A Collection of Letterpress Examples with Specimens of Type, Ornament, Corner Fills, Borders, Twisters, Wrinklers, and Other Freaks of Fancy* (New York: Princeton Architectural, 2009).

8. "Report of the President," *Supplement to The Typographical Journal* 6, no. 6. (1894): 1.

9. U.S. Bureau of the Census, *Manufactures* (Washington: Government Printing Office, 1905). Similar percentages appear to have applied in Britain. Stallybrass notes that the 1907 British Census of Production found that books accounted for only 14 percent of the value produced by the printing trades (table on "Printing and the Manuscript Revolution," 111). Making blank books was counted separately because it was often the work of bookbinders, not of job printers, a reminder that the printing trades were an agglomeration of allied specializations that overlapped in some settings and not in others.

10. James N. Green and Peter Stallybrass, *Benjamin Franklin, Writer and Printer* (New Castle, DE: Oak Knoll, 2006), 88–89 (see also 47–61 on job printing). For a critique of a too-simple dichotomy between manuscript and print, see David McKitterick, *Print, Manuscript and the Search for Order, 1450–1830* (Cambridge: Cambridge University Press, 2003).

11. Alan Liu, "Transcendental Data: Toward a Cultural History and Aesthetics of the New Encoded Discourse," *Critical Inquiry* 31 (Autumn 2004): 49–84.

12. Quoted in Catherine Gallagher, *Nobody's Story: The Vanishing Acts of Women Writers in the Marketplace, 1670–1820* (Berkeley: University of California Press, 1994), 97. See also Jody Greene, *The Trouble with Ownership: Literary Property and Authorial Liability in England, 1660–1730* (Philadelphia: University of Pennsylvania Press, 2005).

13. Gallagher, *Nobody's Story*, 98. There is a longer history of printed punctuation of which these blanks are part; see, for example, Joan DeJean, *The Reinvention of Obscenity: Sex, Lies, and Tabloids in Early Modern France* (Chicago: University of Chicago Press, 2002), 34–35.

14. Classic accounts include Jürgen Habermas, *The Structural Transformation of the Public Sphere: An Inquiry into a Category of Bourgeois Society*, trans. Thomas Burger with Frederick Lawrence (Cambridge, MA: MIT Press, 1989); Benedict Anderson, *Imagined Communities: Reflections on the Origins and Spread of Nationalism*, rev. ed. (London: Verso, 1991); James Carey, *Communication as Culture: Essays on Media and Society* (Boston: Unwin Hyman, 1989), 13–36.

15. Edgar A. Poe, "The Purloined Letter," in *The Gift: A Christmas, New Year, and Birthday Present* (Philadelphia: Carey and Hart, 1845) 59, 49, 47. For Poe's attention to the printed page, see Meredith L. McGill, *American Literature and the Culture of Reprinting, 1834–1853* (Philadelphia: University of Pennsylvania Press, 2003); Leon Jackson, "'The Italics are Mine': Edgar Allan Poe and the Semiotics of Print," in *Illuminating Letters: Typography and Literary Interpretation*, ed. Paul C. Gutjahr and Megan L. Benton (Amherst: University of Massachusetts Press, 2001), 139–61.

16. Poe, "The Purloined Letter," 60, 57, 50.

17. Jacques Derrida, *The Postcard: From Socrates to Freud and Beyond*, trans. Alan Bass (Chicago: University of Chicago Press, 1987), 428.

18. Ibid., 421. Derrida excludes questions of typography from his analysis except perhaps when considering the final quotation of the story and a missing set of quotation marks. Although Jacques Lacan's reading (see below in the text) turns on questions of absence and presence — castration of the mother, in Lacan's universe — Derrida is not so much interested in blanks as enclosures, "the framing of the frames, the interminable supplementarity of the quotation marks" (493).

19. See Barbara Johnson, "The Frame of Reference: Poe, Lacan, Derrida," *Yale French Studies* 55–56 (1977): 457–505.

20. McGill, *American Literature and the Culture of Reprinting*, 157.

21. Ibid., 150.

22. Two works elaborating this centrifugal view are Lloyd Pratt, *Archives of American Time: Literature and Modernity in the Nineteenth Century* (Philadelphia: University of Pennsylvania Press, 2010), and Trish Loughran, *The Republic in Print: Print Culture in the Age of U.S. Nation Building, 1770–1870* (New York: Columbia University Press, 2007).

23. Niklas Luhmann, in a slightly different register, focuses on the social "system"

and its "subsystems," such as politics, economy, education, and law (*The Differentiation of Society*, trans. Stephen Holmes and Charles Larmore [New York: Columbia University Press, 1982], 264). Carl F. Kaestle and Janice A. Radway point to the "integration" of print within "institutions, practices, and associations," "A Framework for the History of Publishing and Reading in the United States, 1880–1940," in *Print in Motion: The Expansion of Publishing and Reading in the United States, 1880–1940*, ed. Carl F. Kaestle and Janice A. Radway (Chapel Hill: published in association with the American Antiquarian Society by the University of North Carolina Press, 2009), 15.

24. Mary Poovey, *Genres of the Credit Economy: Mediating Value in Eighteenth- and Nineteenth-Century Britain* (Chicago: University of Chicago Press, 2008), 3.

25. B. Kafka, *The Demon of Writing*, 111.

26. I'm alluding here to Anderson, *Imagined Communities*, and Carey, *Communication as Culture*.

27. Max Weber, *Sociological Writings*, ed. Wolf Heydebrand and trans. Martin Black with Lance W. Garmer (New York: Continuum, 1994), 79.

28. B. Kafka, *The Demon of Writing*, 117.

29. Michael Hardt, "Affective Labor," *boundary 2* 26, no. 2 (1999): 90.

30. Darren Wershler-Henry, *The Iron Whim: A Fragmented History of Typewriting* (Toronto: McClelland and Stewart, 2005), 6.

31. U.S. House Committee on Standards of Official Conduct, *House Ethics Manual* (2008), 321; http://ethics.house.gov/sites/ethics.house.gov/files/documents/2008 _House_Ethics_Manual.pdf, accessed 20 June 2013.

32. For an analysis of this dynamic for an earlier period, see Konstantin Dierks, "Letter Writing, Stationery Supplies, and Consumer Modernity in the Eighteenth-Century Atlantic World," *Early American Literature* 41, no. 3 (2006): 473–94; see also Konstantin Dierks, *In My Power: Letter Writing and Communications in Early America* (Philadelphia: University of Pennsylvania Press, 2009). On the way greeting cards "work," see David M. Levy, *Scrolling Forward: Making Sense of Documents in the Digital Age* (New York: Arcade, 2001), 85, 91–96.

33. Quoted in Virginia Jackson, *Dickinson's Misery: A Theory of Lyric Reading* (Princeton, NJ: Princeton University Press, 2005), 133.

34. *Boston Gazette*, 24 February 1766. I relied on Joseph M. Adelman for this example, "The Business of Politics: Printers and the Emergence of Political Communication Networks, 1765–1776," PhD diss., Johns Hopkins University, 2010.

35. *Primrose v. Western Union Telegraph Co.*, 154 U.S. 1 (1894). The decision gives an account of many previous cases about related issues.

36. Alenda Chang, "Contract or Charter? The End-User License Agreement and the Textual Warranting of Virtual Worlds," paper presented at the annual meeting of the Modern Language Association of America, San Francisco, 29 December 2008.

37. *Baker v. Selden*, 101 U.S. 99, Transcript of Record (filed January 13, 1877), 93, U.S. Supreme Court Records and Briefs, Library of Congress, Washington, DC. I should add that graft here is described in terms that make clear it is a reaction to

bureaucratic objectification: men who treat other men with sympathy are none-theless treating the state without it.

38. Ibid., 94.

39. See Meredith L. McGill, "Copyright," in *The Industrial Book, 1840–1880*, ed. Scott E. Casper, Jeffrey D. Groves, Stephen W. Nissenbaum, and Michael Winship (Chapel Hill: Published in association with the American Antiquarian Society by the University of North Carolina Press, 2007), 3:158–78. McGill calls this decision "a pivot between nineteenth- and twentieth-century thinking about copyright" (176), noting: "The court contrasted the opacity of aesthetic language with the ideal transparency of commercial speech, the intransitivity of aesthetic appreciation with the iterability of scientific truth, theory with practice, and the uniqueness and physicality of the embodiment of ideas in writing with the elusive nature of disseminated habits and routines — a catalog of opposing terms that have come to underwrite the legal dichotomy between expression and idea" (177). For a readable narrative history of *Baker v. Selden*, see Paula Samuelson, "The Story of *Baker v. Selden*: Sharpening the Distinction between Authorship and Invention," in *Intellectual Property Stories*, ed. Jane C. Ginsburg and Rochelle Cooper Drefuss (New York: Foundation, 2006), 159–93.

40. *Baker v. Selden*, 101 U.S. 99 (1879).

41. Transcript of record in *Baker v. Selden*, 64–65.

42. *Baker v. Selden*, 101 U.S. 99 (1879). Williams made not a few of the court's jesuitical elaborations — the oddly self-defeating complexity of the examples in its decision — look beside the point. As Meredith L. McGill has written, "despite the court's assurance of the soundness of their decision, they nonetheless felt compelled to lay out their process of reasoning, unfolding examples which undermine as much as they lend support to the court's ruling" ("Fugitive Objects: Securing Public Property in United States Copyright Law," October 2000, unpublished manuscript).

43. Pasko, *American Dictionary of Printing and Bookmaking*, 310.

44. Ibid., 311.

45. S. M. Weatherly, *The Young Job Printer: A Book of Instructions in Detail on Job Printing for Beginners* (Chicago, 1889), 5.

46. Alastair Johnston writes that typefounders "profited from selling spacing material with their founts, enjoying the 'fat of quads' (to use Edward Rowe Mores' felicitous expression) . . . for blank spacers were as assiduously composed by the typesetter as textual matter, leading to the expression 'a fat take,' meaning a copy with a lot of blank space to set" (*Alphabets to Order: The Literature of Nineteenth-Century Typefounders' Specimens* [New Castle, DE: Oak Knoll, 2000], 123). Michael Winship noted to me that "most job work was charged and compositors paid by time, rather than by the amount composed," a practice typical in book and newspaper work of the period.

47. William Dean Howells, *The World of Chance: A Novel* (New York: Harper and Brothers, 1893), 162.

48. Nathan Rosenberg, "Technological Change in the Machine Tool Industry, 1840–

1910," *Journal of Economic History* 23, no. 4 (1963): 425–26. See also David A. Hounshell, *From the American System to Mass Production, 1800–1932* (Baltimore, MD: Johns Hopkins University Press, 1984).

49. The most notable among them in this context is probably William H. Leffing-well, author of *Scientific Office Management* (Chicago: A. W. Shaw, 1917); see 195–202 on "Saving Thousands with Standardized Forms." Leffingwell was responsible for extending Taylorist practices — already redolent with blank forms — to the modern office. As Alan Liu notices, Leffingwell himself drew the analogy to machine tools when he compared the standardized business form to the jigs of a factory floor (Liu, "Transcendental Data," 70).

50. "Specimens of Fine Printing," *Printers' Circular* 5 (March 1870): 19.

51. My thinking in this paragraph is indebted to Philip Scranton, who uses the 1909 U.S. Census of Manufactures in *Endless Novelty: Specialty Production and American Industrialization, 1865–1925* (Princeton, NJ: Princeton University Press, 1997), 12–16.

52. Ibid., 21.

53. Ibid., 18.

54. Becker and Clark, *Little Tools of Knowledge*.

55. Oscar H. Harpel, *Harpel's Typograph, Or Book of Specimens, Containing Useful Information and a Collection of Examples of Letterpress Job Printing, Arranged for the Assistance of Master Printers, Amateurs, Apprentices, and Others* (Cincinnati, OH, 1870); John L. Phillips, *"The Art Preservative": 100 Fancy Specimens of Job Printing and a Collection of Valuable Papers, for the Use of Job Printers and Apprentices* (Springfield, IL, 1875). Resemblances from one generation of printers' manuals to the next have been mapped by Stephen O. Saxe, foreword to Rummonds, *Nineteenth-Century Printing Practices and the Iron Handpress*, 1:xxiii–xxx. After the example of Harpel, job printers in the United Kingdom and the United States collaborated to collect a series of specimens in the *International Printers' Specimen Exchange* (1880–97); see Clouse and Voulangas, *The Handy Book of Artistic Printing*, 24–29.

56. Harpel, *Harpel's Typograph*, 3.

57. *List of Prizes Awarded at the Vienna Universal Exposition* (1873), New York Public Library, New York, NY. There were five winners in this category, two of which were for artificial dentures.

58. Maurice Rickards, *Collecting Printed Ephemera* (Oxford: Phaidon, 1988), 7. See also Maurice Rickards, *Encyclopedia of Ephemera: A Guide to the Fragmentary Documents of Everyday Life for the Collector, Curator, and Historian* (New York: Routledge, 2000); and Martin Andrews, "The Importance of Ephemera," in *A Companion to the History of the Book*, ed. Simon Eliot and Jonathan Rose (Malden, MA: Blackwell, 2007), 434–50.

59. Harpel, *Harpel's Typograph*, 248–49.

60. Ibid., 4. See Walker Rumble's blog for a series of fascinating posts from 2009 on Harpel and the *Typograph* ("Posts Tagged 'Oscar Harpel,'" accessed 26 May 2013, http://rumble101.wordpress.com/tag/oscar-harpel). Rumble notes that one of

Harpel's agendas was to challenge chromolithography, showing how good relief printing in color could be with the benefits of skilled workmanship and a platen press that offered "light 'kiss' impressions" ("On Dents," 2 October 2009). See also Walker Rumble, *The Swifts: Printers in the Age of Typesetting Races* (Charlottesville: University of Virginia Press, 2003), chapter 8.

61. Advertisement, "Something You Ought to Have!" *Printers' Circular* 5 (January 1871): 471. In addition to carrying Harpel's advertisements, the *Printers' Circular* covered the design and production of *Harpel's Typograph* in occasional notices, such as "Harpel's Typograph," in *Printers' Circular* 5 (September 1870): 287 and (November 1870): 381. This volume survives in the collections of the New York Public Library, New York, NY.

62. Quoted first is *New Haven Evening Register*, 23 November 1881; next is *Cincinnati Commercial*, 14 November 1881; and the two final quotes are from "Poet and Printer," *Cincinnati Daily Gazette*, 15 November 1881. The most extensive of these obituaries draw without acknowledgment on the brief autobiography Harpel included in *Poets and Poetry of Printerdom* (Cincinnati, OH, 1875); thus, Harpel appears to have had the distinction of having written his own obituary.

63. The rise and fall of "artistic printing" has been traced in Clouse and Voulangas, *The Handy Book of Artistic Printing*. See also Ellen Mazur Thomson, *The Origins of Graphic Design in America, 1870–1920* (New Haven, CT: Yale University Press, 1997); Doug Clouse, *MacKellar, Smiths & Jordan: Typographic Tastemakers of the Late Nineteenth Century* (New Castle, DE: Oak Knoll, 2008).

64. *Williams' Cincinnati Directory, Embracing a Full Alphabetical Record of the Names of the Inhabitants of Cincinnati* (Cincinnati, OH, June 1870). One-third of Cincinnatians were foreign born, 55,000 of them German. With a total population of 350,000, Chicago had a higher percentage of foreign-born residents, of whom 65,000 were German. See the U.S. Bureau of the Census, *Ninth Census* (1870), Vol. III, *Statistics of the Wealth and Industry of the United States*, especially 23, 37–38, 49; and Vol. I, *Statistics of the Population of the United States* (Washington: Government Printing Office, 1872). For an extended meditation on the place and space of publishing, see Aurora Wallace, *Media Capital: Architecture and Communications in New York City* (Urbana: University of Illinois Press, 2012).

65. I say "probably" because of the seventy-two from beyond Cincinnati, twenty-nine (40 percent) are concentrated within a twenty-five-page section (164–89). It turns out that just as the book was about to be bound, water damaged "over four complete signatures, of eight pages each"; Harpel was forced "to reprint them all, or partially as the case may be" (see "Harpel's Typograph," *Printers' Circular* 5 [November 1870]: 381). The signatures were reassembled, probably with new specimens (Harpel hardly would have kept standing type for already printed pages) and perhaps with contributions — in some form — from other job printers. I'm guessing that the out-of-town specimens appear in the replacement signatures, because that offers an explanation for their idiosyncratic concentration in these pages. But nothing is sure. In any event, it's hard to reconcile *Harpel's Typo-*

graph with Jack Golden's observation that "it reproduces hundreds of examples of contemporary letterpress printing submitted by printers from all over the United States" ("Historical Introduction to the Art and Technique of Printed Ephemera," in *Graphic Americana: The Art and Technique of Printed Ephemera*, ed. Dale Roylance [Princeton, NJ: Princeton University Library, 1992], 9. We have no locations for thirty-six samples in *Harpel's Typograph*; the bulk of them are visiting cards, which were circulated in society rather than the commercial marketplace.

66. Despite his subtitle, Phillips printed approximately 124 specimens in eighty-six pages. Of these thirty-seven — mostly visiting cards — gave no location; eighty indicated Springfield or an Illinois state entity; and seven were from elsewhere in Illinois.

67. Harpel, *Harpel's Typograph*, 241; see also 13.

68. Ibid., 244. See also Theodore Low DeVinne's *The Printers' Price List: A Manual* (New York, 1871); Roger B. Daniels and Jesse Beeler, "An Archival Investigation of a Late 19th Century Accounting Information System: The Use of Decision Aids in the American Printing Industry," *Accounting Historians Journal* 28, no. 1 (June 2001): 3–18.

69. See Ellen Mazur Thomson, "Early Graphic Design Periodicals in America," *Journal of Design History* 7, no. 2 (1994): 113–26.

70. The volume was announced under this title in the "Printers' Doings," *Typographic Advertiser* 19, no. 4 (1874): 564 and announced under a slightly different title in the *Printers' Circular*, according to Rumble, "Posts Tagged 'Oscar Harpel,'" "Inside Glimpses."

71. Charles Hamilton, Business Records, 1860–1906, vol. 10, Work and Expense Book, 1875–1905, American Antiquarian Society, Worcester, MA. I am grateful to Michael Winship for introducing me to this collection and sharing some of his findings from it. Winship finds that Hamilton had an average annual profit of about $1,450 in 1879–1905.

72. Michael Winship, "The Art Preservative: From the History of the Book Back to Printing History," *Printing History* 17, no. 1 (1995): 18.

73. Ibid., 22.

74. These customers are from the catalog of the American Antiquarian Society, which can be searched by imprint.

75. Charles Hamilton, Business Records, 1860–1906, The Quotation and Day Book (1885–95) includes a few transcribed items of correspondence.

76. EBSCO Information Services, *American Antiquarian Society (AAS) Historical Periodicals Collection*, Series 5 (1886–1877), described at http://ebscohost.com /archives/featured-archives/american-antiquarian-society, accessed 20 June 2013.

77. "Oscar H. Harpel Again Arrested for Counterfeiting Tickets," *Cincinnati Commercial*, 20 May 1871.

78. Ibid.

79. Ibid.

80. David Henkin, *City Reading: Written Words and Public Spaces in Antebellum New York* (New York: Columbia University Press, 1998), 17, 14.

81. Stephen Mihm, *A Nation of Counterfeiters: Capitalists, Con Men, and the Making of the United States* (Cambridge, MA: Harvard University Press, 2007), 101.

82. Walter Benjamin, *The Work of Art in the Age of Its Technological Reproducibility, and Other Writings on Media*, ed. Michael W. Jennings, Brigid Doherty, and Thomas Y. Levin, trans. Edmund Jephcott et al. (Cambridge, MA: Belknap Press of Harvard University Press, 2008), 171.

83. On corruption as the story of this era, see Richard White, *Railroaded: The Transcontinentals and the Making of Modern America* (New York: W. W. Norton, 2011), xxi–xxxiv; see also Scott A. Sandage, *Born Losers: A History of Failure in America* (Cambridge, MA: Harvard University Press, 2006).

84. John Moxon, *Mechanick Exercises on the Whole Art of Printing*, 2 vols. (London, 1683–84).

85. McKitterick, *Print, Manuscript and the Search for Order*, 147. McKitterick is making the case here on the basis of the books actually printed.

86. Harpel, *Harpel's Typograph*, 8.

87. McKitterick, *Print, Manuscript and the Search for Order*, 1. See also Barbara A. Brannon, "The Laser Printer as an Agent of Change: Fixity and Fluxion in the Digital Age," in *Agent of Change: Print Culture Studies after Elizabeth L. Eisenstein*, ed. Sabrina Alcorn Baron, Eric N. Lindquist, and Eleanor F. Shevlin (Amherst: University of Massachusetts Press, 2007), 353–64.

88. James J. Brenton, ed., *Voices from the Press: A Collection of Sketches, Essays, and Poems by Practical Printers* (New York: Charles B. Norton, 1850).

89. On the variable distance between authoring and publishing, see L. Jackson, "'The Italics Are Mine,'" 41; Leon Jackson, *The Business of Letters: Authorial Economies in Antebellum America* (Stanford, CA: Stanford University Press, 2008).

90. See L. Jackson, "'The Italics Are Mine.'"

91. Adrian Johns, "The Identity Engine: Printing and Publishing at the Beginning of the Knowledge Economy." The role of publisher was in formation during the nineteenth century, as booksellers began to specialize in retail.

92. Thomas MacKellar, *The American Printer: A Manual of Typography, Containing Complete Instructions for Beginners as Well as Practical Instructions for Managing Every Department of a Printing Office*, 6th ed. (Philadelphia: MacKellar, Smiths and Jordan, 1871), 183.

93. Theodore Low DeVinne, *Manual of Printing Office Practice* (1883; reprint, New York: Ars Typographica, 1926).

94. N. P. Willis, "Title," in Brenton, *Voices from the Press*, 306.

95. Harpel, *Harpel's Typograph*, 17.

96. Harlan H. Ballard, "Amateur Newspapers," *St. Nicholas Magazine*, 1882, 717–27. Lara Cohen directed me to this item and generously shared her knowledge of the amateur press.

97. Elizabeth M. Harris, *Personal Impressions: The Small Printing Press in Nineteenth-Century America* (Boston: David R. Godine, 2004), 22; see also 14, 19.

98. American Antiquarian Society, "Amateur Newspapers," accessed May 26, 2013, http://www.americanantiquarian.org/amateurnews.htm. An even larger collection is being processed in Special Collections at the University of Wisconsin's Memorial Library in Madison.

99. This and other relevant collections are described in Harris, *Personal Impressions*.

100. Stephen Duncombe dates the zines tradition to science fiction fans of the 1930s (*Notes from Underground: Zines and the Politics of Alternative Culture*, 2nd ed. [Bloomington, IN: Microcosm, 2008], 11). Lara Cohen and Mikki Smith have been thinking about amateurdom and using the American Antiquarian Society collections; both have been generous in discussing their work with me.

101. See James Beniger, *The Control Revolution: Technological and Economic Origins of the Information Society* (Cambridge, MA: Harvard University Press, 1989).

CHAPTER TWO. THE TYPESCRIPT BOOK

1. Robert C. Binkley, *Methods of Reproducing Research Materials* (Ann Arbor, MI: Edwards Brothers, 1931), title page and "Distribution of This Survey" (138). The term "tentative" is from the foreword to Robert C. Binkley, *Manual on Methods of Reproducing Research Materials* (Ann Arbor, MI: Edwards Brothers, 1936), iii. Unlike the 1936 work, the 1931 one was reproduced with a reduction ratio of 1:2 (that is, half-size).

2. Binkley, *Methods of Reproducing Research Materials*, 138.

3. ProQuest, once owned by Xerox, is now owned by the Cambridge Information Group, a private company. It is a frequent partner with Google in the development of new resources and has diversified beyond scholarly resources into library services of many types. See ProQuest, "About Us," accessed 26 May 2013, http://www.proquest.com/en-US/aboutus/default.shtml.

4. Robert C. Binkley, *Selected Papers of Robert C. Binkley*, ed. Max H. Fisch (Cambridge, MA: Harvard University Press, 1948), 170.

5. Ibid., 171. See also Robert C. Binkley, "Do the Records of Science Face Ruin?" *Scientific American* 140 (January 1929): 28–30.

6. Minutes, 17–18 February 1930, Box 75, Records of the Joint Committee on Materials for Research, Library of Congress, Washington, DC (hereafter Joint Committee Records).

7. A summary of Binkley's life and career was prepared at the time of his death and may be found in Box 83, Joint Committee Records. Much helpful information may also be gained from "Robert C. Binkley, 1897–1940: Life, Works, Ideas," accessed 26 May 2013, http://www.wallandbinkley.com/rcb/. The work of the Joint Committee and of Binkley has also been described in Kenneth Carpenter, "Toward a New Cultural Design: The American Council of Learned Societies, the Social Science Research Council, and Libraries in the 1930s," in *Institutions of Reading: The Social Life of Libraries in the United States*, ed. Thomas Augst and Kenneth Carpenter (Amherst: University of Massachusetts Press, 2007), 283–309.

8. Willard McCarty, "What Is Humanities Computing? Toward a Definition of the Field," 16 February 1998, accessed 23 August 2010, http://www.cch.kcl.ac.uk /legacy/teaching/dtrt/class1/mccarty_humanities_computing.pdf.

9. Susan Hockey, "The History of Humanities Computing," in *A Companion to the Digital Humanities*, ed. Susan Schreibman, Ray Siemens, and John Unsworth (Malden, MA: Blackwell, 2004), 4. A more nuanced account of the emergence of the digital humanities is rendered by the essays in Willard McCarty, ed., *Text and Genre in Reconstruction: Effects of Digitalization on Ideas, Behaviours, Products and Institutions* (Cambridge: Open Book, 2010).

10. Jerome J. McGann, *Radiant Textuality; Literature after the World Wide Web* (New York: Palgrave, 2001); Alan Liu, *Laws of Cool: Knowledge Work and the Culture of Information* (Chicago: University of Chicago Press, 2004).

11. William Stott, *Documentary Expression and Thirties America* (New York: Oxford University Press, 1974).

12. Alan Liu, "Transcendental Data: Toward a Cultural History and Aesthetics of the New Encoded Discourse," *Critical Inquiry* 31 (Autumn 2004): 65–69.

13. Carpenter, "Toward a New Cultural Design," 299.

14. Robert C. Binkley, letter to Robert T Crane, 30 January 1936, Box 33, Joint Committee Records. Details on the publication are in Boxes 33 and 45, Joint Committee Records.

15. Robert C. Binkley, "New Tools for Men of Letters," *Yale Review* 24 (March 1935): 519–37. Rick Prelinger introduced me to this article and through it Robert Binkley, and I remain grateful to him. Additionally helpful in explaining "how the New Deal state came to express itself . . . in the idiom of the archival record" was Laura Helton, "Bibliography, Mimeography, and Ten Thousand List-Makers: Transmitting Historical Texts circa 1939," unpublished manuscript. I am grateful for Helton's insights.

16. Robert C. Binkley, letter to Norman Gras, 8 February 1940, Box 80, Joint Committee Records. See also "Report on the Need for Materials in Research in the Fields of the Humanities and the Social Sciences," September 1930, Box 75; and Carpenter, "Toward a New Cultural Design," 303.

17. Joint Committee on Materials for Research, "Circular Number I," December 1930, Box 32, Joint Committee Records.

18. Franklin F. Holbrook, *Survey of Activities of American Agencies in Relation to Materials for Research in the Social Sciences and the Humanities* (Washington and New York: Social Science Research Council and American Council of Learned Societies, 1932), vii.

19. Minutes, 17–18 February 1930, Box 75, Joint Committee Records.

20. See Carpenter, "Toward a New Cultural Design," 286; Alex Csiszar, "Seriality and the Search for Order: Scientific Print and Its Problems during the Late Nineteenth Century," *History of Science* 48, nos. 3–4 (2010): 399–434.

21. Binkley, *Manual on Methods of Reproducing Research Materials*, 198.

22. Peter Novick, *That Noble Dream: The "Objectivity Question" and the American Historical Profession* (Cambridge: Cambridge University Press, 1988), 141.

23. Binkley, *Methods of Reproducing Research Materials*, 125.

24. "Conference on the Reproduction and Distribution of Research Materials," 5 November 1932, and "Project for the Production and Distribution of Materials for Research," Box 75, Joint Committee Records; Binkley, *Methods of Reproducing Research Materials*, 131–34; Carpenter, "Toward a New Cultural Design," 301. The default alternative to a publication service of some kind was the university press. See Joseph S. Meisel, "American University Presses, 1929–1979," *Book History* 13 (2010) 122–53; Andrew Abbot, "Publication and the Future of Knowledge," plenary lecture at the annual meeting of the Association of American University Presses, Montreal, Canada, 27 June 2008, accessed 26 May 2013, http://home.uchicago.edu/~aabbott/Papers/aaup.pdf.

25. Binkley, *Manual on Methods of Reproducing Research Materials*, vii.

26. Jonathan Kahana, *Intelligence Work: The Politics of American Documentary* (New York: Columbia University Press, 2008), 23.

27. Stott, *Documentary Expression and Thirties America*, 72.

28. Kahana, *Intelligence Work*, 26; see also 23.

29. Warren I. Susman, *Culture as History: The Transformation of American Society in the Twentieth Century* (New York: Pantheon, 1984), 166.

30. Mark Goble, *Beautiful Circuits: Modernism and the Mediated Life* (New York: Columbia University Press, 2010), 232. Goble discusses Lewis Mumford's *Technics and Civilization* (1934) and the form and content of history in this period, chapter 4.

31. Quoted in ibid., 225.

32. Henry Steele Commager, preface to *Documents of American History*, ed. Henry Steele Commager (New York: F. S. Crofts, 1935), 1:vii–viii.

33. On Lange, see Library of Congress, "Destitute pea pickers in California. Mother of seven children. Age thirty-two. Nipomo, California," accessed 26 May 2013, http://www.loc.gov/pictures/item/fsa1998021539/PP. On Agee, see Stott, *Documentary Expression and Thirties America*, 264.

34. See Novick, *That Noble Dream*, especially chapters 6–9.

35. Binkley, "New Tools for Men of Letters," 519, 537.

36. Ibid., 519.

37. Walter Benjamin, *The Work of Art in the Age of Its Technological Reproducibility, and Other Writings on Media*, ed. Michael W. Jennings, Brigid Doherty, and Thomas Y. Levin, trans. Edmund Jephcott et al. (Cambridge, MA: Belknap Press of Harvard University Press, 2008), 22–24.

38. Ibid., 22, emphasis in the original.

39. Binkley, *Manual on Methods of Reproducing Research Materials*, 1.

40. Goble, *Beautiful Circuits*, 238.

41. Robert C. Binkley, letter to Robert T. Crane, 5 October 1934, Box 33, Joint Committee Records.

42. National Gallery of Art, Washington, DC, see http://www.nga.gov/collection/gallery/iad.htm, accessed 21 June 2013.

43. Goble, *Beautiful Circuits*, 289.

44. Binkley, *Manual on Methods of Reproducing Research Materials*, 107.
45. Nicholson Baker, *Double Fold: Libraries and the Assault on Paper* (New York: Random House, 2001). Baker's book is a screed against "preservation microfilming," in which Binkley comes off badly. On Binkley and microfilm generally, see also Alan Marshall Meckler, *Micropublishing: A History of Scholarly Micropublishing in America, 1938–80* (Westport, CT: Greenwood, 1982), chapter 2.
46. The present of documentary feels obsessive because, as Kahana puts it, "the self-evidence of social reality is itself ideological" (*Intelligence Work*, 24).
47. Binkley, *Manual on Methods of Reproducing Research Materials*, 183.
48. Robert C. Binkley, carbon typescript to Clara Newth de Villa S., 25 February 1938, Box 32, Joint Committee Records.
49. Binkley, *Manual on Methods of Reproducing Research Materials*, 62.
50. Ibid., 18. See also Binkley, "New Tools for Men of Letters," 526, 528.
51. Binkley, "New Tools for Men of Letters," 529.
52. Witness the fate of Columbia University Press's Gutenberg-e and the ACLS's current Humanities E-Book project, which collects mostly old titles, not new. See Robert Darnton, "The Library: Three Jeremiads," *New York Review of Books*, 23 December 2010, 22–26.
53. This is from Adobe, "ITC American Typewriter Std," accessed 24 June 2013, http://store1.adobe.com/cfusion/store/html/index.cfm?store=OLS-US&event=displayFontPackage&code=1338. For an account of the meaning of the look of typewriting circa 1883, see my "Mississippi MSS: Twain, Typing, and the Moving Panorama of Textual Production," in *Residual Media*, ed. Charles R. Acland (Minneapolis: University of Minnesota Press, 2007), 329–43.
54. Binkley, "New Tools for Men of Letters," 528.
55. David M. Levy puts this in what are perhaps the simplest terms in *Scrolling Forward: Making Sense of Documents in the Digital Age* (New York: Arcade, 2001), 152. See Johanna Drucker, *SpecLab: Digital Aesthetics and Projects in Speculative Computing* (Chicago: University of Chicago, 2009) chapter 3; Matthew G. Kirschenbaum, *Mechanisms: New Media and the Forensic Imagination* (Cambridge: MIT Press, 2008); and N. Katherine Hayles, *How We Became Posthuman: Virtual Bodies in Cybernetics, Literature, and Informatics* (Chicago: University of Chicago Press, 1999).
56. Binkley, "New Tools for Men of Letters," 527.
57. I'm being anachronistic, I know, but the executability of computer code has been the subject of some fascinating recent work. See, for instance, Wendy Hui Kyong Chun, *Programmed Visions: Software and Memory* (Cambridge, MA: MIT Press, 2011), 22–29. "Follow copy" tells a typesetter to, well, follow the copy at hand.
58. Binkley, "New Tools for Men of Letters," 528.
59. John Guillory, "The Memo and Modernity," *Critical Inquiry* 31, no. 1 (2004): 111, emphasis in the original.
60. Binkley, *Manual on Methods of Reproducing Research Materials*, 2.
61. Ibid., 93.
62. McGann, *Radiant Textuality*, 54.

63. Binkley, *Manual on Methods of Reproducing Research Materials*, 196.

64. "Reviews, criticisms, etc.," Box 45, Joint Committee Records.

65. Robert C. Binkley, letter to Julian P. Boyd, librarian of the Historical Society of Pennsylvania, 20 September 1939, "General Correspondence, Misc. B," Box 32, Joint Committee Records.

66. Ibid.

67. On the historical semantics of servers and serving, see Markus Krajewski, "Ask Jeeves: Servants and Search Engines," trans. Charles Marcrum II, *Grey Room* 38 (Winter 2010): 6–19.

68. Vernon D. Tate, "The Gentlemen's Agreement and the Problem of Copyright," *Journal of Documentary Reproduction* 2, no. 1 (1939): 29. "The Gentlemen's Agreement" probably took its name from an episode in U.S. diplomacy, but *The Gentleman's Agreement* was also the title of a film with Vivien Leigh that opened in London in June 1935. On the history of "The Gentlemen's Agreement" and for an evaluation of its legacy, see Peter B. Hirtle, "Research, Libraries, and Fair Use: The Gentlemen's Agreement of 1935," 2006, accessed 25 June 2013, http://dspace.library.cornell.edu/bitstream/1813/2719/1/Research_Libraries_and_Fair_Use.pdf.

69. Quoted in Binkley, *Manual on Methods of Reproducing Research Materials*, 138.

70. M. Llewellyn Raney, introduction to *Microphotography for Libraries*, ed. M. Llewellyn Raney (Chicago: American Library Association, 1936), v.

71. Vernon D. Tate, "Criteria for Measuring the Effectiveness of Reading Devices," in *Microphotography for Libraries*, ed. M. Llewellyn Raney (Chicago: American Library Association, 1936), 15. For a comparable taxonomy of reading on screen, see Abigail J. Sellen and Richard H. R. Harper, *The Myth of the Paperless Office* (Cambridge, MA: MIT Press, 2002), 83.

72. Ultimately the film was arranged a bit differently than the STC, but STC numbers were used to identify images on the film. Power describes how this happened in "Report of Progress on Filming English Books before 1550," winter 1938, reproduced on reel 1, Power, Eugene Barnum, Papers, 1937–70, University of Michigan Library, Ann Arbor, MI (hereafter Power Papers).

73. Power comments on the profit motive in Eugene B. Power, *Edition of One: The Autobiography of Eugene B. Power, Founder of University Microfilms* (Ann Arbor, MI: University Microfilms International, 1990), 249, 315. On dissertations, see ibid., 165–68. For an overview of scholarly microfilms in this period, see Meckler, *Micropublishing*, chapters 2–3.

74. Robert C. Binkley, "History for a Democracy," *Minnesota History* 18, no. 1 (1937): 23–24.

75. Binkley, "New Tools for Men of Letters," 530–31.

76. Binkley, "History for a Democracy," 10.

77. Ibid., 11.

78. Robert C. Binkley, "The Cultural Program of the W.P.A.," *Harvard Educational Review* 9, no. 2 (1939): 159–60.

79. Quoted in Edward Francis Barrese, "The Historical Records Survey: A Nation

Acts to Save Its Memory," PhD diss., George Washington University, 1980, 134. The HRS produced almost two thousand publications (ibid., 54). See also William F. McDonald, *Federal Relief Administration and the Arts* (Columbus: Ohio State University Press, 1969).

80. U.S. Works Progress Administration (Ohio), *Annals of Cleveland* (1937). This information about multigraphing appears on the title pages.

81. Robert S. Lynd, review of *Annals of Cleveland: 1818–1935*, *American Sociological Review* 3, no. 4 (1938): 594–97.

82. Barrese, "The Historical Records Survey," 141.

83. Liu, "Transcendental Data," 63.

84. Binkley, "The Cultural Program of the W.P.A.," 156–57.

85. Benjamin, *The Work of Art in the Age of Its Technological Reproducibility*, 33–34.

86. Ibid., 34.

87. Ibid., emphasis in the original.

88. On the relatively staid politics of the digital humanities, see Alan Liu, "Where Is Cultural Criticism in the Digital Humanities?," January 2011, accessed 27 May 2013, http://liu.english.ucsb.edu/where-is-cultural-criticism-in-the-digital -humanities/. The digital humanities has been laudably active politically in the area of open access.

89. Benjamin, *The Work of Art in the Age of Its Technological Reproducibility*, 20–21.

90. Power, *Edition of One*, 26, 27. The same moment is captured in "Notes on Conversation with T. R. Schellenberg," January 1935, reel 1, Power Papers.

91. Chadwyck-Healey, "About EEBO," accessed 24 June 2013, http://eebo.chadwyck .com/marketing/about.htm.

92. Social Science Research Network, home page, accessed 27 May 2013, www.ssrn .com.

93. Answers, "Edwards Brothers, Inc.," accessed 24 June 2013, http://www.answers .com/topic/edwards-brothers-inc. Despite the persistence of this listing, Edwards Brothers became part of Edwards Brothers Malloy in 2012; see http:// www.edwardsbrothersmalloy.com/.

94. Tim Causer, "Welcome to Transcribe Bentham," accessed 27 May 2013, www.ucl .ac.uk/transcribe-bentham; "Zooniverse: Real Science Online," accessed October 2012, www.zooniverse.org/projects.

95. John McMillian, *Smoking Typewriters: The Sixties Underground Press and the Rise of Alternative Media in America* (New York: Oxford University Press, 2011), 13.

CHAPTER THREE. XEROGRAPHERS OF THE MIND

1. Brian Cantwell Smith, *On the Origin of Objects* (Cambridge, MA: MIT Press, 1998), 300–301.

2. David Owen, *Copies in Seconds: Chester Carlson and the Birth of the Xerox Machine* (New York: Simon and Schuster, 2004), 223. See also Eva Hemmungs Wirtén, *No Trespassing: Authorship, Intellectual Property Rights, and the Boundaries of Globalization* (Toronto: University of Toronto Press, 2004), 64.

3. Christopher Kelty, *Two Bits: The Cultural Significance of Free Software and the Internet* (Durham, NC: Duke University Press, 2008), 132. Hillel Schwartz notes that "xerography would be the tinder to The Pentagon Papers of 1972" (*The Culture of the Copy: Striking Likenesses, Unreasonable Facsimiles* [New York: Zone, 1996], 238.

4. George Soros, "Soros: In Revolutionary Times the Impossible Becomes Possible," 27 July 2009, accessed 24 June 2013, http://edition.cnn.com/2009/WORLD/europe/07/27/aoc.soros.opensociety/.

5. D. F. McKenzie, *Making Meaning: "Printers of the Mind" and Other Essays*, ed. Peter D. McDonald and Michael F. Suarez (Amherst: University of Massachusetts Press, 2002), 21.

6. For one account of the papers, including statements by participants, see John Prados and Margaret Pratt Porter, "Creating the Papers," in *Inside the Pentagon Papers*, ed. John Prados and Margaret Pratt Porter (Lawrence: University Press of Kansas, 2004), 12–50.

7. Daniel Ellsberg, "Interview for 'Hearts and Minds' 1972," typed transcript, 107, Box 64, Neil Sheehan Papers, Library of Congress, Washington, DC (hereafter Sheehan Papers).

8. David Rudenstine, *The Day the Presses Stopped: A History of the Pentagon Papers Case* (Berkeley: University of California Press, 1996), 119.

9. For example, Max Frankel, "Impact in Washington; Pentagon Papers a Major Fact of Life for All Three Branches of Government," *New York Times*, 25 June 1971.

10. *New York Times v. United States*, 403 U.S. 713; *The Pentagon Papers as Published by the New York Times, Based on Investigative Reporting by Neil Sheehan, Written by Neil Sheehan, Hedrick Smith, E. W. Kenworthy, and Fox Butterfield*, articles and documents edited by Gerald Gold, Allan M. Siegal, and Samuel Abt (New York: Bantam, 1971).

11. See, for instance, Wilson McWilliams, "Washington Plans Aggressive War," *New York Times*, 26 September 1971.

12. On the multiple editions, see H. Bradford Westerfield, "What Use Are Three Versions of the Pentagon Papers?," *American Political Science Review* 69, no. 2 (1975): 685–89. A fourth version now exists, since the bulk of the papers were declassified in 2011 and published online (National Archives, "Pentagon Papers," accessed February 2013, http://www.archives.gov/research/pentagon-papers/).

13. Michel Foucault, "What Is an Author?" in Michel Foucault, *The Foucault Reader*, ed. Paul Rabinow (New York: Pantheon, 1984), 108.

14. Jerome J. McGann, *The Textual Condition* (Princeton, NJ: Princeton University Press, 1991), 13.

15. Fred P. Graham, "A Hearing Today," *New York Times*, 17 June 1971. Of course, the newspapers later covered the Ellsberg trial, so they acknowledged that the papers were copies at that point.

16. According to the indictment, one of the seven "overt acts" committed to "effect the objects" of the conspiracy was that "on or about October 4, 1969, defendants Ellsberg and Russo, and co-conspirator Sinay operated a Xerox copy machine at

8101 Melrose Avenue, Los Angeles, California." The indictment is reprinted as Appendix B in Meiklejohn Civil Liberties Institute, *Pentagon Papers Case Collection: Annotated Procedural Guide and Index*, ed. Ann Fagan Ginger and the Meiklejohn Institute Staff (Berkeley, CA: Meiklejohn Civil Liberties Institute, 1975), 164–71.

17. For copying as appropriation, see Schwartz, *The Culture of the Copy*, chapter 6. Schwartz notes that "the more instantaneous the copy, the more complete the confusion" between "copy" as a noun and "copy" as a verb: no wonder that "Xerox" came to mean both (235).

18. Daniel Ellsberg, *Secrets: A Memoir of Vietnam and the Pentagon Papers* (New York: Viking, 2002), 331, 371. See also Tom Wells, *Wildman: The Life and Times of Daniel Ellsberg* (New York: Palgrave, 2001). Wells, not Ellsberg, mentions the lines and page numbers that were lost (323). Ellsberg refers to this "declassification" in scare quotes.

19. I haven't been able to determine the process used, but it was probably offset. The original photocopies—as it were—in the Sheehan Papers remain classified, despite repeated publication and now declassification of the Pentagon Papers; repeated requests for access have gone unheeded. Westerfield notes that the edition published by the Government Printing Office was offset from "indifferently Xeroxed originals" ("What Use Are Three Versions of the Pentagon Papers?," 687–88).

20. Rudenstine, *The Day the Presses Stopped*, 37.

21. Ibid., 42.

22. John Brooks, "Profiles: Xerox, Xerox, Xerox, Xerox," *New Yorker*, 1 April 1967, 52, 55. Brooks gives two figures per copy, six and nine seconds.

23. Ellsberg, "Interview for 'Hearts and Minds' 1972," 122. On the pathology of copying see Rowan Wilken, "The Practice and 'Pathologies' of Photocopying," *Déjà Vu: antiTHESIS* 17 (2007): 126–43.

24. Quoted in "Project—New Technology and the Law of Copyright: Reprography and Computers," *UCLA Law Review* 15 (1967–68): 943.

25. Gladstone Associates, "Market Supports for Future Development in Harvard Square: An Assessment of Alternatives," prepared for the Harvard Square Task Force (September 1975), 2–13, Loeb Design Library, Harvard University, Cambridge, MA.

26. Harvard University, Report of the President of Harvard College and Reports of Departments, University Library, 1959–1960, 1960–1961, 1961–1962, and 1963–1964. Harvard University Archives online, accessed 20 April 2009, http://hul.harvard.edu/huarc/refshelf/AnnualReports.htm. In addition to the new Xerox 914 machines, Harvard had a central Photographic Department that used Copyflo (a xerographic process that prints from microfilm exposures, marketed by Haloid Xerox starting in 1955).

27. Thomas Augst, "Faith in Reading: Public Libraries, Liberalism, and the Civil Religion," in *Institutions of Reading: The Social Life of Libraries in the United States*, ed. Thomas Augst and Kenneth Carpenter (Amherst: University of Mas-

sachusetts Press, 2007), 154. Notably Augst is writing about public circulating libraries like the Boston Public Library, not private libraries like Harvard's.

28. Quoted in Wirtén, *No Trespassing*, 66.

29. See Schwartz, *The Culture of the Copy*, 235. See also Geoffrey C. Bowker, *Memory Practices in the Sciences* (Cambridge, MA: MIT Press, 2005), 15.

30. Brooks, "Profiles," 58, emphasis in the original.

31. Quoted in John Dessauer, *My Years with Xerox: The Billions Nobody Wanted* (Garden City, NY: Doubleday, 1971), xiv–xv.

32. Matthew G. Kirschenbaum elaborates this point with regard to digital documents in "The .txtual Condition" in *Comparative Textual Media*, ed. N. Katherine Hayles and Jessica Pressman (University of Minnesota Press, forthcoming).

33. Richard H. Ullman, "The Pentagon's History as 'History,'" *Foreign Policy* 4 (1971): 154.

34. Max Weber, *Sociological Writings*, ed. Wolf Heydebrand and trans. Martin Black with Lance W. Garmer (New York: Continuum, 1994), 61.

35. On reading as self-ownership, see Augst, "Faith in Reading," 154. David M. Levy attributes an earlier ownership of files (by departments in companies) to the uses of carbon paper (*Scrolling Forward: Making Sense of Documents in the Digital Age* [New York: Arcade, 2001], 71).

36. Ellsberg, *Secrets*, 305. Ellsberg also describes working at the copying with his son, Russo, and Russo's girlfriend as a happy family scene. It's hard not to read this psychoanalytically when, of course, Ellsberg was in or had been in analysis.

37. Brooks, "Profiles," 57.

38. Daniel Ellsberg, "Escalating in a Quagmire," paper prepared for the annual meeting of the American Political Science Association, Los Angeles, CA, 8–12 September 1970, emphasis in the original, Box 64, Sheehan Papers.

39. Both of Ellsberg's letters are dated 8 June 1966 (Box 27, Sheehan Papers), emphases are in the originals. At this point Ellsberg was working for John McNaughton at the American Embassy in Vietnam. He was urging both McNamara and Rostow to meet with his friend John Vann for a real insider's view of the situation in Indochina.

40. Neil Sheehan, introduction to *The Pentagon Papers as Published by the New York Times*, xii, xiii.

41. Serguei Alex Oushakine, "The Terrifying Mimicry of Samizdat," *Public Culture* 13, no. 2 (2001), 204, 203, emphasis in the original. As Oushakine elaborates in this riveting account, during the late 1960s, samizdat "became dominated by *political* documents" — petitions, open letters, pamphlets, and trial transcripts, rather than the more well-known (in the West) artistic expressions (195, emphasis in the original). Oushakine argues that this Soviet protest writing worked by echoing and thereby amplifying the rhetoric of the state apparatus, forming a sort of "mimetic resistance" in lieu of an oppositional discourse, which remained unthinkable in Russia until the late 1970s (192). Elena Razlogova sent me this terrific article, and I'm grateful for her thinking on samizdat and xerography.

42. Transportation Security Administration, "How to Get through the Line

Faster," accessed 25 June 2013, http://www.tsa.gov.traveler-information/how-get -through-line-faster.

43. See Lisa Lynch, "The G Word: Guantanamo, the 'Gulag' Backlash, and the Language of Human Rights," *Politics and Culture*, no. 1 (2007), accessed 25 June 2013, http://www.politicsandculture.org/2009/10/02/lisa-lynch-on-the-g-word/.

44. Oushakine, "The Terrifying Mimicry of Samizdat," 192.

45. "Project," 943.

46. Borge Varmer, "Photoduplication of Copyrighted Material by Libraries," *Studies Prepared for the Subcommittee on Patents, Trademarks, and Copyrights* (1959), accessed 25 June 2013, http://www.copyright.gov/history/studies/study15.pdf.

47. "Excerpts from Ehrlichman's Testimony," *New York Times*, 26 July 1973. See also Walter Rugaber, "A Sudden Decision," *New York Times*, 28 April 1973.

48. National Security Archive, "Veto Battle 30 Years Ago Set Freedom of Information Norms," 23 November 2004, accessed June 2011, http://www.gwu.edu /~nsarchiv/NSAEBB/NSAEBB142/index.htm.

49. See Kelty, *Two Bits*, chapter 4. For a recent retelling, see Warren Toomey, "The Strange Birth and Long Life of UNIX" *IEEE Spectrum*, 28 November 2011, accessed January 2012, http://spectrum.ieee.org/computing/software/the-strange -birth-and-long-life-of-unix/0.

50. Kelty, *Two Bits*, 132. This last quotation is from the back cover of the book version of the commentary, published in 1996 under the title *Lions' Commentary on UNIX 6th Edition*. Despite the fact that UNIX version 6 is no longer in use, programmers still enthuse about this book. It is available for $39.95 from Amazon, where it has nine enthusiastic reviews and where used copies go for $38.95 (as of 2010).

51. Ibid.

52. Wirtén, *No Trespassing*, 58. The story is also told in detail in Owen, *Copies in Seconds*.

53. Peter H. Salus, *A Quarter Century of UNIX* (Reading, MA: Addison Wesley, 1994), 34–36.

54. See Dennis M. Ritchie and Ken Thompson, "The UNIX Time-Sharing System," *Communications of the ACM* 17, no. 7 (1974): 365–75.

55. Frederick P. Brooks Jr., *The Mythical Man-Month: Essays on Software Engineering*, corrected ed. (Reading, MA: Addison-Wesley, 1982), 134.

56. Ken Thompson and Dennis Ritchie, "Unix Programmer's Manual," accessed 25 May 2006, http://cm.bell-labs.com/cm/cs/who/dmr/mainintro.html. See also Salus, *A Quarter Century of UNIX*, chapter 6.

57. Christopher Kelty, "Geeks, Social Imaginaries, and Recursive Publics," *Cultural Anthropology* 20, no. 2 (2005): 198. On bootstrapping, see also Bowker, *Memory Practices in the Sciences*, 141.

58. F. Brooks, *The Mythical Man-Month*, 62. On the uses of documentation, see also Julian E. Orr, *Talking about Machines: An Ethnography of a Modern Job* (Ithaca, NY: Cornell University Press, 1996), 105–13. Orr's study is based on fieldwork conducted in the late 1980s.

59. John Lions, "A Commentary on the Sixth Edition UNIX Operating System," 1977, accessed 24 June 2013, http://warsus.github.io/lions-/.

60. J. Lions, "Preface," in "A Commentary on the Sixth Edition UNIX Operating System," 1977, accessed 24 June 2013, http://warsus.github.io/lions-/.

61. Douglas C. Engelbart, "Quarterly Technical Letter Report 6," 28 November 1967, Box 2, Douglas C. Engelbart Papers, 1953–1998 (MO638), Stanford University Libraries, Stanford, CA. See also Kelty, *Two Bits*, 198.

62. Wikipedia, "Living Document," accessed 1 July 2011, http://en.wikipedia.org /wiki/Living_document. "Functional documents" is the phrase used in Request for Comments 115: R. W. Watson and J. B. North, "Some Network Information Center Policies on Handling Documents," April 1971, accessed 24 June 2013, http://www.rfc-editor.org/rfc/rfc115.txt.

63. J. Brooks, "Profiles," 47.

64. I've written elsewhere on documents as distinct from format, as Latourian "matters of concern," made meaningful in the social networks of their potential circulation (Lisa Gitelman, *Always Already New: Media, History, and the Data of Culture* [Cambridge, MA: MIT Press, 2006], chapter 4).

65. See Matthew G. Kirschenbaum, *Mechanisms: New Media and the Forensic Imagination* (Cambridge, MA: MIT Press, 2008); Michael Buckland "What Is a Digital Document?" 1998, http://people.ischool.berkeley.edu/~buckland/digdoc .html, accessed 25 June 2013.

66. J. Brooks, "Profiles," 52, 55.

67. Virginia Jackson, *Dickinson's Misery: A Theory of Lyric Reading* (Princeton, NJ: Princeton University Press, 2005), 6.

68. See Schwartz, *The Culture of the Copy*, 238–41.

69. Alan Dundes and Carl R. Pagter, *Urban Folklore from the Paperwork Empire* (Austin, TX: American Folklore Society, 1975); Paul Smith, "Models from the Past: Proto-Photocopy-Lore," in *The Other Print Tradition: Essays on Chapbooks, Broadsides, and Related Ephemera*, ed. Cathy Lynn Preston and Michael J. Preston (New York: Garland, 1995), 183–222. Chris Kelty and Patricia Crain both pointed me to this material and suggested its relevance.

70. Dundes and Pagter's *Urban Folklore* was republished twice as Alan Dundes and Carl R. Pagter, *Work Hard and You Shall Be Rewarded: Urban Folklore from the Paperwork Empire* (Detroit, MI: Wayne State University Press, 1992). They also published *When You're up to Your Ass in Alligators: More Urban Folklore from the Paperwork Empire* (Detroit, MI: Wayne State University Press, 1987); *Never Try to Teach a Pig to Sing: Still More Urban Folklore from the Paperwork Empire* (Detroit, MI: Wayne State University Press, 1991); *Sometimes the Dragon Wins: Yet More Urban Folklore from the Paperwork Empire* (Syracuse, NY: Syracuse University Press, 1996); and *Why Don't Sheep Shrink When It Rains? A Further Collection of Photocopier Folklore* (Syracuse, NY: Syracuse University Press, 2000).

71. See Dundes and Pagter, *Work Hard and You Shall Be Rewarded*, preface. It's clear that notoriety and respect may have been coextensive aims. See also Regina

Béndiz and Rosemary Lévy Zumwalt, eds., *Folklore Interpreted: Essays in Honor of Alan Dundes* (New York: Garland, 1995).

72. Dundes and Pagter, *Urban Folklore*, xvii–xix.

73. Ibid., xxi.

74. Ibid., xiii, xx, xxi.

75. Cathy Lynn Preston, introduction to *The Other Print Tradition*, xvii. Preston draws productively on Michel de Certeau's elaboration of *la perruque* (*The Practice of Everyday Life*, trans. Steven F. Rendall [Berkeley: University of California Press, 1981], 25–26).

76. Alan Liu, *Laws of Cool: Knowledge Work and the Culture of Information* (Chicago: University of Chicago Press, 2004), 99.

77. Susan Stewart, *Crimes of Writing: Problems in the Containment of Representation* (Durham, NC: Duke University Press, 1994), 66.

78. *Williams & Wilkins Co. v. United States*, 487 F.2d 1345 (1973).

79. Ibid. Librarian Herbert Putnam was quoted within Judge Davis's decision.

80. For the extended career of "The Gentlemen's Agreement," see Peter B. Hirtle, "Research, Libraries, and Fair Use: The Gentlemen's Agreement of 1935," 2006, accessed 25 June 2013, http://dspace.library.cornell.edu/bitstream/1813/2719/1/Research_Libraries_and_Fair_Use.pdf.

81. *Sony Corp. of America v. Universal City Studios*, 464 U.S. 417 (1984).

82. On *Williams & Wilkins* and subsequent litigation, see Wirtén, *No Trespassing*, 68–75.

83. Joshua M. Greenberg, *From Betamax to Blockbuster: Video Stores and the Invention of Movies on Video* (Cambridge, MA: MIT Press, 2008), 45.

84. Ibid., 27.

85. Lucas Hilderbrand, *Inherent Vice: Bootleg Histories of Videotape and Copyright* (Durham, NC: Duke University Press, 2009), 186.

86. For this argument, see Will Straw, "Embedded Memories," in *Residual Media*, ed. Charles R. Acland (Minneapolis: University of Minnesota Press, 2007), 3–31.

87. Kate Eichhorn, "Breach of Copy/Rights: The University Copy District as Abject Zone," *Public Culture* 18, no. 3 (2006): 551–71.

CHAPTER FOUR. NEAR PRINT AND BEYOND PAPER:
KNOWING BY *.PDF

1. Bamber Gascoigne, *How to Identify Prints: A Complete Guide to Manual and Mechanical Processes from Woodcut to Ink Jet* (New York: Thames and Hudson, 1986), 10.

2. On the epideictic here, I'm following Robert S. Nelson, "The Slide Lecture, of the Work of Art History in the Age of Mechanical Reproduction," *Critical Inquiry* 26 (Spring 2000): 414–34.

3. Roland Barthes, *Camera Lucida: Reflections on Photography*, trans. Richard Howard (New York: Hill and Wang, 1981), 4.

4. See Chuck Kleinhans, ed., "In Focus: Visual Culture, Scholarship, and Sexual

Images," *Cinema Journal* 46 (Summer 2007): 96–132. This is a selection of brief articles accompanied by a CD containing images. No printed illustrations appear. It's "a decent enough compromise," notes the journal's editor, Jon Lewis, in a headnote to the selection, but "it's hard to miss the irony: a special section on the difficulty of illustrating essays on sexual representations that itself proved to be difficult to illustrate" (96).

5. Rather, this is partly about images, you might say, and partly about pictures. For an inspiring and far more exacting set of reflections on similar subjects, see W. J. T. Mitchell, *Picture Theory: Essays on Verbal and Visual Representation* (Chicago: University of Chicago Press, 1994), especially 35–82.

6. Adrian Johns, *The Nature of the Book: Print and Knowledge in the Making* (Chicago: University of Chicago Press, 1998), 3. According to Johns, Elizabeth Eisenstein's "fixity" and Bruno Latour's "immutability" end up as "attributes of credibility and persuasion that actually took much work to [construct and] maintain" (18). Immutability itself is agonistic, you might say in Latour's terms, and "we may consider fixity not as an inherent quality but as a transitive one" (19). Johns continues: "I do not question that print enabled the stabilization of texts, to some extent. . . . I do, however, question the character of the link between the two" (36).

7. Ibid., 36, 19.

8. Anne Friedberg, *The Virtual Window, from Alberti to Microsoft* (Cambridge, MA: MIT Press, 2006), 19.

9. Patrick Henry, "Book Production Technology since 1945," in *The Enduring Book: Print Culture in Postwar America*, ed. David Paul Nord, Joan Shelley Rubin, and Michael Schudson (Chapel Hill: published in association with the American Antiquarian Society by the University of North Carolina Press, 2009), 62.

10. Jay David Bolter and Richard Grusin, *Remediation: Understanding New Media* (Cambridge, MA: MIT Press, 1999). PDFs can of course be edited and revised using software designed for that purpose.

11. Kenneth Goldsmith, *Uncreative Writing: Managing Language in the Digital Age* (New York: Columbia University Press, 2011), 156.

12. Wikipedia, "Portable Document Format," accessed 17 July 2012, http://en .wikipedia.org/wiki/Portable_Document_Format.

13. I explore this question in Lisa Gitelman, *Always Already New: Media, History, and the Data of Culture* (Cambridge, MA: MIT Press, 2006), chapter 4.

14. "Processural," I believe, is a coinage by N. Katherine Hayles. See "Materiality Has Always Been in Play, An Interview with N. Katherine Hayles by Lisa Gitelman," 2002, accessed 26 June 2013, http://iowareview.uiowa.edu/TIRW/TIRW _Archive/tirweb/feature/hayles/interview.htm.

15. Jaron Lanier, *You Are Not a Gadget: A Manifesto* (New York: Alfred A. Knopf, 2010), 13.

16. Robert C. Binkley, "New Tools for Men of Letters," *Yale Review* 24 (March 1935): 519.

17. Jonathan Sterne, *MP3: The Meaning of a Format* (Durham, NC: Duke University Press, 2012), 7.

18. See Thomas Streeter, "Why, Really, Do We Love Steve Jobs?," 13 October 2011, accessed 26 June 2013, http://inthesetimes.com/article/12100/why_really_do _we_love_steve_jobs/.

19. Darren Wershler, "The Pirate as Archivist," paper presented at the Network Archaeologies conference, Miami, OH, 20–22 April 2012. I'm grateful to Darren for sharing a .txt file of his talk.

20. For an overview, see Laurens Leurs, "The History of PDF," 17 September 2001, accessed May 2012, http://www.prepressure.com/pdf/basics/history.

21. Wikipedia, "Portable Document Format," accessed 17 July 2012, http://en .wikipedia.org/wiki/Portable_Document_Format; see also Adobe Systems, "PDF Reference and Adobe Extensions to the PDF Specification," accessed 26 June 2013, http://www.adobe.com/devnet/pdf/pdf_reference.html.

22. U.S. Census Bureau, "Portable Document Format (PDF)," accessed 30 July 2011, http://www.census.gov/main/www/pdf.html.

23. Matthew G. Kirschenbaum, *Mechanisms: New Media and the Forensic Imagination* (Cambridge, MA: MIT Press, 2008), 133. In fact, print editions achieved this sameness relatively late; see David McKitterick, *Print, Manuscript and the Search for Order, 1450–1830* (Cambridge: Cambridge University Press, 2003).

24. Bonnie Mak, *How the Page Matters* (Toronto: University of Toronto Press, 2011), 3–5. On imposing, see John Moxon, *Mechanick Exercises on the Whole Art of Printing* (London, 1683–84), 2:223–33.

25. Charles P. Bourne and Trudi Bellardo Hahn, *A History of Online Information Services, 1963–1976* (Cambridge, MA: MIT Press, 2003), 64, 65.

26. Ibid., 326.

27. Ivan Edward Sutherland, "Sketchpad, A Man-Machine Graphical Communication System," PhD diss., Massachusetts Institute of Technology, 1963.

28. Thierry Bardini, *Bootstrapping: Douglas Engelbart, Coevolution, and the Origins of Personal Computing* (Stanford, CA: Stanford University Press, 2000), 84. See also Michael Hiltzik, *Dealers of Lightning: Xerox PARC and the Dawn of the Computer Age* (New York: Harper Collins, 1999), 90–91.

29. Ivan Edward Sutherland, "Sketchpad, A Man-Machine Graphical Communication System," PhD diss., Massachusetts Institute of Technology, 1963, 70–71.

30. Ivan Edward Sutherland, "Sketchpad: A Man-Machine Graphical Communication System," *AFIPS Proceedings* 23 (1963): 335.

31. For versions of this story, see Bardini, *Bootstrapping*; Hiltzik, *Dealers of Lightning*; M. Mitchell Waldrop, *The Dream Machine: J. C. R. Licklider and the Revolution That Made Computing Personal* (New York: Viking, 2001).

32. Otto Friedrich, "The Computer Moves In," *Time* (3 January 1983), accessed 26 June 2013, http://www.time.com/time/magazine/article/0,9171,953632,00 .html.

33. Chuq Von Rospach, *Bull and Coo Journal* 1, no. 1 (November 1989). This fanzine

was part of *Fantasy Amateur* 53, no. 1 (November 1989), also known as "FAPA Mailing No. 209." It was consulted in the Paskow Science Fiction Collection (Science Fiction and Fantasy), Temple University, Special Collections Research Center, Philadelphia, PA.

34. *Instant Print/Copy Shop, AEA Business Manual No. x1298* (Irvine, CA: Entrepreneur, 1984, 1987, 1988), consulted at the New York Public Library.

35. Johanna Drucker, "From A to Screen," in *Comparative Textual Media*, ed. N. Katherine Hayles and Jessica Pressman (Minneapolis: University of Minnesota Press, forthcoming).

36. Ibid. For a detailed account of the related "font wars," see Thomas W. Phinney, "TrueType & PostScript Type 1: What's the Difference?," version 1.51, 1 October 1997, accessed 5 June 2012, http://www.truetype-typography.com/articles/ttvst1 .htm.

37. Pamela Pfiffner, *Inside the Publishing Revolution: The Adobe Story* (Berkeley, CA: Peachpit, 2003), 53.

38. Susan Lammers, "John Warnock — 1986," Programmers at Work, accessed July 2011, programmersatwork.wordpress.com/john-warnock.

39. "John Warnock's 'Camelot' Signaled Birth of PDF," *Planet PDF*, 18 January 2002, accessed 26 June 2013, http://www.planetpdf.com/enterprise/article .asp?ContentID=6519. *Planet PDF* published it on 18 January 2002 as a PDF that was created on 5 May 1995, so its provenance is murky.

40. Abigail J. Sellen and Richard H. R. Harper, *The Myth of the Paperless Office* (Cambridge, MA: MIT Press, 2002), 6.

41. J. Warnock, "The Camelot Project," 1991, accessed 25 June 2013, http://www .planetpdf.com/planetpdf/pdfs/warnock_camelot.pdf.

42. See Jonathan Coopersmith, "Facsimile's False Starts," *IEEE Spectrum* 30, no. 2 (February 1993): 46–49; Jonathan Coopersmith, "Texas Politics and the Fax Revolution," *Information Systems Research* 7 (March 1996): 37–51; Jennifer S. Light, "Facsimile: A Forgotten 'New Medium' from the 20th Century," *New Media and Society* 8, no. 3 (2006): 355–78.

43. J. Warnock, "The Camelot Project."

44. On documents' careers, see Richard H. R. Harper, *Inside the IMF: An Ethnography of Documents, Technology, and Organisational Action* (San Diego, CA: Academic, 1998), 2.

45. Thomas Streeter, *The Net Effect: Romanticism, Capitalism, and the Internet* (New York: New York University Press, 2011), 119.

46. Pfiffner, *Inside the Publishing Revolution*, 140.

47. Tim Bienz and Richard Cohn, *Portable Document Format Reference Manual* (Reading, MA: Addison-Wesley, 1993), 11. See also Patrick Ames, *Beyond Paper: The Official Guide to Adobe Acrobat* (Mountain View, CA: Adobe, 1993), 8–11; Pfiffner, *Inside the Publishing Revolution*, 139.

48. PDF documents — in distinction from the PDF files that describe them — got "smart" about their own internal structures after PDF 1.3 introduced logical structure facilities in 2000.

49. See Jonathan Sterne, "The MP3 as Cultural Artifact," *New Media and Society* 8 (October 2006): 825–42.

50. There is actually a whole family of specific PDF standards, one of which is for archives. See National Digital Information Infrastructure and Preservation Program, "Sustainability of Digital Formats: Planning for Library of Congress Collections," 7 March 2007, accessed August 2009, http://www.digitalpreservation .gov/formats/intro/intro.shtml. "Lossy" encoding compresses files by discarding some of the data they contain; archivists prefer lossless compression.

51. Bienz and Richard Cohn, *Portable Document Format Reference Manual*; Ames, *Beyond Paper*.

52. Shoshana Zuboff, *In the Age of the Smart Machine: The Nature of Work and Power* (New York: Basic, 1984), 125.

53. Ames, *Beyond Paper*, 45–47, 85.

54. Ibid., 93.

55. Streeter, *The Net Effect*, 124 (emphasis in the original). A related point about the uneven penetration of technological change had been made before by Alvin Toffler in *The Third Wave* (New York: William Morrow, 1980), 207–8.

56. Jacques Derrida, *Paper Machine*, trans. Rachel Bowlby (Stanford, CA: Stanford University Press, 2005), 29.

57. These generalizations by me and others are supported and elaborated by ethnographic accounts, including Harper, *Inside the IMF*; Zuboff, *In the Age of the Smart Machine*; and Sellen and Harper, *The Myth of the Paperless Office*. For a thorough reading of alienated white-color labor in the postwar era, see Alan Liu, *Laws of Cool: Knowledge Work and the Culture of Information* (Chicago: University of Chicago Press, 2004), chapters 1–3.

58. Ames, *Beyond Paper*, 24, 26.

59. Adobe Systems, "PDF as a Standard for Archiving," accessed August 2011, www .adobe.com/enterprise/pdfs/pdfarchiving.pdf.

60. See Webopedia, "All about Adobe PDF," accessed October 2012, http://www .webopedia.com/DidYouKnow/Computer_Science/2005/pdf.asp.

61. Ames, *Beyond Paper*, 16.

62. Sellen and Harper, *The Myth of the Paperless Office*, 103 (emphasis in the original). I include smelling in the list above because of John Seely Brown and Paul Duguid, *The Social Life of Information* (Cambridge, MA: Harvard Business Review Press, 2000), 173. See also Ames, *Beyond Paper*, 37.

63. Michele White, "The Hand Blocks the Screen: A Consideration of the Ways the Interface is Raced," *Electronic Techtonics: Thinking at the Interface*, ed. HASTAC (HASTAC, 2008), 119, 117.

64. Ibid.

65. Andrew Piper, *Book Was There: Reading in Electronic Times* (Chicago: University of Chicago Press, 2012), 154.

66. William H. Sherman, *Used Books: Marking Readers in Renaissance England* (Philadelphia: University of Pennsylvania Press, 2008), 43. Manicules were later reinvented as a printers' typographical device.

67. Ibid., 30.

68. Quoted in Friedberg, *The Virtual Window*, 19. See also Piper, *Book Was There*, chapters 1–2.

69. They "hobble, douse, and dull every leap of intuition and every spark of talent" (Primo Levi, *The Periodic Table*, trans. Raymond Rosenthal [New York: Schocken, 1984], 155).

70. Bardini writes: "The personal computer interface started with the hand, not the brain (or the eyes, for that matter). The computer became 'personal' the moment when it came into the hand's reach, via a prosthesis that the user could forget as soon as it was there" (*Bootstrapping*, 53).

71. This reading is dramatically at odds with theorizations like those of de Certeau as well as with research conducted elsewhere in Silicon Valley during the 1990s. See Anne Balsamo, *Designing Culture: The Technological Imagination at Work* (Durham, NC: Duke University Press, 2011), chapter 2. Even the innovators behind microfilm had a more nuanced taxonomy of reading, as I describe in chapter 2.

72. Sellen and Harper, *The Myth of the Paperless Office*, 83.

73. John Warnock, foreword to Ames, *Beyond Paper*, 10.

74. Markus Krajewski, *Paper Machines: About Cards and Catalogs, 1548–1929* (Cambridge, MA: MIT Press, 2011), 143. Krajewski is writing here about a different context.

75. Alan Liu, "Transcendental Data: Toward a Cultural History and Aesthetics of the New Encoded Discourse," *Critical Inquiry* 31 (Autumn 2004): 63.

76. Benjamin, *The Work of Art in the Age of Its Technological Reproducibility*, 33–34.

77. I'm thinking very generally here of Neal Stephenson, "In the Beginning Was the Command Line," accessed 24 June 2013, http://www.cryptonomicon.com /beginning.html. See also David Golumbia, *The Cultural Logic of Computation* (Cambridge, MA: Harvard University Press, 2009), especially 163–77.

78. Wershler, "The Pirate as Archivist." Wershler explains that CBZ and CBR files are made by manually changing the suffixes on RAR and ZIP archives.

79. Jakob Nielsen, "PDF: Unfit for Human Consumption," 14 July 2003, accessed 22 July 2012, http://www.useit.com/alertbox/20030714.html. In "Avoid PDF for On-Screen Reading," Nielsen gives design tips for using PDFs on the web (10 June 2001, accessed 22 July 2012, http://www.useit.com/alertbox/20010610 .html).

80. Anton Ertl, "What Is the PDF Format Good For?," modified 7 December 2006, accessed 24 July 2012, http://www.complang.tuwien.ac.at/anton/why-not-pdf .html.

81. The quote is from 29 November 2001, accessed 4 October 2012 via web.archiv .org, http://www.google.com/help/faq_filetypes.html. Today's Google FAQ contains the same language, from 2011.

82. See John Willinsky, Alex Garnett, and Angela Pan Wong, "Refurbishing the Camelot of Scholarship: How to Improve the Digital Contribution of the PDF Research Article," *Journal of Electronic Publishing* 15, no. 1 (2012), http://dx.doi .org/10.3998/3336451.0015.102.

83. Ibid., note 22.

84. See Matthew G. Kirschenbaum, "The .txtual Condition," in *Comparative Textual Media*, ed. N. Katherine Hayles and Jessica Pressman (Minneapolis: University of Minnesota Press, forthcoming).

85. Matthew G. Kirschenbaum, "The Word as Image in an Age of Digital Reproduction," in *Eloquent Images: Word and Image in the Age of New Media*, ed. Mary E. Hocks and Michelle R. Kendrick (Cambridge, MA: MIT Press, 2003), 138.

86. Ibid., 139.

87. Hito Steyerl, "In Defense of the Poor Image," November 2009, accessed 30 May 2013, http://www.e-flux.com/journal/in-defense-of-the-poor-image/.

88. On databases and their subjects, see, for instance, Mark Poster, "Databases as Discourse; or, Electronic Interpellations," in *Computers, Surveillance, and Privacy*, ed. David Lyon and Elia Zureik (Cambridge, MA: MIT Press, 1994), 175–92; Rita Raley, "Dataveillance and Counterveillance," in *"Raw Data" Is an Oxymoron*, ed. Lisa Gitelman (Cambridge, MA: MIT Press, 2013), 121–46.

89. Allegory is the meat of computational "layers" and of interface, according to Alexander R. Galloway, *The Interface Effect* (Cambridge: Polity, 2012), 54.

AFTERWORD: AMATEURS RUSH IN

1. Henry Jenkins, *Convergence Culture: Where Old and New Media Collide* (New York: New York University Press, 2006); Andrew Keen, *The Cult of the Amateur: How Today's Internet Is Killing Our Culture* (New York: Doubleday, 2007). Keen decries "the pajama army" (47).

2. Oscar Harpel, *Harpel's Typograph, Or Book of Specimens, Containing Useful Information and a Collection of Examples of Letterpress Job Printing, Arranged for the Assistance of Master Printers, Amateurs, Apprentices, and Others* (Cincinnati, OH: 1870); Robert C. Binkley, "New Tools for Men of Letters," *Yale Review* 24 (March 1935): 519–37.

3. In posing this question in this way, I wish to acknowledge a way that zines have a history — within the lives of their creators, readers, and collectors — that cannot be my purpose here. I have been influenced by Janice Radway, "Zines, Half-Lives, and Afterlives: On the Temporalities of Social and Political Change," *PMLA* 126, no. 1 (2011): 140–50; Anna Poletti, *Intimate Ephemera: Reading Young Lives in Australian Zine Culture* (Melbourne, Australia: University of Melbourne Press, 2008); and work in progress by Kate Eichhorn.

4. Oscar Harpel, *Poets and Poetry of Printerdom: A Collection of Original, Selected, and Fugitive Lyrics Written by Persons Connected with Printing* (Cincinnati, OH: 1875).

5. The sequence and chronology of the words' coinage are murky. A search of EBSCO's American Antiquarian Society Periodicals Collection shows the earliest use of "amateurdom" (in scare quotes) in the 1 November 1872 "Wish Correspondents" listings in *Our Boys & Girls Monthly*. "Printerdom" was used once in 1868 in the *Typographic Advertiser*, published by the Philadelphia type foundry

MacKellar, Smiths, & Jordan, where Thomas MacKellar may have been influenced by Harpel, with whom he corresponded.

6. An even larger collection, the Library of Amateur Journalism, is being processed at the University of Wisconsin. For a history of it, see Kenneth W. Faig Jr., "Passion, Controversy, and Vision: A History of the Library of Amateur Journalism," 2005, accessed January 2013, http://www.thefossils.org/laj_hist.pdf. An 1869 ad for the Novelty Job Printing Press located in Google Books mentions only merchants and druggists, but the ad appeared in *Our Young Folks: An Illustrated Magazine for Boys and Girls*.

7. Amateurdom's chroniclers are careful to acknowledge earlier amateurs but stress the organization of amateur press associations as an important moment of origin.

8. Harlan H. Ballard, "Amateur Newspapers," *St. Nicholas*, July 1882, 717–27; Thomas Harrison, *The Career and Reminiscences of an Amateur Journalist, and a History of Amateur Journalism* (Indianapolis, IN: Thomas G. Harrison, 1883).

9. Harrison, *The Career and Reminiscences of an Amateur Journalist*, 15. Subsequent references to this work will be noted parenthetically in the pages that follow.

10. Ballard, "Amateur Newspapers." For additional information about amateurs' postal troubles, see John Travis Nixon, *History of the National Amateur Press Association, Compiled by John Travis Nixon* (Crowley, LA: John T. Nixon, 1900), 56, 95.

11. For a more nuanced account, see Leon Jackson, *The Business of Letters: Authorial Economies in Antebellum America* (Stanford, CA: Stanford University Press, 2008).

12. See W. J. Rorabaugh, *The Craft Apprentice: From Franklin to the Machine Age in America* (New York: Oxford University Press, 1986.) On the platen press, see Harold E. Sterne, *A Catalogue of Nineteenth Century Printing Presses* (New Castle, DE: Oak Knoll, 2001), 119–20; Ralph Green, "A History of the Platen Jobber," reprinted in Ralph Green, *Works of Ralph Green* (Cincinnati, OH: Ye Olde Printery, 1981). Job printing in this period has been considered most recently in Doug Clouse and Angela Voulangas, *The Handy Book of Artistic Printing: A Collection of Letterpress Examples with Specimens of Type, Ornament, Corner Fills, Borders, Twisters, Wrinklers, and Other Freaks of Fancy* (New York: Princeton Architectural, 2009).

13. Quoted in Elizabeth M. Harris, *Personal Impressions: The Small Printing Press in Nineteenth-Century America* (Boston: David R. Godine, 2004), 9. The quote is from a Golding Press advertisement from 1882.

14. Karen Sánchez-Eppler, *Dependent States: The Child's Part in Nineteenth-Century American Culture* (Chicago: University of Chicago Press, 2005), 153.

15. Harrison notes (12) that amateur papers were often started in January (perhaps as the result of a Christmas present or a New Year's resolution), making them a bourgeois counterpart to the long tradition of the carrier's address, the New Year's solicitations by printers' apprentices.

16. Sánchez-Eppler, *Dependent States*, 169.

17. Miranda Joseph, *Against the Romance of Community* (Minneapolis: University of Minnesota Press, 2002), 73.

18. "Cooperative individuality" is an insight of Stephen Duncombe about later zines (*Notes from Underground: Zines and the Politics of Alternative Culture*, 2nd ed. [Bloomington, IN: Microcosm, 2008], 189) and seems apt here as well, as does Janice Radway's notice of girl zine-makers as "intersubjects," "constituted in relation to and therefore always together with others" ("Zines, Half-Lives, and After-lives," 148).

19. See Pat Pflieger, "American Children's Periodicals, 1789–1872," accessed December 2012, http://www.merrycoz.org/bib/intro.htm. Among the most important titles were *Our Young Folks: An Illustrated Magazine for Boys and Girls*, which started in 1865 and was reinvented at *St. Nicholas* in 1873, and *Oliver Optic's Magazine: Our Boys and Girls*, a weekly started in 1867. The number of magazines exploded in these years. See Frank Luther Mott, *A History of American Magazines, 1741–1930*, 5 vols. (Cambridge, MA: Belknap Press of Harvard University Press, 1958–68). Mott estimates "a scant 700 periodicals for 1865, somewhat over 1,200 for 1870, twice that many for 1880, and some 3,300 for 1885" (3:5).

20. The connection is also indicated in Will A. Fiske and Will A. Innes, *The Amateur Directory for 1875* (Grand Rapids, MI: Will A. Innes, 1875).

21. "Our Letter Bag," *Oliver Optic's Magazine: Our Boys and Girls* 2, no. 27 (1867): 327.

22. Michelle H. Phillips, "Along the 'Paragraph Wires': Child-Adult Mediation in *St. Nicholas Magazine*," *Children's Literature* 37 (2009): 86.

23. Jared Gardner, *The Rise and Fall of Early American Magazine Culture* (Urbana: University of Illinois Press, 2012), 109.

24. John Neubauer, *The Fin-de-Siècle Culture of Adolescence* (New Haven, CT: Yale University Press, 1992), 86.

25. Truman Joseph Spencer, "The History of Amateur Journalism" (1947, unpublished manuscript), 169. This work was "prepared and published as an enterprise of The Fossils, Inc.," and a copy exists at the New York Public Library. It is also excerpted on the website of the Fossils (accessed January 2013, http://www.the-fossils.org/horvat/aj/organizations/uapa.htm). I am guessing that Spencer has confused *Golden Hours* (1869–80) and *Golden Days*, since the latter was the one that published in the 1890s.

26. See Fredric Wertham, *The World of Fanzines: A Special Form of Communication* (Carbondale: Southern Illinois University Press, 1973), 39–40; Bob Tucker, "The Neo-Fan's Guide," 1955, accessed January 2013, http://efanzines.com/Neofans Guide1/index.htm. See also John Cheng, *Astounding Wonder: Imagining Science and Science Fiction in Interwar America* (Philadelphia: University of Pennsylvania Press, 2012). Poletti rightly notes that this pattern holds for today's zines — except when it doesn't (*Intimate Ephemera*, 23).

27. R. E. Krab, *Chronicles of Amateurdom in Arkansas* (Judsonia, AK: W. Riley Jr., 1883); *The Amateurs' Guide for 1870* (1870); Marvin Eames Stow, "Trojan," in *Universal History of Amateurdom* (Batavia, NY: M. D. Mix, 1877). These amateur papers were consulted at the American Antiquarian Society, Worcester, MA.

28. H. P. Lovecraft, *Miscellaneous Writings*, ed. S. T. Joshi (Sauk City, WI: Arkham House, 1995), 451. See also 431–38 for Lovecraft's "United Amateur Press Association: Exponent of Amateur Journalism."

29. Ibid., 451–52.

30. Ibid., 431–32.

31. Ibid., 435.

32. Ibid., 433.

33. See Susan J. Douglas, *Inventing American Broadcasting, 1899–1922* (Baltimore, MD: Johns Hopkins University Press, 1987), chapter 6. Douglas's estimate of "several hundred thousand" is from an item in the *New York Times* in 1912 (198). That year was a watershed in amateur radio because of the sinking of the *Titanic* and the subsequent passage of the Radio Act. Radio operators were still called and called themselves "amateurs" after licenses became required in 1934; eventually they were also called "hams."

34. Nixon, *History of the National Amateur Press Association*, chapter 14.

35. Truman J. Spencer, *A Cyclopedia of the Literature of Amateur Journalism* (Hartford, CT: Truman J. Spencer, 1891).

36. Lovecraft, *Miscellaneous Writings*, 443–44.

37. Ibid., 444.

38. On antimodernism, I'm thinking of T. J. Jackson Lears, *No Place of Grace: Antimodernism and the Transformation of American Culture, 1880–1920* (Chicago: University of Chicago Press, 1994). On the magazines, see Richard Ohmann, *Selling Culture: Magazines, Markets, and Class at the Turn of the Twentieth Century* (London: Verso, 1996). On criticism and critical authority, see Ian Small, *Conditions for Criticism: Authority, Knowledge, and Literature in the Late Nineteenth Century* (Oxford: Clarendon Press of Oxford University Press, 1991), 57.

39. "More newsy than literary" is a quotation from a mimeographed "literary newsette," published by Willametta Keffer of Roanoke, a member of the National Amateur Press Association, in the 1940s and 1950s. *Literary Newsette* No. 350 (20 February 1954), Paskow Science Fiction Collection (Science Fiction and Fantasy), Temple University, Special Collections Research Center, Philadephia, PA (hereafter Paskow Collection).

40. Ohmann, *Selling Culture*, 7–9. Amateur point-to-point radio was increasingly pushed into a tiny band on the spectrum, as commercial broadcasting was solidified and protected by regulatory legislation in 1912, 1927, and 1934.

41. Cheng, *Astounding Wonder*, 18.

42. Sam Moskowitz, *The Immortal Storm: A History of Science Fiction Fandom* (1954; reprint, Westport, CT: Hyperion, 1973).

43. Ibid., 26, 251.

44. Francis Towner Laney, "Syllabus for a Fanzine," *Spacewarp* 42 (September 1950), accessed January 2013, http://www.fanac.org/fanzines/Syllabus/Syllabus01 .html; "The Neo-Fan's Guide," ed., Bob Tucker, September 1955, accessed 25 June 2013, http://efanzines.com/NeofansGuide1; and *Fanzine Index* No. 3, February 1958, ed. Bob Pavlat, Paskow Collection.

45. This accounting is based on Pavlat, *Fanzine Index* No. 3, which lists fanzines whose titles were in the part of the alphabet from mid-*F* through *L* up to 1953. I counted each title only once (that is, I didn't count individual issues), except where the index notes that a title switched media, and then I counted it again (and again, if necessary). Ditto and hectograph are identified as different media, but the distinction between them is blurred, and I didn't notice any fanzines identified as ditto. I treat these terms as synonymous. "Other" includes hand-written, offset, and rubber-stamped fanzines. This is a very rough estimate.

46. Moskowitz, *The Immortal Storm*, 104–5. To qualify this somewhat with an example or two: the Paskow Collection has the *Fantasy Amateur* 53, no. 1 (November 1989), which encloses the Fantasy Amateur Press Association's Mailing No. 209. The titles contained in the mailing include one ditto fanzine (a throwback, its editor admits), plenty of mimeographs as well as Xeroxed typescripts, and one new fanzine, *Bull and Coo Journal* 1, no. 1, by Chuck Von Rospach, explaining and promoting desktop publishing. The 1960s ascendance of photo-offset is noted in ODD *Magazine* 20 (Summer 1969), but back in 1950 ODD's "So You Want to Publish a Fanzine" (Warren Baldwin) urges mimeograph as "the wisest choice." ODD itself started as a mimeograph, went photo-offset, and returned to mimeograph.

47. Lee Hoffman, *Science Five Fiction Yearly* 8 (November 1986), Paskow Collection.

48. Quoted in Moskowitz, *The Immortal Storm*, 21.

49. See Cheng, *Astounding Wonder*, 60. See also Jared Gardner, *Projections: Comics and the History of Twenty-First Century Storytelling* (Stanford, CA: Stanford University Press, 2012).

50. F. Towner Laney, "Syllabus for a Fanzine," *Spacewarp* 42 (1950) 11, accessed 12 December 2012, http://www.fanac.org/fanzines/Syllabus/Syllabus01.html?.

51. Fandom debated this point indefatigably.

52. Fan studies is up to its "third wave," at the same time that Web 2.0's supposed ascendance of niche over mass consumption threatens to make fandom "into regular consumption"—that is, to turn us all into fans. See Jonathan Gray, Cornel Sandvoss, and C. Lee Harrington, "Introduction: Why Study Fans?," in *Fandom: Identities and Communities in a Mediated World*, ed. Jonathan Gray, Cornel Sandvoss, and C. Lee Harrington (New York: New York University Press, 2007), 7, 16; this last is Henry Jenkins's point, elaborated in his conclusion to this volume, "Afterword: The Future of Fandom," 357–64.

53. Michael Warner, *Publics and Counterpublics* (New York: Zone, 2002).

54. I elaborate this point in *Always Already New: Media, History, and the Data of Culture* (Cambridge, MA: MIT Press, 2006), chapter 4.

55. Susan Sontag, *On Photography* (New York: Farrar, Straus, and Giroux, 1977), 21.

56. Alvin Toffler, *The Third Wave* (New York: William Morrow, 1980), 286, 368–69.

Acland, Charles R. "Introduction: Residual Media." In *Residual Media*, edited by Charles R. Acland, xiii–xxvii. Minneapolis: University of Minnesota Press, 2007.

Adelman, Joseph M. "The Business of Politics: Printers and the Emergence of Political Communications Networks, 1765–1776." PhD diss. Johns Hopkins University, 2010.

Ames, Patrick. *Beyond Paper: The Official Guide to Adobe Acrobat*. Mountain View, CA: Adobe, 1993.

Anderson, Benedict. *Imagined Communities: Reflections on the Origins and Spread of Nationalism*. Rev. ed. London: Verso, 1991.

Andrews, Martin. "The Importance of Ephemera." In *A Companion to the History of the Book*, edited by Simon Eliot and Jonathan Rose, 434–50. Malden, MA: Blackwell, 2007.

Appadurai, Arjun. *Modernity at Large: Cultural Dimensions of Globalization*. Minneapolis: University of Minnesota Press, 1996.

Auger, C. P. *Information Sources in Grey Literature*. 2nd ed. London: Bowker-Saur, 1989.

Augst, Thomas. *The Clerk's Tale: Young Men and Moral Life in Nineteenth-Century America*. Chicago: University of Chicago Press, 2003.

———. "Faith in Reading: Public Libraries, Liberalism, and the Civil Religion." In *Institutions of Reading: The Social Life of Libraries in the United States*, edited by Thomas Augst and Kenneth Carpenter, 148–83. Amherst: University of Massachusetts Press, 2007.

Baker, Nicholson. *Double Fold: Libraries and the Assault on Paper*. New York: Random House, 2001.

Ballard, Harlan H. "Amateur Newspapers." *St. Nicholas Magazine*, July 1882, 717–27.

Balsamo, Anne. *Designing Culture: The Technological Imagination at Work*. Durham, NC: Duke University Press, 2011.

Bardini, Thierry. *Bootstrapping: Douglas Engelbart, Coevolution, and the Origins of Personal Computing*. Stanford, CA: Stanford University Press, 2000.

Barnouw, Erik. *Documentary: A History of the Non-Fiction Film*. Oxford: Oxford University Press, 1974.

Barrese, Edward Francis. "The Historical Records Survey: A Nation Acts to Save Its Memory." PhD diss., George Washington University, 1980.

Barthes, Roland. *Camera Lucida: Reflections on Photography*. Translated by Richard Howard. New York: Hill and Wang, 1981.

Becker, Carl. "Everyman His Own Historian." *American Historical Review* 37 (January 1932): 221–36.

Becker, Peter, and William Clark, eds. *Little Tools of Knowledge: Historical Essays on Academic and Bureaucratic Practices*. Ann Arbor: University of Michigan Press, 2001.

Béndiz, Regina, and Rosemary Lévy Zumwalt, eds. *Folklore Interpreted: Essays in Honor of Alan Dundes*. New York: Garland, 1995.

Beniger, James. *The Control Revolution: Technological and Economic Origins of the Information Society*. Cambridge, MA: Harvard University Press, 1989.

Benjamin, Walter. *The Work of Art in the Age of Its Technological Reproducibility, and Other Writings on Media*. Edited by Michael W. Jennings, Brigid Doherty, and Thomas Y. Levin. Translated by Edmund Jephcott et al. Cambridge, MA: Belknap Press of Harvard University Press, 2008.

Berlant, Lauren. *The Female Complaint: The Unfinished Business of Sentimentality in American Culture*. Durham, NC: Duke University Press, 2008.

Bienz, Tim, and Richard Cohn. *Portable Document Format Reference Manual*. Reading, MA: Addison-Wesley, 1993.

Binkley, Robert C. "The Cultural Program of the W.P.A." *Harvard Educational Review* 9, no. 2 (1939): 156–74.

———. "Do the Records of Science Face Ruin?" *Scientific American* 140 (January 1929): 28–30.

———. "History for a Democracy." *Minnesota History* 18, no. 1 (1937): 1–27.

———. *Manual on Methods of Reproducing Research Materials*. Ann Arbor, MI: Edwards Brothers, 1936.

———. *Methods of Reproducing Research Materials*. Ann Arbor, MI: Edwards Brothers, 1931.

———. "New Tools for Men of Letters." *Yale Review* 24 (March 1935): 519–37.

———. "The Problem of Perishable Paper." In Robert C. Binkley, *Selected Papers of Robert C. Binkley*, edited by Max H. Fisch (Cambridge, MA: Harvard University Press, 1948), 169–78.

Bolter, Jay David, and Richard Grusin. *Remediation: Understanding New Media*. Cambridge, MA: MIT Press, 1999.

Bourne, Charles P., and Trudi Bellardo Hahn. *A History of Online Information Services, 1963–1976*. Cambridge, MA: MIT Press, 2003.

Bowker, Geoffrey C. *Memory Practices in the Sciences*. Cambridge, MA: MIT Press, 2005.

Brannon, Barbara A. "The Laser Printer as an Agent of Change: Fixity and Fluxion in the Digital Age." In *Agent of Change: Print Culture Studies after Elizabeth L. Eisenstein*, edited by Sabrina Alcorn Baron, Eric N. Lindquist, and Eleanor F. Shevlin, 353–64. Amherst: University of Massachusetts Press, 2007.

Brenton, James J., ed. *Voices from the Press: A Collection of Sketches, Essays, and Poems by Practical Printers*. New York: Charles B. Norton, 1850.

Briet, Suzanne. *What Is Documentation? English Translation of the Classic French Text*. Translated by Ronald E. Day, Laurent Martinet, and Hermina G. B. Anghelescu. Lanham, MD: Scarecrow, 2006.

Brooks, Frederick P., Jr. *The Mythical Man-Month: Essays on Software Engineering*. Corrected ed. Reading, MA: Addison-Wesley, 1982.

Brooks, John. "Profiles: Xerox, Xerox, Xerox, Xerox." *New Yorker*, 1 April 1967, 46–90.

Brown, Bill. "Thing Theory." *Critical Inquiry* 28 (Autumn 2001): 1–22.

Brown, John Seely, and Paul Duguid. *The Social Life of Information*. Cambridge, MA: Harvard Business Review Press, 2000.

Campbell-Kelly, Martin. "Informational Technology and Organizational Change in the British Census, 1801–1911." *Information Systems Research* 7 (March 1996): 22–36.

Carey, James. *Communication as Culture: Essays on Media and Society*. Boston: Unwin Hyman, 1989.

Carpenter, Kenneth. "Toward a New Cultural Design: The American Council of Learned Societies, the Social Science Research Council, and Libraries in the 1930s." In *Institutions of Reading: The Social Life of Libraries in the United States*, edited by Thomas Augst and Kenneth Carpenter, 283–309. Amherst: University of Massachusetts Press, 2007.

Chang, Alenda. "Contract or Charter? The End-User License Agreement and the Textual Warranting of Virtual Worlds." Paper presented at the annual meeting of the Modern Language Association of America, San Francisco, CA, 29 December 2008.

Charpin, Dominique. *Reading and Writing in Babylon*. Translated by Jane Marie Todd. Cambridge, MA: Harvard University Press, 2010.

Cheng, John. *Astounding Wonder: Imagining Science and Science Fiction in Interwar America*. Philadelphia: University of Pennsylvania Press, 2012.

Chun, Wendy Hui Kyong. *Programmed Visions: Software and Memory*. Cambridge, MA: MIT Press, 2011.

Clanchy, M. T. *From Memory to Written Record: England 1066–1307*. 2nd ed. Oxford: Blackwell, 1993.

Clouse, Doug. *MacKellar, Smiths & Jordan: Typographic Tastemakers of the Late Nineteenth Century*. New Castle, DE: Oak Knoll, 2008.

Clouse, Doug, and Angela Voulangas. *The Handy Book of Artistic Printing: A Collection of Letterpress Examples with Specimens of Type, Ornament, Corner Fills, Borders, Twisters, Wrinklers, and Other Freaks of Fancy*. New York: Princeton Architectural, 2009.

Cohen, Ralph. "History and Genre." *New Literary History* 17, no. 2 (1986): 203–18.

Commager, Henry Steele. Preface to *Documents of American History*, edited by Henry Steele Commager (New York: F. S. Crofts, 1935), 1:vii–viii.

Coopersmith, Jonathan. "Facsimile's False Starts." *IEEE Spectrum* 30, no. 2 (February 1993): 46–49.

————. "Texas Politics and the Fax Revolution." *Information Systems Research* 7 (March 1996): 37–51.

Crain, Patricia. "New Histories of Literacy." In *A Companion to the History of the Book*, edited by Simon Eliot and Jonathan Rose, 467–79. Malden, MA: Blackwell, 2007.

————. *The Story of A: The Alphabetization of America from The New England Primer to The Scarlet Letter*. Stanford, CA: Stanford University Press, 2002.

Crary, Jonathan. *Techniques of the Observer: On Vision and Modernity in the Nineteenth Century*. Cambridge, MA: MIT Press, 1990.

Csiszar, Alex. "Seriality and the Search for Order: Scientific Print and Its Problems during the Late Nineteenth Century." *History of Science* 48, nos. 3–4 (2010): 399–434.

Daniels, Roger B., and Jesse Beeler. "An Archival Investigation of a Late 19th Century Accounting Information System: The Use of Decision Aids in the American Printing Industry." *Accounting Historians Journal* 28, no. 1 (June 2001): 3–18.

Darnton, Robert. "The Library: Three Jeremiads." *New York Review of Books*, 23 December 2010, 22–26.

Daston, Lorraine, ed. *Biographies of Scientific Objects*. Chicago: University of Chicago Press, 2000.

————, ed. *Things That Talk: Object Lessons from Art and Science*. New York: Zone, 2004.

De Certeau, Michel. *The Practice of Everyday Life*. Translated by Steven F. Rendall. Berkeley: University of California Press, 1981.

DeJean, Joan. *The Reinvention of Obscenity: Sex, Lies, and Tabloids in Early Modern France*. Chicago: University of Chicago Press, 2002.

Denning, Michael. *The Cultural Front: The Laboring of American Culture in the Twentieth Century*. London: Verso, 1996.

Derrida, Jacques. *Paper Machine*. Translated by Rachel Bowlby. Stanford, CA: Stanford University Press, 2005.

————. *The Postcard: From Socrates to Freud and Beyond*. Translated by Alan Bass. Chicago: University of Chicago Press, 1987.

Dessauer, John. *My Years with Xerox: The Billions Nobody Wanted*. Garden City, NY: Doubleday, 1971.

DeVinne, Theodore Low. *Manual of Printing Office Practice*. 1883. Reprint, New York: Ars Typographica, 1926.

————. *The Printers' Price List: A Manual*. New York, 1871.

Dierks, Konstantin. *In My Power: Letter Writing and Communications in Early America*. Philadelphia: University of Pennsylvania Press, 2009.

————. "Letter Writing, Stationery Supplies, and Consumer Modernity in the Eighteenth-Century Atlantic World." *Early American Literature* 41, no. 3 (2006): 473–94.

Douglas, Susan J. *Inventing American Broadcasting, 1899–1922*. Baltimore, MD: Johns Hopkins University Press, 1987.

Downey, Greg. "Commentary: The Place of Labor in the History of Information-

Technology Revolutions." *International Review of Social History* 48, no. S11 (2003): 225–61.

———. "Virtual Webs, Physical Technologies, and Hidden Workers." *Technology and Culture* 42 (April 2001): 209–35.

Drucker, Johanna. "Entity to Event: From Literal, Mechanistic Materiality to Probabilistic Materiality." *Paralax* 15, no. 4 (2009): 7–17.

———. "From A to Screen." In *Comparative Textual Media*, edited by N. Katherine Hayles and Jessica Pressman. Minneapolis: University of Minnesota Press, forthcoming.

———. *SpecLab: Digital Aesthetics and Projects in Speculative Computing*. Chicago: University of Chicago Press, 2009.

Duncombe, Stephen. *Notes from Underground: Zines and the Politics of Alternative Culture*. 2nd ed. Bloomington, IN: Microcosm, 2008.

Dundes, Alan, and Carl R. Pagter. *Urban Folklore from the Paperwork Empire*. Austin, TX: American Folklore Society, 1975.

———. *Work Hard and You Shall Be Rewarded: Urban Folklore from the Paperwork Empire*. Detroit, MI: Wayne State University Press, 1992.

Dworkin, Craig. *No Medium*. Cambridge, MA: MIT Press, 2013.

Eichhorn, Kate. "Breach of Copy/Rights: The University Copy District as Abject Zone." *Public Culture* 18, no. 3 (2006): 551–71.

Ellsberg, Daniel. *Secrets: A Memoir of Vietnam and the Pentagon Papers*. New York: Viking, 2002.

Fiske, Will A. and Will A. Innes, *The Amateur Directory for 1875*. Grand Rapids, MI: Will A. Innes, 1875.

Foucault, Michel. "What Is an Author?" In Michel Foucault, *The Foucault Reader*, edited by Paul Rabinow, 101–20. New York: Pantheon, 1984.

Friedberg, Anne. *The Virtual Window, from Alberti to Microsoft*. Cambridge, MA: MIT Press, 2006.

Frohmann, Bernd. "The Documentality of Mme. Briet's Antelope." In *Communication Matters: Materialist Approaches to Media, Mobility, and Networks*, edited by Jeremy Packer and Stephen B. Crofts Wiley, 173–82. New York: Routledge, 2012.

Gallagher, Catherine. *Nobody's Story: The Vanishing Acts of Women Writers in the Marketplace, 1670–1820*. Berkeley: University of California Press, 1994.

Galloway, Alexander R. *The Interface Effect*. Cambridge: Polity, 2012.

———. *Protocol: How Control Exists after Decentralization*. Cambridge, MA: MIT Press, 2006.

Gardner, Jared. *Projections: Comics and the History of Twenty-First Century Storytelling*. Stanford, CA: Stanford University Press, 2012.

———. *The Rise and Fall of Early American Magazine Culture*. Urbana: University of Illinois Press, 2012.

Garvey, Ellen Gruber. "'facts and FACTS': Abolitionists' Database Innovations." In *"Raw Data" Is an Oxymoron*, edited by Lisa Gitelman, 89–102. Cambridge, MA: MIT Press, 2013.

Gascoigne, Bamber. *How to Identify Prints: A Complete Guide to Manual and Mechanical Processes from Woodcut to Ink Jet*. New York: Thames and Hudson, 1986.

Ginzburg, Carlo. *Clues, Myths, and the Historical Method*. Translated by John Tedeschi and Anne C. Tedeschi. Baltimore, MD: Johns Hopkins University Press, 1989.

Gitelman, Lisa. *Always Already New: Media, History, and the Data of Culture*. Cambridge, MA: MIT Press, 2006.

———. "Mississippi MSS: Twain, Typing, and the Moving Panorama of Textual Production." In *Residual Media*, edited by Charles R. Acland, 329–43. Minneapolis: University of Minnesota Press, 2007.

Goble, Mark. *Beautiful Circuits: Modernism and the Mediated Life*. New York: Columbia University Press, 2010.

Golden, Jack. "Historical Introduction to the Art and Technique of Printed Ephemera." In *Graphic Americana: The Art and Technique of Printed Ephemera*, edited by Dale Roylance, 9–10. Exhibition catalogue. Princeton, NJ: Princeton University Library, 1992.

Goldsmith, Kenneth. *Uncreative Writing: Managing Language in the Digital Age*. New York: Columbia University Press, 2011.

Golumbia, David. *The Cultural Logic of Computation*. Cambridge, MA: Harvard University Press, 2009.

Grafton, Anthony. *The Footnote: A Curious History*. Cambridge, MA: Harvard University Press, 1997.

Gray, Jonathan, Cornel Sandvoss, and C. Lee Harrington. "Introduction: Why Study Fans?" In *Fandom: Identities and Communities in a Mediated World*, edited by Jonathan Gray, Cornel Sandvoss, and C. Lee Harrington, 1–16. New York: New York University Press, 2007.

Green, James N., and Peter Stallybrass. *Benjamin Franklin, Writer and Printer*. New Castle, DE: Oak Knoll, 2006.

Green, Ralph. "A History of the Platen Jobber." Reprinted in Ralph Green, *Works of Ralph Green*. Cincinnati, OH: Ye Olde Printery, 1981.

Greenberg, Joshua M. *From Betamax to Blockbuster: Video Stores and the Invention of Movies on Video*. Cambridge, MA: MIT Press, 2008.

Greene, Jody. *The Trouble with Ownership: Literary Property and Authorial Liability in England, 1660–1730*. Philadelphia: University of Pennsylvania Press, 2005.

Groebner, Valentin. *Who Are You? Identification, Deception, and Surveillance in Early Modern Europe*. Translated by Mark Kyburz and John Peck. New York: Zone, 2007.

Guillory, John. "Genesis of the Media Concept." *Critical Inquiry* 36, no. 2 (2010): 321–63.

———. "The Memo and Modernity." *Critical Inquiry* 31, no. 1 (2004): 108–32.

Guyer, Jane I. *Marginal Gains: Monetary Transactions in Atlantic Africa*. Chicago: University of Chicago Press, 2004.

Habermas, Jürgen. *The Structural Transformation of the Public Sphere: An Inquiry into a Category of Bourgeois Society*. Translated by Thomas Burger with Frederick Lawrence. Cambridge, MA: MIT Press, 1989.

Hardt, Michael. "Affective Labor." *boundary 2* 26, no. 2 (1999): 89–100.

Hariman, Robert and John Louis Lucaites. *No Caption Needed: Iconic Photographs, Public Culture, and Liberal Democracy*. Chicago: University of Chicago Press, 2007.

Harpel Oscar H. *Harpel's Typograph, Or Book of Specimens, Containing Useful Information and a Collection of Examples of Letterpress Job Printing, Arranged for the Assistance of Master Printers, Amateurs, Apprentices, and Others*. Cincinnati, OH: 1870.

———. *Poets and Poetry of Printerdom: A Collection of Original, Selected, and Fugitive Lyrics Written by Persons Connected with Printing*. Cincinnati, OH: 1875.

Harper, Richard H. R. *Inside the IMF: An Ethnography of Documents, Technology, and Organisational Action*. San Diego, CA: Academic, 1998.

Harris, Elizabeth M. *Personal Impressions: The Small Printing Press in Nineteenth-Century America*. Boston: David R. Godine, 2004.

Harrison, Thomas G. *The Career and Reminiscences of an Amateur Journalist, and a History of Amateur Journalism*. Indianapolis, IN: Thomas G. Harrison, 1883.

Hayles, N. Katherine. *How We Became Posthuman: Virtual Bodies in Cybernetics, Literature, and Informatics*. Chicago: University of Chicago Press, 1999.

———. *How We Think: Digital Media and Contemporary Technogenesis*. Chicago: University of Chicago Press, 2012.

Helton, Laura. "Bibliography, Mimeography, and Ten Thousand List-Makers: Transmitting Historical Texts circa 1939." Unpublished manuscript.

Henkin, David. *City Reading: Written Words and Public Spaces in Antebellum New York*. New York: Columbia University Press, 1998.

Henry, Patrick. "Book Production Technology since 1945." In *The Enduring Book: Print Culture in Postwar America*, edited by David Paul Nord, Joan Shelley Rubin, and Michael Schudson, 54–71. Chapel Hill: published in association with the American Antiquarian Society by the University of North Carolina Press, 2009.

Hilderbrand, Lucas. *Inherent Vice: Bootleg Histories of Videotape and Copyright*. Durham, NC: Duke University Press, 2009.

Hiltzik, Michael. *Dealers of Lightning: Xerox PARC and the Dawn of the Computer Age*. New York: Harper Collins, 1999.

Hockey, Susan. "The History of Humanities Computing." In *A Companion to the Digital Humanities*, edited by Susan Schreibman, Ray Siemens, and John Unsworth, 3–19. Malden, MA: Blackwell, 2004.

Hofmeyr, Isabel. *Gandhi's Printing Press: Experiments in Slow Reading*. Cambridge, MA: Harvard University Press, 2013.

———. *The Portable Bunyan: A Transnational History of "The Pilgrim's Progress."* Princeton, NJ: Princeton University Press, 2004.

Holbrook, Franklin F. *Survey of Activities of American Agencies in Relation to Materials for Research in the Social Sciences and the Humanities*. Washington and New York: Social Science Research Council and American Council of Learned Societies, 1932.

Hounshell, David A. *From the American System to Mass Production, 1800–1932*. Baltimore, MD: Johns Hopkins University Press, 1984.

Howells, William Dean. *The World of Chance: A Novel*. New York: Harper and Brothers, 1893.

Huhtamo, Erkki, and Jussi Parikka, eds. *Media Archaeology: Approaches, Applications, and Implications*. Berkeley: University of California Press, 2011.

Hull, Matthew S. *Government of Paper: The Materiality of Bureaucracy in Urban Pakistan*. Berkeley: University of California Press, 2012.

Jackson, Leon. *The Business of Letters: Authorial Economies in Antebellum America*. Stanford, CA: Stanford University Press, 2008.

———. "'The Italics Are Mine': Edgar Allan Poe and the Semiotics of Print." In *Illuminating Letters: Typography and Literary Interpretation*, edited by Paul C. Gutjahr and Megan L. Benton, 139–61. Amherst: University of Massachusetts Press, 2001.

Jackson, Virginia. *Dickinson's Misery: A Theory of Lyric Reading*. Princeton, NJ: Princeton University Press, 2005.

Jenkins, Henry. "Afterword: The Future of Fandom." *Fandom: Identities and Communities in a Mediated World*. Edited by Jonathan Gray, Cornel Sandvoss, and C. Lee Harrington, 357–64. New York: New York University Press, 2007.

———. *Convergence Culture: Where Old and New Media Collide*. New York: New York University Press, 2006.

Johns, Adrian. *The Nature of the Book: Print and Knowledge in the Making*. Chicago: University of Chicago Press, 1998.

Johnson, Barbara. "The Frame of Reference: Poe, Lacan, Derrida." *Yale French Studies* 55–56 (1977): 457–505.

Johnston, Alastair. *Alphabets to Order: The Literature of Nineteenth-Century Typefounders' Specimens*. New Castle, DE: Oak Knoll, 2000.

Joseph, Miranda. *Against the Romance of Community*. Minneapolis: University of Minnesota Press, 2002.

Kaestle, Carl F., and Janice A. Radway. "A Framework for the History of Publishing and Reading in the United States, 1880–1940." In *A History of the Book in America. Volume 4. Print in Motion: The Expansion of Publishing and Reading in the United States, 1880–1940*, edited by Carl F. Kaestle and Janice A. Radway, 7–21. Chapel Hill: published in association with the American Antiquarian Society by the University of North Carolina Press, 2009.

Kaestle, Carl F., and Janice A. Radway, eds. *Print in Motion: The Expansion of Publishing and Reading in the United States, 1880–1940*. Chapel Hill: published in association with the American Antiquarian Society by the University of North Carolina Press, 2009.

Kafka, Ben. *The Demon of Writing: Powers and Failures of Paperwork*. New York: Zone, 2012.

Kafka, Franz. *Franz Kafka: The Office Writings*. Edited by Stanley Corngold, Jack Greenberg, and Benno Wagner. Translated by Eric Patton with Ruth Hein. Princeton, NJ: Princeton University Press, 2008.

Kahana, Jonathan. *Intelligence Work: The Politics of American Documentary*. New York: Columbia University Press, 2008.

Keen, Andrew. *The Cult of the Amateur: How Today's Internet Is Killing Our Culture*. New York: Doubleday, 2007.

Kelty, Christopher. "Geeks, Social Imaginaries, and Recursive Publics." *Cultural Anthropology* 20, no. 2 (2005): 185–214.

———. *Two Bits: The Cultural Significance of Free Software and the Internet*. Durham, NC: Duke University Press, 2008.

Kirschenbaum, Matthew G. *Mechanisms: New Media and the Forensic Imagination*. Cambridge, MA: MIT Press, 2008.

———. "The .txtual Condition." In *Comparative Textual Media*, edited by N. Katherine Hayles and Jessica Pressman. Minneapolis: University of Minnesota Press, forthcoming.

———. "The Word as Image in an Age of Digital Reproduction." In *Eloquent Images: Word and Image in the Age of New Media*, edited by Mary E. Hocks and Michelle R. Kendrick, 137–56. Cambridge, MA: MIT Press, 2003.

Kleinhans, Chuck, ed. "In Focus: Visual Culture, Scholarship, and Sexual Images." *Cinema Journal* 46 (Summer 2007): 96–132.

Krajewski, Markus. "Ask Jeeves: Servants and Search Engines." Translated by Charles Marcrum II. *Grey Room* 38 (Winter 2010): 6–19.

———. *Paper Machines: About Cards and Catalogs, 1548–1929*. Cambridge, MA: MIT Press, 2011.

Lanier, Jaron. *You Are Not a Gadget: A Manifesto*. New York: Alfred A. Knopf, 2010.

Latour, Bruno. "Drawing Things Together." In *Representation and Scientific Practice*, edited by Michael Lynch and Steve Woolgar, 19–68. Cambridge: MIT Press, 1990 [1988].

Lears, T. J. Jackson. *No Place of Grace: Antimodernism and the Transformation of American Culture, 1880–1920*. Chicago: University of Chicago Press, 1994.

Leffingwell, William H. *Scientific Office Management*. Chicago: A. W. Shaw, 1917.

Levi, Primo. *The Periodic Table*. Translated by Raymond Rosenthal. New York: Schocken, 1984.

Levy, David M. *Scrolling Forward: Making Sense of Documents in the Digital Age*. New York: Arcade, 2001.

Light, Jennifer S. "Facsimile: A Forgotten 'New Medium' from the 20th Century." *New Media and Society* 8, no. 3 (2006): 355–78.

Liu, Alan. *Laws of Cool: Knowledge Work and the Culture of Information*. Chicago: University of Chicago Press, 2004.

———. "Transcendental Data: Toward a Cultural History and Aesthetics of the New Encoded Discourse." *Critical Inquiry* 31 (Autumn 2004): 49–84.

Loughran, Trish. *The Republic in Print: Print Culture in the Age of U.S. Nation Building, 1770–1870*. New York: Columbia University Press, 2007.

Lovecraft, H. P. *Miscellaneous Writings*. Edited by S. T. Joshi. Sauk City, WI: Arkham House, 1995.

Luhmann, Niklas. *The Differentiation of Society.* Translated by Stephen Holmes and Charles Larmore. New York: Columbia University Press, 1982.

Lynd, Robert S. Review of *Annals of Cleveland: 1818–1935. American Sociological Review* 3, no. 4 (1938): 594–97.

MacKellar, Thomas. *The American Printer: A Manual of Typography, Containing Complete Instructions for Beginners as Well as Practical Instructions for Managing Every Department of a Printing Office.* 6th ed. Philadelphia: MacKellar, Smiths and Jordan, 1871.

Mak, Bonnie. *How the Page Matters.* Toronto: University of Toronto Press, 2011.

Marx, Leo. "Technology: The Emergence of a Hazardous Concept." *Social Research* 64 (Fall 1997): 965–88.

McCarty, Willard, ed. *Text and Genre in Reconstruction: Effects of Digitalization on Ideas, Behaviours, Products and Institutions.* Cambridge: Open Book, 2010.

McDonald, William F. *Federal Relief Administration and the Arts.* Columbus: Ohio State University Press, 1969.

McDowell, Paula. "Mediating Media Past and Present: Toward a Genealogy of 'Print Culture' and 'Oral Tradition.'" In *This Is Enlightenment,* edited by Clifford Siskin and William Warner, 229–46. Chicago: University of Chicago Press, 2010.

McGann, Jerome J. *Radiant Textuality: Literature after the World Wide Web.* New York: Palgrave, 2001.

———. *The Textual Condition.* Princeton, NJ: Princeton University Press, 1991.

McGill, Meredith L. *American Literature and the Culture of Reprinting, 1834–1853.* Philadelphia: University of Pennsylvania Press, 2003.

———. "Copyright." In *The Industrial Book, 1840–1880,* edited by Scott E. Casper, Jeffrey D. Groves, Stephen W. Nissenbaum, and Michael Winship, 3:158–78. Chapel Hill: Published in association with the American Antiquarian Society by the University of North Carolina Press, 2007.

———. "Fugitive Objects: Securing Public Property in United States Copyright Law." October 2000. Unpublished manuscript.

McKenzie, D. F. *Bibliography and the Sociology of Texts.* London: British Library, 1986.

———. *Making Meaning: "Printers of the Mind" and Other Essays.* Edited by Peter D. McDonald and Michael F. Suarez. Amherst: University of Massachusetts Press, 2002.

McKitterick, David. *Print, Manuscript and the Search for Order, 1450–1830.* Cambridge: Cambridge University Press, 2003.

McLuhan, Marshall. *The Gutenberg Galaxy: The Making of Typographic Man.* Toronto: University of Toronto Press, 1962.

McLuhan, Marshall, and Quentin Fiore. *The Medium Is the Massage: An Inventory of Effects.* New York: Bantam, 1967.

McMillian, John. *Smoking Typewriters: The Sixties Underground Press and the Rise of Alternative Media in America.* New York: Oxford University Press, 2011.

Meckler, Alan Marshall. *Micropublishing: A History of Scholarly Micropublishing in America, 1938–80.* Westport, CT: Greenwood, 1982.

Meiklejohn Civil Liberties Institute. *Pentagon Papers Case Collection: Annotated Pro-*

cedural Guide and Index, edited by Ann Fagan Ginger and the Meiklejohn Institute Staff. Berkeley, CA: Meiklejohn Civil Liberties Institute, 1975.

Meisel, Joseph S. "American University Presses, 1929–1979." *Book History* 13 (2010): 122–53.

Mihm, Stephen. *A Nation of Counterfeiters: Capitalists, Con Men, and the Making of the United States*. Cambridge, MA: Harvard University Press, 2007.

Miller, Carolyn R. "Genre as Social Action." *Quarterly Journal of Speech* 70 (1984): 151–67.

Mitchell, W. J. T. *Picture Theory: Essays on Verbal and Visual Representation*. Chicago: University of Chicago Press, 1994.

———. *What Do Pictures Want? The Lives and Loves of Images*. Chicago: University of Chicago Press, 2005.

MLA Handbook for Writers of Research Papers. 7th ed. New York: Modern Language Association of America, 2009.

Moskowitz, Sam. *The Immortal Storm: A History of Science Fiction Fandom*. 1954. Reprint, Westport, CT: Hyperion, 1973.

Mott, Frank Luther. *A History of American Magazines, 1741–1930*. 5 vols. Cambridge, MA: Belknap Press of Harvard University Press, 1958–68.

Moxon, John. *Mechanick Exercises on the Whole Art of Printing*. 2 vols. London, 1683–84.

Nelson, Robert S. "The Slide Lecture, of the Work of Art History in the Age of Mechanical Reproduction." *Critical Inquiry* 26 (Spring 2000): 414–34.

Neubauer, John. *The Fin-de-Siècle Culture of Adolescence*. New Haven, CT: Yale University Press, 1992.

Nichols, Bill. *Introduction to Documentary*. 2nd ed. Bloomington: Indiana University Press, 2010.

Nixon, John Travis. *History of the National Amateur Press Association, Compiled by John Travis Nixon*. Crowley, LA: John T. Nixon, 1900.

Novick, Peter. *That Noble Dream: The "Objectivity Question" and the American Historical Profession*. Cambridge: Cambridge University Press, 1988.

Nunberg, Geoffrey. "Farewell to the Information Age." In *The Future of the Book*, edited by Geoffrey Nunberg, 103–29. Berkeley: University of California Press, 1996.

———. "The Places of Books in the Age of the Electronic Publication." *Representations* 42 (Spring 1993): 13–37.

Ohmann, Richard. *Selling Culture: Magazines, Markets, and Class at the Turn of the Twentieth Century*. London: Verso, 1996.

Orr, Julian E. *Talking about Machines: An Ethnography of a Modern Job*. Ithaca, NY: Cornell University Press, 1996.

Oushakine, Serguei Alex. "The Terrifying Mimicry of Samizdat." *Public Culture* 13, no. 2 (2001): 191–214.

Owen, David. *Copies in Seconds: Chester Carlson and the Birth of the Xerox Machine*. New York: Simon and Schuster, 2004.

Parikka, Jussi. *What Is Media Archaeology?* Cambridge: Polity, 2012.

Pasko, W. W. *American Dictionary of Printing and Bookmaking, Containing a History of These Arts in Europe and America, with Definitions of Technical Terms and Biographical Sketches*. New York: Howard Lockwood, 1894.

The Pentagon Papers as Published by the New York Times, Based on Investigative Reporting by Neil Sheehan, Written by Neil Sheehan, Hedrick Smith, E. W. Kenworthy, and Fox Butterfield. Articles and documents edited by Gerald Gold, Allan M. Siegal, and Samuel Abt. New York: Bantam, 1971.

Peters, John Durham. "Technology and Ideology: The Case of the Telegraph Revisited." In *Thinking with James Carey: Essays on Communications, Transportation, History*, edited by Jeremy Packer and Craig Robertson, 137–56. New York: Peter Lang, 2006.

Pfiffner, Pamela. *Inside the Publishing Revolution: The Adobe Story*. Berkeley, CA: Peachpit, 2003.

Phillips, John L. *"The Art Preservative": 100 Fancy Specimens of Job Printing and a Collection of Valuable Papers, for the Use of Job Printers and Apprentices*. Springfield, IL: 1875.

Phillips, Michelle H. "Along the 'Paragraph Wires': Child-Adult Mediation in *St. Nicholas Magazine*." *Children's Literature* 37 (2009): 84–113.

Piper, Andrew. *Book Was There: Reading in Electronic Times*. Chicago: University of Chicago Press, 2012.

———. *Dreaming in Books: The Making of the Bibliographic Imagination in the Romantic Age*. Chicago: University of Chicago Press, 2009.

Poe, Edgar A. "The Purloined Letter." *The Gift: A Christmas, New Year, and Birthday Present*, 41–61. Philadelphia: Carey and Hart, 1845.

Poletti, Anna. *Intimate Ephemera: Reading Young Lives in Australian Zine Culture*. Melbourne, Australia: University of Melbourne Press, 2008.

Pollard, Alfred W. and G. R. Redgrave. *A Short-Title Catalogue of Books Printed in England, Scotland and Ireland: and of English Books Published Abroad, 1475–1640*. London: Bibliographical Society, 1926.

Poovey, Mary. *Genres of the Credit Economy: Mediating Value in Eighteenth- and Nineteenth-Century Britain*. Chicago: University of Chicago Press, 2008.

Poster, Mark. "Databases as Discourse; or, Electronic Interpellations." In *Computers, Surveillance, and Privacy*, edited by David Lyon and Elia Zureik, 175–92. Cambridge, MA: MIT Press, 1994.

Power, Eugene. *Edition of One: The Autobiography of Eugene B. Power, Founder of University Microfilms*. Ann Arbor, MI: University Microfilms International, 1990.

Prados, John, and Margaret Pratt Porter. "Creating the Papers." In *Inside the Pentagon Papers*, edited by John Prados and Margaret Pratt Porter, 12–50. Lawrence: University Press of Kansas, 2004.

Pratt, Lloyd. *Archives of American Time: Literature and Modernity in the Nineteenth Century*. Philadelphia: University of Pennsylvania Press, 2010.

Preston, Cathy Lynn. Introduction to *The Other Print Tradition: Essays on Chapbooks, Broadsides, and Related Ephemera*, edited by Cathy Lynn Preston and Michael J. Preston, ix–xx. New York: Garland, 1995.

Price, Leah. *How to Do Things with Books in Victorian Britain*. Princeton, NJ: Princeton University Press, 2012.

Price, Leah, and Pamela Thurschwell, eds. *Literary Secretaries/Secretarial Culture*. Aldershot, UK: Ashgate, 2005.

"Project—New Technology and the Law of Copyright: Reprography and Computers." *UCLA Law Review* 15 (1967–68): 939–1030.

Rabinowitz, Paula. *They Must Be Represented: The Politics of Documentary*. New York: Verso, 1994.

Radway, Janice. "Zines, Half-Lives, and Afterlives: On the Temporalities of Social and Political Change." *PMLA* 126, no. 1 (2011): 140–50.

Raley, Rita. "Dataveillance and Counterveillance." In *"Raw Data" Is an Oxymoron*, edited by Lisa Gitelman, 121–46. Cambridge, MA: MIT Press, 2013.

Raney, M. Llewellyn. Introduction to *Microphotography for Libraries*, edited by M. Llewellyn Raney, v–xi. Chicago: American Library Association, 1936.

Renov, Michael, ed. *Theorizing Documentary*. New York: Routledge, 1993.

Rheinberger, Hans-Jörg. *Toward a History of Epistemic Things: Synthesizing Proteins in the Test Tube*. Stanford, CA: Stanford University Press, 1997.

Rickards, Maurice. *Collecting Printed Ephemera*. Oxford: Phaidon, 1988.

———. *Encyclopedia of Ephemera: A Guide to the Fragmentary Documents of Everyday Life for the Collector, Curator, and Historian*. New York: Routledge, 2000.

Riles, Annelise. "Introduction: In Response." In *Documents: Artifacts of Modern Knowledge*, edited by Annelise Riles, 1–38. Ann Arbor: University of Michigan Press, 2006.

———. *The Network Inside Out*. Ann Arbor: University of Michigan Press, 2000.

Ritchie, Dennis M., and Ken Thompson. "The UNIX Time-Sharing System." *Communications of the ACM* 17, no. 7 (1974): 365–75.

Robertson, Craig. *The Passport in America: The History of a Document*. New York: Oxford University Press, 2010.

Rorabaugh, W. J. *The Craft Apprentice: From Franklin to the Machine Age in America*. New York: Oxford University Press, 1986.

Rosenberg, Nathan. "Technological Change in the Machine Tool Industry, 1840–1910." *Journal of Economic History* 23, no. 4 (1963): 414–43.

Rudenstine, David. *The Day the Presses Stopped: A History of the Pentagon Papers Case*. Berkeley: University of California Press, 1996.

Rumble, Walker. *The Swifts: Printers in the Age of Typesetting Races*. Charlottesville: University of Virginia Press, 2003.

Rummonds, Richard-Gabriel. *Nineteenth-Century Printing Practices and the Iron Handpress, with Selected Readings*. 2 vols. New Castle, DE: Oak Knoll, 2004.

Saito, Akira. "The Mission and the Administration of Documents: The Case of Mojos from the 18th to the 20th Century." In *Usos del documento y cambios socials en la historia de Bolivia*, edited by Clara López Beltrán and Akira Saito, 27–72. Osaka, Japan: National Museum of Ethnology, 2005.

Salus, Peter H. *A Quarter Century of UNIX*. Reading, MA: Addison Wesley, 1994.

Samuelson, Paula. "The Story of *Baker v. Selden*: Sharpening the Distinction between

Authorship and Invention." In *Intellectual Property Stories*, edited by Jane C. Ginsburg and Rochelle Cooper Dreyfuss, 159–93. New York: Foundation, 2006.

Sánchez-Eppler, Karen. *Dependent States: The Child's Part in Nineteenth-Century American Culture*. Chicago: University of Chicago Press, 2005.

Sandage, Scott A. *Born Losers: A History of Failure in America*. Cambridge, MA: Harvard University Press, 2006.

Saxe, Stephen O. Foreword to Richard-Gabriel Rummonds, *Nineteenth-Century Printing Practices and the Iron Handpress, with Selected Readings*, 1:xxiii–xxx. New Castle, DE: Oak Knoll, 2004.

Schwartz, Hillel. *The Culture of the Copy: Striking Likenesses, Unreasonable Facsimiles*. New York: Zone, 1996.

Scranton, Philip. *Endless Novelty: Specialty Production and American Industrialization, 1865–1925*. Princeton, NJ: Princeton University Press, 1997.

Sellen, Abigail J., and Richard H. R. Harper. *The Myth of the Paperless Office*. Cambridge, MA: MIT Press, 2002.

Sellers, Charles. *The Market Revolution: Jacksonian America, 1815–1846*. New York: Oxford University Press, 1991.

Sheehan, Neil. Introduction to *The Pentagon Papers as Published by the New York Times, Based on Investigative Reporting by Neil Sheehan, Written by Neil Sheehan, Hedrick Smith, E. W. Kenworthy, and Fox Butterfield*. Articles and documents edited by Gerald Gold, Allan M. Siegal, and Samuel Abt, ix–xvii. New York: Bantam, 1971.

Sherman, William H. *Used Books: Marking Readers in Renaissance England*. Philadelphia: University of Pennsylvania Press, 2008.

Shirky, Clay. *Here Comes Everybody: The Power of Organizing without Organizations*. New York: Penguin, 2008.

Small, Ian. *Conditions for Criticism: Authority, Knowledge, and Literature in the Late Nineteenth Century*. Oxford: Clarendon Press of Oxford University Press, 1991.

Smith, Brian Cantwell. *On the Origin of Objects*. Cambridge, MA: MIT Press, 1998.

Smith, Merritt Roe, and Leo Marx, eds. *Does Technology Drive History? The Dilemma of Technological Determinism*. Cambridge MA: MIT Press, 1994.

Smith, Paul. "Models from the Past: Proto-Photocopy-Lore." In *The Other Print Tradition: Essays on Chapbooks, Broadsides, and Related Ephemera*, edited by Cathy Lynn Preston and Michael J. Preston, 183–222. New York: Garland, 1995.

Sontag, Susan. *On Photography*. New York: Farrar, Straus, and Giroux, 1977.

Spencer, Amy. *DIY: The Rise of Lo-Fi Culture*. London: Marion Boyars, 2008.

Spencer, Truman J. *A Cyclopedia of the Literature of Amateur Journalism*. Hartford, CT: Truman J. Spencer, 1891.

Stallybrass, Peter. "Printing and the Manuscript Revolution." In *Explorations in Communication and History*, edited by Barbie Zelizer, 111–18. New York: Routledge, 2008.

Sterne, Harold E. *A Catalogue of Nineteenth Century Printing Presses*. New Castle, DE: Oak Knoll, 2001.

Sterne, Jonathan. "The MP3 as Cultural Artifact." *New Media and Society* 8 (October 2006): 825–42.

———. *MP3: The Meaning of a Format*. Durham, NC: Duke University Press, 2012.

Stewart, Susan. *Crimes of Writing: Problems in the Containment of Representation*. Durham, NC: Duke University Press, 1994.

Stott, William. *Documentary Expression and Thirties America*. New York: Oxford University Press, 1974.

Straw, Will. "Embedded Memories." In *Residual Media*, edited by Charles R. Acland, 3–31. Minneapolis: University of Minnesota Press, 2007.

Streeter, Thomas. *The Net Effect: Romanticism, Capitalism, and the Internet*. New York: New York University Press, 2011.

Susman, Warren I. *Culture as History: The Transformation of American Society in the Twentieth Century*. New York: Pantheon, 1984.

Sutherland, Ivan Edward. "Sketchpad, A Man-Machine Graphical Communication System." PhD diss., Massachusetts Institute of Technology, 1963.

———. "Sketchpad: A Man-Machine Graphical Communication System." *AFIPS Proceedings* 23 (1963): 329–46.

Tanselle, G. Thomas. *Literature and Artifacts*. Charlottesville: Bibliographic Society of the University of Virginia, 1998.

Tate, Vernon D. "Criteria for Measuring the Effectiveness of Reading Devices." In *Microphotography for Libraries*, edited by M. Llewellyn Raney, 13–26. Chicago: American Library Association, 1936.

———. "The Gentlemen's Agreement and the Problem of Copyright." *Journal of Documentary Reproduction* 2, no. 1 (1939): 29–36.

Thomson, Ellen Mazur. "Early Graphic Design Periodicals in America." *Journal of Design History* 7, no. 2 (1994): 113–26.

———. *The Origins of Graphic Design in America, 1870–1920*. New Haven, CT: Yale University Press, 1997.

Toffler, Alvin. *The Third Wave*. New York: William Morrow, 1980.

Ullman, Richard H. "The Pentagon's History as 'History.'" *Foreign Policy* 4 (1971): 150–56.

United States Bureau of the Census. *Manufactures*. Washington, DC: Government Printing Office, 1905.

———. *Ninth Census*. Washington, DC: Government Printing Office, 1872.

Vissman, Cornelia. *Files: Law and Media Technology*. Stanford, CA: Stanford University Press, 2008.

Waldrop, M. Mitchell. *The Dream Machine: J. C. R. Licklider and the Revolution That Made Computing Personal*. New York: Viking, 2001.

Wallace, Aurora. *Media Capital: Architecture and Communications in New York City*. Urbana: University of Illinois Press, 2012.

Warner, Michael. *The Letters of the Republic: Publication and the Public Sphere in Eighteenth-Century America*. Cambridge, MA: Harvard University Press, 1990.

————. *Publics and Counterpublics.* New York: Zone, 2002.

Warnock, John. Foreword to *Beyond Paper: The Official Guide to Adobe Acrobat.* Mountain View, CA: Adobe, 1993.

Warwick, Andrew. *Masters of Theory: Cambridge and the Rise of Mathematical Physics.* Chicago: University of Chicago Press, 2003.

Weatherly, S. M. *The Young Job Printer: A Book of Instructions in Detail on Job Printing for Beginners.* Chicago, 1889.

Weber, Max. *Sociological Writings.* Edited by Wolf Heydebrand and translated by Martin Black with Lance W. Garmer. New York: Continuum, 1994.

Wells, H. G. *World Brain.* Garden City, NY: Doubleday, Doran, 1938.

Wells, Tom. *Wildman: The Life and Times of Daniel Ellsberg.* New York: Palgrave, 2001.

Wershler-Henry, Darren. *The Iron Whim: A Fragmented History of Typewriting.* Toronto: McClelland and Stewart, 2005.

Wertham, Fredric. *The World of Fanzines: A Special Form of Communication.* Carbondale: Southern Illinois University Press, 1973.

Westerfield, H. Bradford. "What Use Are Three Versions of the Pentagon Papers?" *American Political Science Review* 69, no. 2 (1975): 685–89.

White, Michele. "The Hand Blocks the Screen: A Consideration of the Ways the Interface Is Raced." *Electronic Techtonics: Thinking at the Interface,* ed. HASTAC, 117–28. HASTAC, 2008.

White, Richard. *Railroaded: The Transcontinentals and the Making of Modern America.* New York: W. W. Norton, 2011.

Wilken, Rowan. "The Practice and 'Pathologies' of Photocopying." *Déjà Vu: antiTHESIS* 17 (2007): 126–43.

Williams' Cincinnati Directory, Embracing a Full Alphabetical Record of the Names of the Inhabitants of Cincinnati. Cincinnati, OH, June 1870.

Williams, Raymond. *Keywords: A Vocabulary of Culture and Society.* Revised ed. New York: Oxford University Press, 1985.

Winship, Michael. "The Art Preservative: From the History of the Book Back to Printing History." *Printing History* 17, no. 1 (1995): 14–23.

Wirtén, Eva Hemmungs. *No Trespassing: Authorship, Intellectual Property Rights, and the Boundaries of Globalization.* Toronto: University of Toronto Press, 2004.

Yates, JoAnne. *Control through Communication: The Rise of System in American Management.* Baltimore, MD: Johns Hopkins University Press, 1989.

————. *Structuring the Information Age: Life Insurance and Technology in the Twentieth Century.* Baltimore, MD: Johns Hopkins University Press, 2005.

Zielinski, Siegfried. *Deep Time of Media: Toward an Archaeology of Hearing and Seeing by Technical Means.* Translated by Gloria Custance. Cambridge, MA: MIT Press, 2006.

Zuboff, Shoshana. *In the Age of the Smart Machine: The Nature of Work and Power.* New York: Basic, 1984.